EXPLORERS

From Ancient Times to the Space Age

Simon & Schuster Macmillan
1633 Broadway
New York, NY 10019

Library of Congress Catalog Card Number: 98-8809

PRINTED IN THE UNITED STATES OF AMERICA

Printing Number

1 2 3 4 5 6 7 8 9 10

Library of Congress Cataloging-in-Publication Data

Explorers and discoverers: from ancient times to the space age/consulting editors,
    John Logan Allen, E. Julius Dasch, Barry Gough.
        p. cm.
    Includes bibliographical references and index.
    ISBN 0-02-864893-5 (set).—ISBN 0-02-864890-0 (v. 1).—ISBN 0-02-864891-9 (v. 2).—
ISBN 0-02-864892-7 (v. 3)
    1. Explorers—Biography—Dictionaries.   I. Allen, John Logan. 1941–
II. Dasch, E. Julius.   III. Gough, Barry M.
G200.E877   1998
910′.92′2—dc21   98-8809
[B]   CIP

EXPLORERS

From Ancient Times to the Space Age

Volume 3

Consulting Editors

John Logan Allen
Professor of Geography
University of Connecticut

E. Julius Dasch
Manager/Scientist
NASA National Space Grant Program

Barry M. Gough
Professor of History
Wilfrid Laurier University

Macmillan Library Reference USA

Simon & Schuster Macmillan
New York

Simon & Schuster and Prentice Hall International
London   Mexico City   New Delhi   Singapore   Sydney   Toronto

Peary, Robert Edwin

American
b May 6, 1856; Cresson, Pennsylvania
d February 20, 1920; Washington, D.C.
Explored Arctic and Greenland;
claimed to have reached North Pole

Inuit people of the Canadian Arctic, sometimes known as the Eskimo

The Arctic explorer Robert Edwin Peary was honored by Congress with the rank of rear admiral when he retired.

In April 1909, after almost 25 years of exploration in the Arctic region, Robert Edwin Peary claimed to be the first person to have reached the North Pole. However, when Peary returned to the United States to publicize his accomplishment, he learned that Frederick Albert Cook had recently announced that he had reached the pole one year before Peary. Although neither explorer had the solid evidence necessary to support such a claim, Peary generally received credit for the feat. Historians continue to debate the question today. Nevertheless, Peary's several expeditions earned him a reputation as the United States's greatest Arctic explorer.

Passion for Adventure

Like many people in the late 1800s, Peary grew up fascinated by accounts of Arctic exploration. After graduating from Bowdoin College with a degree in civil engineering, he spent two years doing odd jobs in Maine. When he was offered a government position in Washington, D.C., he eagerly accepted the work. In 1881 he took advantage of an opportunity to go to Nicaragua as a civil engineer with the U.S. Navy.

Peary's passion for Arctic exploration, which he called "Arctic fever," was related to his desire for a simple existence apart from modern civilization. In college he wrote about the "restless wild essence of life." Peary believed that the Arctic was one of the last places where "the poetry of the world" had not yet been spoiled by the "pressure of man's foot." According to Peary, in the polar region, the "grand old primal elements" had not yet been mastered.

However, Peary never tried to be a natural part of the Arctic environment, nor did he feel the kinship with the **Inuit** that the American explorer Charles Francis HALL had felt. In his pursuit of the pole, Peary saw the Arctic as something he had to conquer rather than understand. He admired the Inuit and adopted their skills, but he always felt that he was superior to them.

Peary's involvement with the Arctic was connected to his literary career, since he was as much a journalist as an explorer. Much of his income came from contracts to write books and newspaper and magazine articles. Writing in a straightforward style, Peary always made himself the hero at the center of the adventure, and his works were well received. He jealously guarded his plans and findings, refusing to let his assistants publish their own accounts of his journeys. Peary wanted to ensure that he would receive the best possible profit for his stories.

Laying the Foundation

Peary planned his first experience in the Arctic in 1886, after reading Nils Adolf Erik NORDENSKIÖLD's

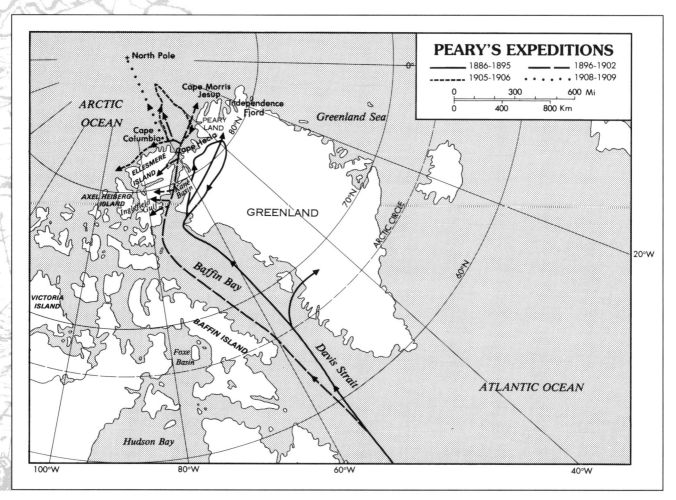

PEARY'S EXPEDITIONS

1886-1895   1896-1902
1905-1906   • • • • • 1908-1909

0   300   600 Mi
0   400   800 Km

On two of his early missions to the Arctic region, Robert Edwin Peary set records for reaching high northern positions.

anthropologist scientist who studies human societies

sledge heavy sled, often mounted on runners, that is pulled over snow or ice

account of his trip to Greenland. Peary obtained a leave from the navy and funds from his mother to explore part of Greenland's west coast. The American explorer and a young Danish companion penetrated 100 miles inland. Nordenskiöld and his assistants had traveled 140 miles, but Peary still boasted that he had gone farther than any other explorer.

Five years later, Peary returned to Greenland. On this expedition, he was accompanied by his new wife, Josephine Diebitsch Peary, and his servant and assistant for all his later Arctic explorations, Matthew HENSON. The group also included Dr. Frederick Cook, who was hired as a surgeon and **anthropologist.** Peary and his party spent the winter on Inglefield Gulf in northwestern Greenland. The explorer and a Norwegian companion, Eivind Astrup, then traveled 500 miles by dog-drawn **sledge** to Independence Fjord, on the country's northeast coast. This journey marked the beginning of Peary's efforts to prove that Greenland was an island.

Slow Progress

Peary's successful sledge trip had doubled the distance covered by Fridtjof NANSEN a few years earlier, and it brought him instant fame. After a lecture tour, he had enough money to fund a new expedition, and the U.S. Navy reluctantly granted him another leave. He returned to Inglefield Gulf in 1893 to retrace much of his previous

Robert Edwin Peary used this photograph to support his claim that he had reached the North Pole in April 1909.

route and to attempt to head north to the pole. But poor weather conditions forced him to end the mission. He stayed in the region the following year with Henson and another assistant, while the rest of the party returned home.

On April 1, 1895, Peary returned to Independence Fjord, but he made no further progress. He did manage to bring back two large meteorites that he had found near Cape York, south of Inglefield Gulf. The rocks had been used by the Inuit as a source of iron. The explorer justified taking their property by saying that he and other white traders provided all the iron goods that the Inuit needed.

In the summers of 1896 and 1897, Peary returned to Greenland in order to bring back a 100-ton meteorite, study Inuit culture, and develop exploration techniques. He brought several Inuit back to the United States for scientific study, but they soon died. While he was at home, he occupied his time by giving lectures and looking for wealthy supporters. His main financial backer, Morris K. Jesup, started the Peary Arctic Club, which supported the explorer's ventures for the next decade. Another of Peary's influential friends then arranged for another leave from the navy, and Peary once again prepared for a trip north.

Pursuit of the Pole

On July 4, 1898, Peary set off on the *Windward* to try another route to the pole, through Kane Basin. While spending the winter there, he became worried that the Norwegian explorer Otto SVER-DRUP might reach the pole before him. Sverdrup was wintering on his ship, the *Fram,* 40 miles to the south. Despite the dangers of traveling during the harsh Arctic winter, Peary headed for Fort Conger, on the east coast of Ellesmere Island. When Peary arrived there, Henson helped him take off his boots, and several frostbitten toes came off with them. Peary had to wait until the spring of 1900 to set out again, but he successfully reached the northernmost point of Greenland on May 13. He named the spot Cape Morris Jesup. Although Peary was unable to proceed over the sea toward the pole, this expedition proved that Greenland was an island.

Peary stayed in the Arctic for another two years, upset by his failure to get near the North Pole. By the spring of 1902, he felt better, and he tried another route to the pole, off Cape Hecla on the north coast of Ellesmere Island. His progress, however, was delayed by open water and slow supply sledges, and he did not meet his objective.

Quick Return

Although his latest attempt to reach the pole had been unsuccessful, Peary was not discouraged. He returned home and raised

depot place where supplies are stored

money to build a ship capable of navigating through Arctic waters. On July 16, 1905, Peary sailed on the 184-foot-long steam vessel *Roosevelt* out of New York and reached the northeastern coast of Ellesmere Island before winter.

The following February, the expedition's support parties left Point Moss, west of Cape Hecla, to set up supply **depots** on the sea ice to the north. On March 6, the rest of the party followed. After some delay caused by a wide channel of water in the ice, Peary, Henson, and some of the Inuit members of the group proceeded north. With their supplies running low and the sledge dogs in poor health, they had to turn back only 180 miles from the pole. Disappointed again, Peary set off to explore the northern coast of Ellesmere Island before heading home. On this journey, he made it to the northern tip of Axel Heiberg Island, where he reported sighting land still farther to the northwest. He named it Crocker Land, but it later turned out not to exist.

The Final Dash to the Pole

Peary's last attempt to reach the pole was a remarkable feat of planning and endurance. Using almost the same route as in 1906, Peary's first supply party left Cape Columbia—the northernmost point on Ellesmere Island—on February 28, 1909. A second party set out soon after, and on March 1, Peary and Henson departed with the remaining group. Peary, Henson, and four Inuit companions made the final dash of more than 130 miles on April 2. The party marched for almost five days with little sleep or rest.

Peary reported reaching camp just 3 miles short of the pole at 10 A.M. on April 6, 1909. In the next 30 hours, he said, he crossed the area that he believed to be the actual pole and then headed back to Cape Columbia. Peary was exhausted—Henson described him as a "dead weight." Still, the party made remarkable time on the return trip, covering 70 miles in one day.

When he returned to New York City to announce his achievement, Peary learned that his former colleague, Frederick Cook, had already claimed to have reached the North Pole. Cook said that his accomplishment had taken place nearly a year earlier. Few people believed Cook, who was soon discredited. But Peary was also unable to prove without a doubt that he had actually reached the North Pole. Peary, who had been obsessed with the Arctic for so long, was greatly upset that critics doubted his claim to fame. Today scholars, navigators, and other experts on the Arctic still debate whether Cook or Peary ever made it to the pole.

Peary's treks deep into the ice-covered Arctic had little scientific value. But they stirred a sense of adventure and glory in a young nation that had ambitions of becoming a world power. In the introduction to Peary's best-selling account of the voyage, President Theodore Roosevelt wrote that "we, his fellow Americans, are his debtors."

SUGGESTED READING Robert M. Bryce, *Cook and Peary: The Polar Controversy, Resolved* (Stackpole Books, 1997); John Goodsell, *On Polar Trails: The Peary Expedition to the North Pole, 1908-1909* (Eakin, 1983); Wally Herbert, *The Noose of Laurels: Robert E. Peary and the Race to the North Pole* (Atheneum, 1989); William R. Hunt, *To Stand at the Pole: The Dr. Cook-Admiral Peary Controversy* (Stein and Day, 1982).

Pérez Hernández, Juan Josef

Spanish
b 1725?; Majorca, Spain
d November 2, 1775; at sea off California coast
Explored northwest coast of North America

New Spain region of Spanish colonial empire that included the areas now occupied by Mexico, Florida, Texas, New Mexico, Arizona, California, and various Caribbean islands

latitude distance north or south of the equator

An officer in the Spanish navy, Juan Josef Pérez Hernández led one of the first groups of Spanish colonists from Mexico to what is now California. He later commanded an expedition up the west coast of North America, reaching as far north as what is now Nootka Sound off Vancouver Island.

Searching for New Lands to Settle

Little is known of Pérez before 1767, when he arrived for naval duty in San Blas, **New Spain.** During the next few years, the Spanish became concerned about reports that the Russians were expanding eastward from their colonies in Alaska's Aleutian Islands. To strengthen their claims in North America, the Spanish decided to push their settlements farther north, from Baja (Lower) California to what was then called Alta (Upper) California. In 1769 Pérez commanded the ship that carried some of the first colonists to San Diego and Monterey. For the next several years, he traveled regularly to those ports with supplies for the colonists.

In 1774 Spain sent an expedition to explore the coastline north of Alta California and to look for any signs of Russian settlers. Pérez was put in charge of the mission, with Estéban José MARTÍNEZ as his second-in-command. Pérez was given sealed instructions and was ordered not to read them until he was at sea. After he left Monterey in June 1774 on the *Santiago,* he learned that he was to sail at least as far as 60° north **latitude.** On his return trip, he was to keep as close to shore as possible and land whenever he could do so safely. He was not to establish any settlements, but he was to note likely sites for future colonies and claim them for Spain. Pérez was also instructed to avoid any settlements or ships of other nations, treat well any Indians he met, and study the Indians' customs.

Pérez first sailed northwest until he reached a latitude of 50° and then turned directly north. On July 18, he sighted land near what is now the border between Canada and Alaska. The next day, he anchored off the northernmost island of the present-day Queen Charlotte Islands. There the *Santiago* was greeted by three canoes of Haida Indians seeking to trade with the Spanish. Although Pérez did not understand the Haida language and could not ask the Indians about their customs, he recorded detailed observations of them in his journal. Pérez was prevented from going ashore by a lack of wind and a current that dragged the ship seaward.

After spending four days in the area, Pérez sailed north again, reaching a latitude of 55°. He sighted what is now Cape Muzon on Dall Island, off the southeastern tip of Alaska. Strong winds and currents kept him from sailing farther north, so he decided to head back without reaching 60° north latitude. He had failed to take formal possession of any lands for Spain, though he did note that he was in a maze of islands that were populated with Indians who seemed eager to trade.

Southward Explorations

While exploring in the north, Pérez had been reluctant to get too close to shore because he feared that reefs would damage the

Santiago. He exercised the same caution on his voyage home. The expedition sailed along the west coast of what is now Vancouver Island, which Pérez and his crew thought was part of the mainland. On August 8, they dropped anchor at the mouth of a large bay, later named Nootka Sound. Once again local Indians came out to the ship to trade, and one of them stole some silver spoons from the crew. Four years later, when British Captain James COOK entered the sound, he bought the spoons, which he said proved that the Spanish had been there before him. Pérez reported that this bay would be a strategic site for a Spanish settlement, which was later established there.

After a failed attempt to land at Nootka, Pérez continued south. He eventually passed what is now called the Strait of Juan de Fuca but did not take notice of it. While near the strait, Pérez did see a snow-capped mountain, which he named Sierra Nevada de Santa Rosalia. The peak, in the present-day state of Washington, is now called Mount Olympus.

At this point, the crew was eager to return to New Spain. The men had begun to suffer from **scurvy.** Bad weather and the fear of uncharted waters also made the crew homesick, so Pérez proceeded south as quickly as possible.

Although the **viceroy** of New Spain was not pleased that Pérez had not claimed any territory for Spain, he recommended that Pérez receive a reward. Pérez then set out as second-in-command under his countryman Bruno de HEZETA on another difficult expedition to northern waters. The trip ruined his health. He died soon after the voyage and was buried at sea in November 1775.

SUGGESTED READING Warren L. Cook, *Flood Tide of Empire: Spain and the Pacific Northwest, 1543–1819* (Yale University Press, 1973).

scurvy disease caused by a lack of vitamin C and once a major cause of death among sailors; symptoms include internal bleeding, loosened teeth, and extreme fatigue

viceroy governor of a Spanish colony in the Americas

Pigafetta, Antonio Francesco

Italian
b 1491?; Vicenza, Italy
d 1534?; Malta
Kept record of Magellan's attempt to sail around the world

circumnavigation journey around the world

mutiny rebellion by a ship's crew against the officers

Antonio Francesco Pigafetta was one of the few men who successfully completed Ferdinand MAGELLAN's intended **circumnavigation.** He supported the captain during attempted **mutinies** and was at his side when Magellan was killed in the Philippine Islands. Pigafetta's detailed journal was the only written record of the historic and dangerous three-year voyage.

Born into a noble Italian family, Pigafetta was well educated and well traveled, and he had a flair for languages. His experience and his connections earned him a place as an observer on Magellan's 1519 westward expedition from Seville, Spain, to the Spice Islands (also known as the Moluccas). On the voyage, Pigafetta became a devoted admirer of Magellan. While defending the commander in the Philippines, Pigafetta was struck in the face by a poisoned arrow. He described this incident and other adventures in his journal.

Pigafetta and 17 other crew members returned to Seville on September 8, 1522, completing the first circumnavigation in just under three years. He reported on the voyage to King Charles I of Spain and later to officials in Venice, Paris, Lisbon, and Rome. The French version of his account was published in 1523. The following year, Pigafetta joined the Knights Hospitalers, a religious and military group. He died in 1530 while defending the Greek island of Rhodes from Turks.

SUGGESTED READING Paula Spurlin Paige, translator, *The Voyage of Magellan: The Journal of Antonio Pigafetta* (Prentice-Hall, 1969).

Pike, Zebulon Montgomery

American
b January 5, 1779; Trenton, New Jersey
d April 27, 1813; Toronto, Canada
Explored Rocky Mountains in central Colorado

headwaters source of a river

Zebulon Pike's ideas about the Southwest were not always accurate, but they helped to shape U.S. policy in the region for many years after his death.

A career soldier, Zebulon Montgomery Pike carried out two major explorations while serving in the U.S. Army. On his first expedition, in 1805, Pike traveled northward along the Mississippi River in search of its source. The following year, he led a mission to the **headwaters** of the Arkansas River and into the southern Rocky Mountains, where he tried but failed to climb the peak that now bears his name.

The Origin of the Mighty River

While still a boy, Pike joined his father's army unit as a cadet; he became a first lieutenant by the age of 20. For several years, he served on the western frontier of the United States. In 1805 his commanding officer, General James Wilkinson, ordered him to take a group of 20 soldiers up the Mississippi River to find its source. Pike had two other goals on this mission. He was instructed to inform the Indians of the area that they had come under the authority of the U.S. government. Under Jay's Treaty of 1794, Great Britain had agreed to withdraw from the land that is now Ohio, Indiana, Illinois, Michigan, Wisconsin, and Minnesota. Pike was also ordered to warn any British fur traders he encountered on his journey that they were now in American territory.

Pike and his party traveled up the Mississippi in a small riverboat. When winter came, they hurriedly built a fort. Some of the men stayed there, but Pike and the others continued north on foot, dragging their supplies over the snow on sleds. After reaching Leech Lake, which Pike mistakenly thought was the source of the Mississippi, the soldiers returned to St. Louis on April 30, 1806.

A Web of Intrigue

Pike began his second and final expedition a few months later. While historians agree on the events that took place during this journey, they differ on the motives that lay behind it. Pike was again given orders by General Wilkinson, who was commanding general of the U.S. Army as well as governor of the newly acquired Louisiana Territory. It was later revealed that Wilkinson was being bribed by the Spanish, who wanted to know what the Americans planned to do with the Louisiana lands. Wilkinson was also connected with schemes devised by Aaron Burr, a former U.S. vice president. Burr was accused of wanting to establish an empire in the Southwest. Most historians think that Pike did not know of Wilkinson's questionable dealings. Pike apparently believed that he was acting out of loyalty to his country.

On this expedition, Pike was ordered to locate the headwaters of the Arkansas and Red Rivers. According to the United States, the upper Red River was the boundary between the Louisiana Territory

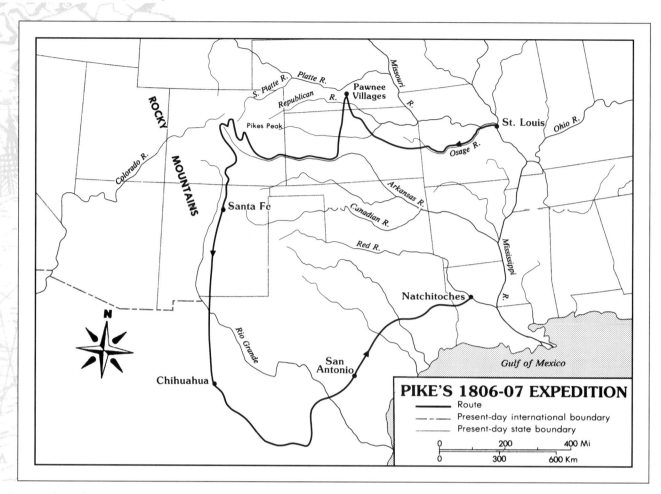

PIKE'S 1806-07 EXPEDITION
- ——— Route
- – – – Present-day international boundary
- ——— Present-day state boundary

| 0 | 200 | 400 Mi |
| 0 | 300 | 600 Km |

After his journey through Mexico, Zebulon Pike gave American officials precise details about the number and type of Spanish troops he saw.

New Spain region of Spanish colonial empire that included the areas now occupied by Mexico, Florida, Texas, New Mexico, Arizona, California, and various Caribbean islands

and **New Spain.** Pike was also instructed to bring back any information about New Spain that might be useful to the United States. He was not given permission, however, to cross into Spanish territory. Rather, Pike was told to spy without appearing to do so, perhaps by pretending to have become lost inside New Spain.

To add to the confusion, Wilkinson seems to have told the Spanish about Pike's planned route. A force of 600 Spaniards, led by Facundo Melgares, marched north from what is now New Mexico to Pawnee Indian villages in Kansas, where Pike was scheduled to stop. Melgares warned the Pawnee not to have any dealings with the Americans and then returned with his troops to New Mexico.

Into the Rockies

In the meantime, Pike had set out from St. Louis on July 15, 1806. He first returned some Osage Indian captives to their villages on what is now the western border of Missouri. Then his expedition traveled north to the Pawnee villages, where the Americans received a hostile reception. From there he headed south until he reached the Arkansas River and then followed it westward into the Rocky Mountains.

On November 15, the party sighted a mountain that looked like "a small blue cloud." The peak was actually 120 miles away, and it took more than a week for the soldiers to get close to it. Determined

tributary stream or river that flows into a larger stream or river

gangrene decay of a part of the body, caused by lack of blood circulation

to reach the top, Pike started to climb the mountain with three men. But Pike had misjudged the mountain's height and the difficulty of the terrain around it. The explorers were wearing summer uniforms—the only clothes they had. After almost four days of bitterly cold weather, including a snowstorm, they gave up. Pike called his discovery the Great Mountain, but today it is named Pikes Peak.

The party spent the rest of November and December exploring the Rockies in what is now Colorado. They traveled as far north as the source of the South Platte River and as far south as the Sangre de Cristo Mountains. Pike built a small fort on a **tributary** of the Arkansas River and left some men there. He and 13 others set out in January on a difficult crossing of the Sangre de Cristo range. During this exhausting journey, six men suffered **gangrene** as a result of frostbite. Although Pike had to leave them behind, they were later rescued.

Encounter with the Spanish

Pike and the others pushed on. Two weeks after leaving the Arkansas River, they arrived at a branch of the Rio Grande. They were now well into Spanish territory, north and west of the source of the Red River. Pike wrote that he and his men thought that they had reached the Red, but—as one of them later admitted—everyone knew that they were actually at the Rio Grande.

The party built a small log fort at this site. One member of the group, a friend of General Wilkinson's, then headed down the Rio Grande to Santa Fe to collect a trading debt. He notified the Spanish authorities that American troops were in Spanish territory, and by February 26, 1807, Pike and his men had been arrested.

To be captured by the Spanish seems to have been part of Pike's plan. He and his men were taken to Santa Fe and then to the governor in Chihuahua, so that Pike had an excellent chance to carry out his unofficial spying mission. Although Pike's papers were seized, the Spanish treated him well, and eventually they escorted him back to the United States.

His days as an explorer were over, but Pike continued his military service. During the War of 1812, he died in a battle against British troops near Toronto, Canada, on April 27, 1813.

Pike's Legacy

Prior to his death, Pike published his report of the march to Santa Fe and Chihuahua. Pike described the plains of the Southwest as a barren land with little water and no timber. He thought that the land could not support American settlements, but he also believed that keeping America's population east of the Mississippi River would help to preserve the country's unity. The myth of a Great American Desert discouraged settlers from moving to the area for the next 30 to 40 years.

Based on his observations, Pike proposed that the best route from the Atlantic Ocean to the Pacific Ocean lay across the Southwest, from the Arkansas River to the Colorado River. Pike also noted the opportunity for trade with Santa Fe and what is now northern

Mexico. The ideas that Pike set forth in his report influenced the way Americans thought about the Southwest for years to come.

SUGGESTED READING Zebulon Montgomery Pike, *The Journals of Zebulon Montgomery Pike, with Letters and Related Documents*, edited by Donald Jackson, 2 volumes (University of Oklahoma Press, 1966); Dale Van Every, *The Final Challenge* (William Morrow, 1964).

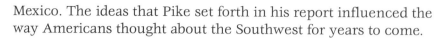

Pineda, Alonso Alvarez de. See *Alvarez de Pineda, Alonso*.

Pinzón, Martín Alonso

Spanish
b 1440?; Palos, Spain
d 1493; Palos, Spain
***Explored island of Great Inagua;
discovered Hispaniola***

Martín Alonso Pinzón's discovery of Hispaniola and its gold mines lured many other explorers to the Americas in search of riches.

Martín Alonso Pinzón was commander of the *Pinta* during Christopher COLUMBUS's historic voyage of discovery in 1492. Lured by tales of gold, Pinzón later deserted Columbus to explore an island called Babeque (present-day Great Inagua of the Bahamas). He eventually discovered Hispaniola and the gold mines of Cibao.

Growing Up on the Water

Martín Pinzón was born in 1440 to a wealthy family of Spanish shipowners. He and his younger brothers, Vicente Yáñez PINZÓN and Francisco Martín Pinzón, were skilled navigators who participated actively in trading voyages. While trading in West Africa and the Mediterranean region, Martín Pinzón gained much information about sea routes and amassed a great fortune.

Pinzón may have preceded Columbus in suggesting a crossing of the Atlantic Ocean to find a new route to Asia. One story indicates that he examined a map showing a voyage across the Atlantic to Japan long before Columbus won support for an expedition to the Indies. In any case, Pinzón eagerly supported Columbus's mission and helped him to gather crewmen, supplies, and financial backing.

A Spirit of Independence

Columbus's fleet departed from Palos, Spain, on August 3, 1492. Pinzón, aided by his brother Francisco, commanded the *Pinta*, while their brother Vicente captained the *Niña*. On October 12, when the *Pinta*'s lookout first sighted land, it was Martín Pinzón who gave Columbus the good news.

A month later, however, Pinzón and the *Pinta* abandoned the other two ships to search for an island called Babeque. An Indian guide had told him that the beaches there were littered with gold. Pinzón did not find that gold, though he did find the island, but he went on to discover Hispaniola (the island now occupied by Haiti and the Dominican Republic). After anchoring the *Pinta* there, he went inland and became the first European to discover gold in the mountain ranges that the Indians called Cibao.

Pinzón later learned from Indians about the shipwreck of the *Santa Maria*. He rejoined Columbus, who was at Hispaniola on the *Niña*. Although Columbus forgave him for his disloyalty, Pinzón then tried to reach Spain before his leader, so that he could take credit for the discoveries of the voyage. Columbus arrived first, however. A disappointed Pinzón returned home to Palos in April 1493 and died shortly afterward.

SUGGESTED READING John Frye, *Los Otros: Columbus and the Three Who Made His Enterprise of the Indies Succeed* (E. Mellen Press, 1992).

Pinzón, Vicente Yáñez

Spanish
b 1463; Palos, Spain
d after 1523; ?
Explored Central America and South America

Vicente Yáñez Pinzón was appointed governor of the lands he had discovered in Central America, but he never took formal possession of them for Spain.

After sailing on the famous first voyage of Christopher COLUMBUS in 1492, Vicente Yáñez Pinzón led several expeditions of his own to Central America and South America. Like his former commander, Pinzón attempted to find a water route leading west to Asia. In 1500 Pinzón reached northeastern Brazil, and he may have been the first European to discover that country.

Brazilian Explorations

Pinzón was one of three brothers who accompanied Columbus and helped finance his journey. Pinzón commanded the *Niña*. Unlike his more rebellious older brother, Martín Alonso PINZÓN, Vicente Pinzón remained loyal to their leader throughout the voyage. When the mission was completed in 1493, Pinzón decided to launch his own expedition.

Pinzón sailed from his hometown of Palos in 1499, and he reported reaching a cape near what is now Recife in northeastern Brazil in January 1500. If his report is accurate, he arrived months before Pedro Álvares CABRAL, so that Pinzón was the first European to explore Brazil. However, the date of Pinzón's arrival has been disputed by Brazilian and Portuguese historians who recognize Cabral as the country's discoverer. Other historians believe that the Italian explorer Amerigo VESPUCCI preceded both Pinzón and Cabral in reaching Brazil.

Traveling northwest along the coast, Pinzón noticed that the sea had changed color. He tasted the water and found that it was fresh, not salty. He followed the freshwater until he reached some islands at the mouth of what is now called the Amazon River. Fearful of its strong currents and tides, Pinzón did not attempt to enter the great river. Before he left, however, he raided Indian settlements along the Amazon and took dozens of prisoners. Some historians say that Pinzón's hostile acts may have caused the Indians to attack later European explorers of the Amazon region. After stopping at Hispaniola (the island now occupied by Haiti and the Dominican Republic) and the Bahamas, Pinzón returned to Spain.

Uncharted Territory

In 1502 Pinzón again explored the coast of Brazil, just north of his original landfall. The two-year journey also took him back to Hispaniola, where he encountered Columbus. The Italian explorer had gone there after his rescue from Jamaica, where two of his ships had been damaged.

On his next expedition, in 1506, Pinzón was accompanied by Juan de Solís. The two explorers traveled to the coastal area of Central America that had already been visited by Columbus. The Spaniards went on to explore all of the Yucatán peninsula and proceeded south to Trujillo, in what is now Honduras. Pinzón was appointed governor of these lands and is credited by some historians with the discovery of Honduras.

Two years later, Pinzón was sent by Spain to make another attempt to find a body of water that would take him west from Europe to the Spice Islands (also known as the Moluccas). Again sailing with Solís, Pinzón headed for the coast of Brazil, but he ended the mission the next year, apparently because of difficulties with his companion. This was Pinzón's last recorded voyage. Very little is known about the remainder of his life.

SUGGESTED READING John Frye, *Los Otros: Columbus and the Three Who Made His Enterprise of the Indies Succeed* (E. Mellen Press, 1992).

Pizarro, Francisco

Spanish
b 1475; Trujillo, Spain
d June 26, 1541; Lima, Peru
***Explored, conquered, and colonized
Peru and Ecuador***

---

conquistador Spanish or Portuguese explorer and military leader in the Americas

Francisco Pizarro was a clever and ruthless **conquistador.** Commanding an armed force of fewer than 200 men, Pizarro conquered the much larger army of the Inca Empire, placing Peru under Spanish rule. His additional conquests extended the Spanish Empire as far south as Chile and assured him a permanent place in South American history.

From Pig Herder to Politician
Pizarro was born in Trujillo in the Spanish province of Estremadura. Little is known of his early life, except that his father was in the army, that he herded pigs as a young man, and that he never received a formal education. In 1502 he went to the islands of the Caribbean in the fleet of Nicolás de Ovando, the recently appointed governor of Hispaniola (the island now occupied by Haiti and the Dominican Republic).

Several years later, Pizarro was a member of Alonso de OJEDA's expedition to the Gulf of Urabá, on the Caribbean coast of what is now Colombia. When Ojeda left the settlement to obtain supplies, Pizarro was placed in charge. In 1513 Pizarro was a captain, and he joined Vasco Nuñez de BALBOA's journey across Panama and was reported to have been the second European to see the Pacific Ocean from the Americas.

From 1519 to 1523, Pizarro served as lieutenant governor under Governor Pedro Arias de Ávila—known as Pedrarias—in the newly founded town of Panamá. Pizarro also became a cattle breeder and trader. He began a partnership with Diego de ALMAGRO, a wandering soldier, and Hernando de Luque, a wealthy priest. Their business prospered and eventually expanded to include mining, agriculture, and slave trading.

Search for South American Riches
The Spanish heard rumors of a great empire called Birú, which they referred to as Peru, along the west coast of South America.

Francisco Pizarro conquered the Inca Empire in South America, placing the region under Spanish control.

viceroy governor of a Spanish colony in the Americas

Pizarro obtained permission from Governor Pedrarias to journey to that region. He received financial backing from Luque and sailed south from Panama in 1524. Almagro followed Pizarro's main force with a support vessel. However, the danger of starvation, as well as heavy losses in battles with Indians along the coast of what is now Colombia, brought an early end to the expedition.

Two years later, Pizarro assembled another force and set out to explore the Colombian coast. He found a small amount of gold; then he headed south while Almagro returned to Panama for reinforcements. Traveling through what is now Ecuador, Pizarro discovered traces of gold and signs of a highly developed society. When Almagro returned, he and Pizarro still felt that their force was too small to launch a major campaign. Almagro went back to Panama for more soldiers while Pizarro waited on the island of Gorgona. Instead of the requested troops, however, the new governor of the Spanish colony of Darién sent two ships to bring back any men who wished to return. Without sufficient forces, Pizarro was ready to give up his quest to find and conquer the rich Indian civilization of the area.

A Crucial Decision

Pizarro then received a secret message from Almagro and Luque urging him to continue his mission. To force his men to make a decision, Pizarro reportedly drew a line in the sand with his sword, pointed south, and said, "Shipmates and friends! There lies the hard way, leading to Peru and wealth." Then he pointed north and said, "That way lies Panama and peace and rest, but also poverty. Take your choice." Pizarro then crossed to the south side of the line, and 13 men followed him.

Pizarro and these men waited seven months for Almagro to return with a ship and supplies. But when Almagro arrived, there were no other soldiers on board—just the ship's crew. This small party sailed south, reaching the city of Tumbes on the edge of the Inca Empire in 1527. The Spaniards found a small amount of gold and more signs of the region's advanced civilization before they returned to Panama.

In the spring of 1528, Pizarro sailed to Spain to present information about the Inca Empire to the royal court. As evidence of his findings, he brought llamas, fine cloth, and items made of gold and silver. These goods impressed King Charles I, and on July 26, 1529, the king appointed him **viceroy** of the province of New Castile. The province extended 600 miles south of Panama, along the newly discovered coast. In this post, Pizarro was given the authority to explore and conquer the vast area occupied by the Inca. At the time, their empire extended more than 2,000 miles from north to south, including what is now Ecuador, Bolivia, Peru, and part of northern Chile.

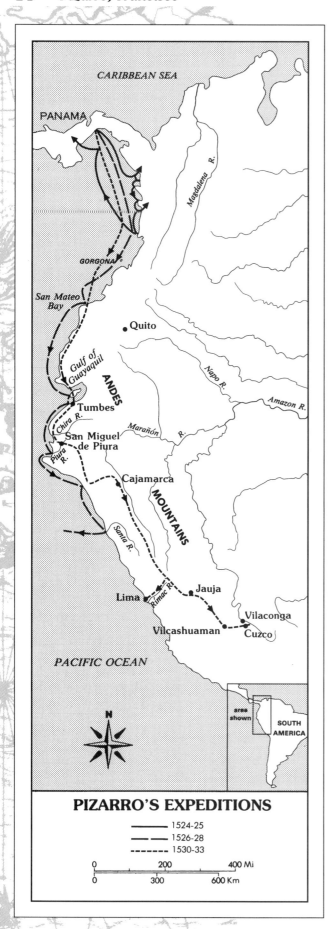

PIZARRO'S EXPEDITIONS

———— 1524-25
— — — 1526-28
- - - - - 1530-33

0   200   400 Mi

0   300   600 Km

In his travels, Francisco Pizarro used part of the Royal Inca Highway, a superb system of roads that covered more than 3,000 miles through the Andes.

Difficulties on the Way to Peru

Pizarro returned to Panama with many new recruits, including his four half brothers. On December 27, 1530, he set sail for Tumbes. Strong headwinds forced him to land at San Mateo Bay on the Ecuadoran coast. The Spaniards then began a long, tiring march south. The party faced food shortages and illness, struggled across flooded rivers, and fought with local Indians.

When Pizarro and his men finally reached Tumbes in 1532, the city was in ruins as a result of a civil war within the Inca Empire. Although the members of the party were disappointed, their spirits soon rose. Sebastián de BENALCÁZAR, an experienced conquistador, arrived by ship with 30 men, and Hernando de SOTO soon followed with supplies, horses, and 100 more volunteers from what is now Nicaragua.

Pizarro left Tumbes in May 1532. He proceeded to the Chira River, explored northwestern Peru, and selected a site for the first Spanish settlement. He founded San Miguel de Piura and left 60 Spaniards as the town's first citizens. Then Pizarro set out with about 60 horsemen and 100 foot soldiers to conquer the Inca Empire.

Benefits of Disease and War

Fortunately for Pizarro, his mission to conquer the Inca came at a time when the Indians were coping with many problems of their own. Between 1525 and 1527, the Inca emperor and most of his royal court had died in an epidemic, probably of smallpox. The Spaniards had carried the disease to South America, and it was widespread among the Inca. After the emperor's death, the Inca lands were divided between his surviving sons. One son, Huascar, ruled the city of Cuzco. The other, Atahualpa, controlled the empire's main army in Quito. War broke out between the brothers, giving the Spaniards an opportunity to take advantage of this instability among the Inca.

Pizarro had planned to attack Cajamarca, but he learned that Atahualpa was camped outside that city with an army of 30,000 men. The Inca chief eventually sent a representative to Pizarro with gold bracelets and other gifts. Pizarro saw a chance to avoid a major battle, so he lured Atahualpa into the city, promising friendly discussion. Instead he captured the Inca chief, who then offered to pay a huge ransom for his freedom. Pizarro accepted the offer, and Atahualpa filled a room with silver and gold for the Spaniards. But in July 1533, Pizarro had Atahualpa executed on charges that he had plotted an attack against the Europeans and had murdered his brother Huascar.

The Conquest Continues

Pizarro then began his march on Cuzco. He and his men traveled 750 miles through the Andes Mountains, crossing raging rivers and enduring the cold temperatures and thin air of the high altitudes. In four battles along the way, the Spanish proved the superiority of their mounted, armored soldiers over Inca warriors, even when the Inca outnumbered them. By the time Pizarro entered Cuzco, the Inca had surrendered to the Spanish army.

On January 6, 1535, Pizarro founded a new city on the Rímac River and named it the City of the Kings (now called Lima, a version of the word Rímac). In order to keep his fellow conquistadors from growing restless and challenging his authority, Pizarro sent them to explore the region. These expeditions reached into areas that are now parts of Ecuador, Colombia, and Chile.

After a few years in Peru, Pizarro's ruthless and scheming ways finally caught up with him. On June 26, 1541, he was murdered in Lima by Almagro's son, who wanted revenge for his father's death at the hands of Pizarro's half brother Hernando.

Although he explored much of northern South America, Pizarro is remembered primarily for his brutal conquest of the Inca. His victory gave Spain new wealth and helped make his country the greatest power of that time. More than any other explorer, Pizarro guaranteed Spain's dominance in South America.

SUGGESTED READING John Hemming, *The Conquest of the Incas* (Macmillan, 1970); Joachim G. Leithauser, *Worlds Beyond the Horizon,* translated by Hugh Merrick (Knopf, 1955); Albert Marrin, *Inca and Spaniard: Pizarro and the Conquest of Peru* (Atheneum, 1989).

Polo, Marco

Italian
b 1254?; Venice (now in Italy)
d 1324; Venice (now in Italy)
Explored central, eastern, and southern Asia

khan title of an Asian ruler

courtier attendant at a royal court

Marco Polo was perhaps the most outstanding European traveler of the Middle Ages. As a teenager traveling with his father and his uncle, he crossed Asia Minor (the peninsula now occupied by Turkey) and central Asia. After entering Cathay (present-day China), the Polos reached the court of Cathay's ruler, Kublai Khan. Marco eventually served the **khan** as a **courtier** and a diplomat. After nearly 25 years of traveling throughout eastern Asia and southern Asia on behalf of the khan, Polo returned to Europe.

The story of Polo's travels might have been lost if he had not been captured and imprisoned by the Genoese, rivals of his native city of Venice. While in prison, Polo dictated an account of his adventures to a fellow inmate named Rusticello, a writer of popular romances. The book of Polo's observations and descriptions of exotic Asian lands was later called *Il milione,* which means "The Million." In English it is known as *The Travels of Marco Polo.* Although the book was a great success and was translated into many languages, *Il milione*

When Marco Polo returned from his long travels, his own family at first refused to believe that he was indeed their long-lost relative.

caravan large group of people traveling together, often with pack animals, across a desert or other dangerous region

was sometimes accused of being merely a collection of tall tales. Since no original copy exists, modern scholars still debate which parts of the book are authentic and which were created by translators.

Like his book, Polo himself has been both criticized and admired. Some scholars are puzzled by his tendency to leave out important details. For instance, Polo never mentioned the Great Wall of China or the unique writing system used in that country. Despite these criticisms, Polo's place in history is well deserved. More than any other European of the time, he replaced ignorance about Asia with information. His story stirred the imagination of later European explorers, who sailed in search of the rich lands he had described.

A Merchant's Son

Polo was born in Venice in about 1254. Like so many other facts about his life, Polo's exact birth date is uncertain. His father, Niccolò, and his uncles were affluent merchants. In the late 1200s, Venice was one of the wealthiest city-states of northern Italy. Its merchant families specialized in trade with Asia, and its ships sailed as far east as the Black Sea.

In 1255 Niccolò Polo and his brother Maffeo left Venice to trade in Constantinople (now Istanbul, Turkey). After six successful years there, they went to the port of Sudak on the Black Sea, where they met their brother, Marco the elder, a well-known trader in the region. From Sudak, the Polos hoped to trade goods between Russia and Europe.

Niccolò and Maffeo then traveled up the Volga River to Sarai, the site of the court of Barka Khan. Barka was king of the western Mongols, a tribe of warring nomads who had settled in Russia. Known as the Golden Horde, they were part of the great Mongol Empire founded by Genghis Khan, whose armies had conquered most of China, central Asia, and Russia during the first half of the 1200s. The Mongol kingdoms now owed their loyalty to Kublai Khan, the grandson of Genghis, who ruled in the city of Cambaluc (present-day Beijing).

Through shrewd trading and the support of Barka Khan, the Polo brothers doubled their wealth. But when war broke out between Barka and a neighboring ruler, the two traders could not return to Sudak. Instead the Polos decided to head farther east.

Success in the East

Niccolò and Maffeo first journeyed to the court of Djagatai Khan in the city of Bukhara (in what is now Uzbekistan). Bukhara was an important stop on the Silk Road, a trade route for merchant **caravans** that carried the treasures of Asia. Since their business was thriving, the Polos stayed there for three years. Then, in early 1265, they joined a caravan of Mongols, who told them that Kublai Khan was inviting foreign traders to his court at Cambaluc. The caravan headed eastward, and before the end of the year, it reached Cambaluc.

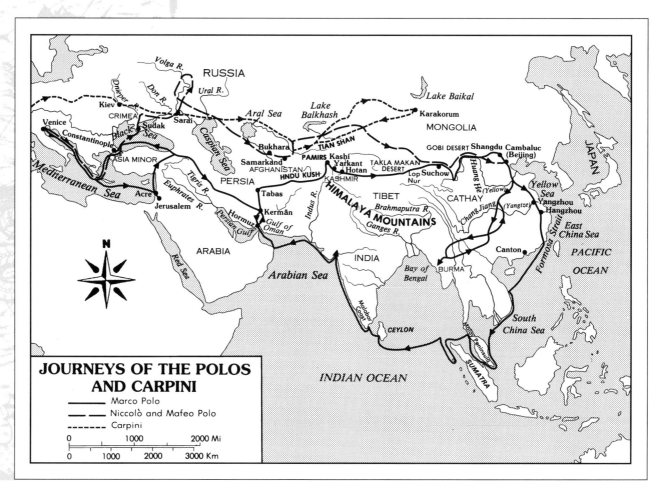

JOURNEYS OF THE POLOS AND CARPINI

——— Marco Polo
— — — Niccolò and Mafeo Polo
- - - - - - Carpini

0	1000		2000 Mi
0	1000	2000	3000 Km

Among the many lands Polo visited was the Gobi Desert. He wrote that illusions played tricks with minds there, and evil spirits lured travelers to their deaths.

The Polo brothers were well received, for Kublai Khan was interested in foreigners and eager to learn more about the lands of the west. The khan asked the two Venetian traders to serve as his representatives to the pope—the head of the Roman Catholic Church. Kublai wanted the pope to send 100 intelligent men to Cambaluc to debate the ideas of Christianity with his royal philosophers. The khan also asked the Polos to bring back oil from the lamp burning at Jesus' tomb in Jerusalem. For their protection, he gave the brothers a golden tablet with his seal on it. The seal guaranteed that they would be treated well as they traveled through lands controlled by the Mongols.

By the time the Polos reached Venice in 1269, Niccolò's wife had died, and his son Marco was now about 15 years old. Father and son spoke to each other for the first time; they then prepared to travel together to Asia.

A Fortunate Beginning

Pope Clement IV had died while the Polos were away. They waited two years for a new pope to be elected and then decided that they had to return to Cathay without the philosophers that Kublai Khan had requested. Niccolò, his son Marco, and Maffeo left for Jerusalem in 1271 to get the lamp oil. There they learned that a new pope,

malaria disease that is spread by mosquitoes in tropical areas

Gregory X, had finally been named. He was a priest formerly known as Teobaldo Visconti—an old friend of the Polos'. Gregory X hoped to open diplomatic relations with Cathay, and he named the Polos as his official ambassadors. He also gave them fine gifts to present to Kublai Khan and ordered two monks to accompany them on their journey.

The Polos departed from Jerusalem and crossed the lands that are now Iran and Iraq to the city of Hormuz on the Persian Gulf. They trekked over snow-covered mountains and sweltering deserts and faced occasional attacks by thieves. When the group arrived at Hormuz, the two monks refused to go farther and turned back. The Polos then headed north to the city of Kerman (in what is now central Iran), then traveled across the edge of the Dasht-e-Lut desert region. They rested at Tabas (now in Iran) before crossing into what is now Afghanistan.

The Venetians spent almost one year in Badakhshan, Afghanistan's northernmost region, possibly to recover from **malaria.** Some scholars suggest that during this period, Marco explored lands to the south, perhaps journeying into Pakistan and India. When their health improved, the Polos continued east to the Pamir Mountains. They marveled as they crossed peaks between 13,000 and 15,000 feet above sea level, in a region that would one day be called the rooftop of the world. There Marco first saw the long-horned mountain sheep that were later named for him, the *Ovis poli.*

Approaching Cathay

From the mountains, the Polos journeyed to Kashi in Chinese Turkistan (now part of Xinjiang province in China). To the east of the city lay the great Takla Makan desert. Marco later described it as a vast wasteland that "looks as if it had never been traversed by man or beast." The Polos next passed along the Silk Road and visited the cities of Yarkant (present-day Shache) and Hotan; then they proceeded to the oasis of Lop Nur. They paused there to rest before crossing the harsh Gobi Desert. In *Il milione,* Marco wrote that they saw no living creatures in that empty ocean of sand, for there was absolutely nothing there to eat.

After a monthlong journey across the desert, the Polos reached the city of Suchow (present-day Jiuquan) at the edge of the Great Wall that separated Cathay from its neighbors. In those days, the wall ran from Suchow to Cambaluc. Polo, however, never mentioned it in his writings. The Polos then continued east through unknown regions that were said to be home to Prester John. This mythical ruler supposedly reigned over a wealthy Christian kingdom somewhere in India or Asia. Although he had no proof, Marco argued that Prester John did indeed exist. This claim motivated later generations of explorers to search unsuccessfully for his kingdom from Africa to central Asia.

As the Polos traveled farther east, following the Huang He (also known as the Yellow River), they were met by representatives of Kublai Khan. The Mongols escorted the Venetians to the emperor's summer court at Shangdu in 1274 or 1275. Although *Il milione* is

never specific about dates, modern scholars generally agree that the Polos remained in China for 16 or 17 years.

Marco and the Khan

It is difficult to obtain accurate biographical information about Marco Polo from his writings, because he did not attempt to create a personal account of his travels. He probably wrote *Il milione* to provide other Italian merchants with a straightforward factual description of Asia. Polo may have allowed Rusticello to add events to make *Il milione* more exciting, but his fellow inmate left out facts of Polo's life and the sequence of his explorations.

Polo was about 20 years old when he arrived in Cathay. By that time, he was an experienced traveler who spoke many foreign languages. He attracted the attention of the emperor, who loved to hear stories of distant lands. Scholars have been able to gather this information from *Il milione.* Details of Polo's personality, however, are more difficult to obtain. Though creative writers and historians have devised many theories about Marco Polo, no one is sure about his true character.

Some scholars claim that Polo was a humorless, matter-of-fact man with little creativity or personality. Others criticize him for reporting legends as established facts and for relating stories about places he had not actually seen. Still, he must have been intelligent and charming, for he soon became one of Kublai Khan's most important courtiers.

Roaming the Empire

During their years in Cathay, Niccolò and Maffeo Polo remained close to the emperor's court, traded goods, and became very wealthy. Meanwhile, Marco roamed the empire in the service of Kublai Khan. He traveled by ship from the Formosa Strait, off China's east coast, to what are now the countries of Myanmar, Laos, Vietnam, and India. Some historians believe that Polo may have played an important role in the empire's trade of salt—a valuable item at the time.

Despite the lack of personal information, Polo provided detailed observations of the many sights he saw. His readers must have been fascinated by his account of Kublai Khan's great wealth. The khan owned huge palaces and vast hunting grounds. He and his court wore expensive clothes, and he was famous for his generosity. When peasants in the region faced starvation as a result of crop failures, Kublai Khan fed them with grain that had been reserved for the court. He was known to give money to the poor, and his people treated him as if he were a god. Polo also described the exotic customs of Cathay. He wrote that the Asian people used paper money—an idea that medieval Europeans, who used metal coins, must have found absurd.

The Busy Waterways of Cathay

Polo also discussed the great technical achievements of the Chinese, such as the Grand Canal, which today stretches for nearly 1,000 miles through eastern China from Hangzhou to Tianjin.

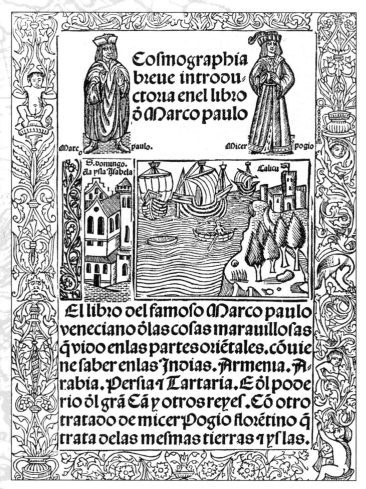

This illustrated page is from a manuscript of Polo's book. No two copies of the oldest existing versions are identical.

Marco believed that the canal had been built on the orders of Kublai Khan. Although the emperor had restored and extended the waterway, its construction had actually begun some 600 years before the Polos first saw it.

Marco was amazed by the heavy shipping traffic on the Huang He and the Chang Jiang (also known as the Yangtze River). He wrote that on the Chang Jiang, "the total volume of traffic exceeds all the rivers of the Christians put together and their seas into the bargain."

Although he marveled at the accomplishments of the Mongols, Polo also remarked on some of their failures. One of these was Cathay's military expedition in 1281 to conquer Japan, a kingdom previously unknown to Europe. The Mongol fleet was destroyed by a typhoon, known in Japanese legend as the *kamikaze,* which means divine wind. Polo reported that Kublai Khan had had the commanders of the expedition put to death.

The Saints and the Peacock Hunter

One of the last major journeys that Polo made for the emperor was to India. Little is known about this mission except that Marco traveled part of the way by ship. The chapters in *Il milione* that deal with India are vague. Polo supplied detailed observations of the customs and beliefs of the various kingdoms there, but it is not clear which regions he actually visited.

One anecdote told by Polo about India mentioned Thomas the Apostle (now known as Saint Thomas), who supposedly preached Christianity there. According to Polo, Thomas was accidentally killed, while saying his prayers, by an arrow shot by a peacock hunter. *Il milione* also contains many details about Hinduism and Buddhism in India, indicating that Polo might have been interested in philosophy and religion.

Polo's descriptions of the various ethnic groups he encountered greatly entertained his readers. However, these accounts led his critics to say that he was too eager to report gossip as fact. Later explorers, however, confirmed much of what he wrote. While he did not visit some of the places he described, such as Java and Japan, Polo did go to regions so remote that they were not visited again by Europeans for hundreds of years.

Taking Leave of the Khan

When Polo returned to Cambaluc from India around 1290, he found his father and uncle anxious to go back to Venice. Although the Polos were wealthy and respected in Asia, they may have grown homesick as the years passed. More important, Kublai Khan was by then in his late 70s. The Venetians concluded that after the khan's death, the new ruler might not be as kind toward European traders.

At first the khan was reluctant to let the Polos leave, but he eventually agreed to their request. He decided to let them travel with a Mongol princess who was about to sail to Persia (now Iran) for her marriage. Since the Polos were experienced sea travelers and had been to the lands to the west, they were considered ideal escorts. They joined a fleet of 14 ships carrying approximately 600 sailors, soldiers, and courtiers, departing sometime around 1292.

Marco Polo does not describe the voyage in detail. The fleet stopped in what is now Vietnam, as well as at several islands around the Malay Peninsula. The travelers spent five months on Sumatra (in present-day Indonesia) to wait out the rainy season before sailing on to Ceylon (now called Sri Lanka). From there the fleet followed the Indian coastline.

The Polos spent some time ashore, though *Il milione* does not indicate how long. Marco reflected upon the wealth he saw, from the pearl industry of Ceylon to the rich merchant cities of India's Malabar Coast. His accounts inspired later generations of explorers to risk any danger to acquire India's immense riches. Not until 200 years later did Vasco da GAMA's voyage around Africa open direct trade between India and western Europe.

The expedition sailed westward along the coast of what is now Pakistan and then reached the city of Hormuz. The Polos traveled by land to Khorasan, Persia, where they left the princess. While in Khorasan, they learned that Kublai Khan had died. His official protection for the Polos continued while they were in lands that pledged loyalty to Cathay. But when the Polos reached Christian territory in what is now Turkey, they were attacked by bandits. The robbers took much of the Polos' hard-earned wealth.

Last Years in Venice

In 1295 the travelers reached Constantinople and sailed at last for Venice. They had been away from home for 24 years. The Polos reportedly amazed their relatives with precious stones and jewels, which they had carried sewn into the linings of their clothes.

Based on official documents, historians have concluded that in 1296 or 1298, Marco was captured during a sea battle with forces from the city of Genoa and was put in jail. In captivity he met the writer Rusticello, and the two men worked together on *Il milione*. In 1299 the war between Venice and Genoa ended, and Polo was released from prison. He returned to Venice, where he continued to trade. He also married and raised a family. He seems to have been fairly wealthy, although many Venetians doubted his tales of Cathay. Polo died in 1324 at the age of 70.

Il milione continued to be a literary success. Readers enjoyed Rusticello's vivid writing style as much as Polo's observations. Over the centuries, the book has been revised many times, and opinions of Polo have changed as well. Whatever the exact truth may be, historians generally agree that his travels were an impressive feat. Polo himself supposedly said on his deathbed: "I did not write half of what I saw."

SUGGESTED READING Mary Hull, *The Travels of Marco Polo* (Lucent Books, 1995); Marco Polo, *The Travels of Marco Polo, A Modern Translation*, edited by Teresa Waugh, translated by Maria Bellonci (Sidgwick and

Ponce de León, Juan

Spanish
b 1460?; San Tervás de Campos, Spain
d July 1521; Havana, Cuba
Discovered Florida;
explored and colonized Puerto Rico

adelantado Spanish leader of a military
expedition to America during the 1500s who
also served as governor and judge

Juan Ponce de León never found the
legendary fountain of youth that he is
famous for seeking.

Jackson, 1984); Rebecca Stefoff, *Marco Polo and the Medieval Explorers* (Chelsea House, 1992); Clint Twist, *Marco Polo: Overland to Medieval China* (Raintree Steck-Vaughn, 1994).

During the time Juan Ponce de León spent in the Americas as a politician and military leader, he explored, colonized, and governed Puerto Rico; he discovered the Bahama Channel between 1508 and 1513. Despite these achievements, it was his discovery of Florida in 1513 that made him a legend in American history. Best known as the man who searched for the mythical fountain of youth, he later tried to establish the first European settlement in Florida. Ponce de León is also remembered for his belief in peaceful conquest and colonization. His nonviolent treatment of Indians was unusual among Spanish explorers of his time.

A Peaceful Approach

Ponce de León was born in about 1460, into a poor but noble family in the northern Spanish province of León. He received a basic military education and served as an attendant to the prince of Castile, who later became King Ferdinand of Castile and Aragon. Ponce de León's career in exploration began when he sailed on Christopher COLUMBUS's second voyage to the Americas, in 1493. In 1502 he joined Nicolás de Ovando on an expedition to Hispaniola (the island now occupied by Haiti and the Dominican Republic).

Ponce de León was then appointed governor of the province of Higüey (in present-day Haiti). He developed the area peacefully and gained great personal wealth in this position. The Indians who lived on the neighboring island of Borinquén invited Ponce de León to visit. In 1508 he explored the island, renamed it San Juan de Puerto Rico, and founded a settlement there. When King Ferdinand heard about Ponce de León's excellent skills as a colonial leader, he made him **adelantado** of Puerto Rico in 1509. Two years later, Ponce de León lost this post due to a conflict with political rivals. He immediately applied to the king for permission to seek the islands of Bimini, which were said to lie north of Cuba. According to local legend, a miraculous fountain of youth existed there. While there is no historical evidence that Ponce de León specifically set out to find the fountain, he may have planned his route based on the stories he had heard.

The Land of Flowers

Ponce de León received approval for his expedition and left Puerto Rico with three ships on March 3, 1513. Sailing northwest, he sighted the North American mainland on March 27. About a week later, he landed just north of the site of the modern-day city of St. Augustine. He and his party stayed on shore until April 8. Ponce de León named the new land Tierra La Florida, meaning Land of Flowers, because he had discovered it on Easter—the holiday known in Spanish as Pascua Florida.

Proceeding south along the east coast of Florida, Ponce de León discovered the Bahama Channel. This waterway proved to be very

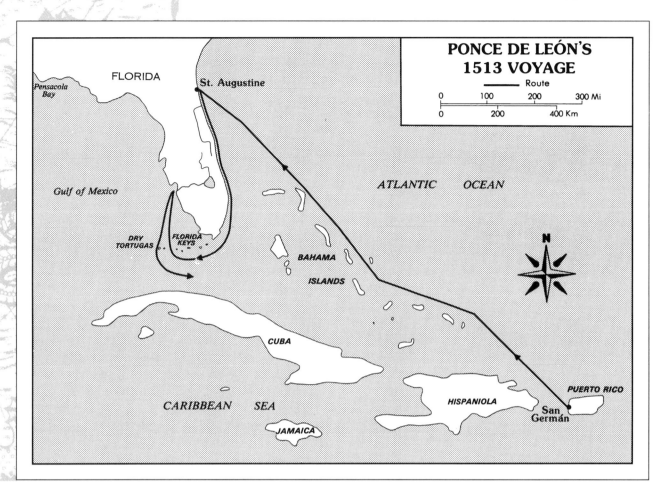

PONCE DE LEÓN'S 1513 VOYAGE

On his voyage to settle the islands of Bimini, Ponce de León discovered Florida on Easter Sunday, 1513.

valuable because it provided a new sea route from the Caribbean Islands to Spain. After passing around the Florida Keys, which he named the Martyrs, he headed up the west coast of Florida. He may have gone as far as what is now called Pensacola Bay before turning south again. He stopped at some islands, which he named the Tortugas (now known as the Dry Tortugas) because of the turtles that he found there; then he returned to Puerto Rico. When Ponce de León arrived in Spain in 1514, he was knighted, given a personal coat of arms, and granted royal permission to colonize Florida and the islands of Bimini.

The Final Voyage

Seven years passed before Ponce de León set out to colonize Florida. He departed from Puerto Rico with 200 men in 1521. They landed on the west coast of Florida, either near the mouth of the Caloosahatchee River or on Sanibel Island. But when they tried to establish a settlement there, the Spaniards were attacked by Indians. Ponce de León was seriously wounded during the battle, and the Spaniards abandoned their mission. The expedition sailed as far as Havana, Cuba, where Ponce de León died from his injuries.

An outstanding explorer and governor, Ponce de León is remembered for his kindness to the Indians of Haiti and Puerto Rico. To this day, Puerto Ricans honor his memory. Many places in Puerto

Rico and Florida proudly bear his name. The words on Ponce de León's gravestone describe his courage and determination: "This narrow grave contains the remains of a man who was a lion by name and much more so by his deeds."

SUGGESTED READING Anthony Q. Devereux, *Juan Ponce de León, King Ferdinand, and the Fountain of Youth* (Reprint Company, 1993); Father Jerome, *Juan Ponce de León* (Abbey Press, 1962); Douglas T. Peck, *Ponce de León and the Discovery of Florida: The Man, the Myth, and the Truth* (Pogo Press, 1993).

Pond, Peter

American
b January 18, 1740; Milford, Connecticut
d 1807; Boston, Massachusetts?
Explored central Canada

portage transport of boats and supplies overland between waterways

Peter Pond was a fur trader who explored the northern reaches of Canada for the North West Company. In the spring of 1778, he set out to find Lake Athabasca, a body of water then known only to Indians. On this expedition, he became the first non-Indian to complete the 13-mile **portage** that connects the Churchill-Saskatchewan River system with the Mackenzie River. Pond's maps of northwest Canada greatly influenced the travels of later explorers.

Exploring for Trade

Pond entered the fur trade in 1765 and spent several years based in Detroit, Michigan. Later he moved farther north and established a trading post on the North Saskatchewan River. When one of his competitors, the Hudson's Bay Company, set up a post farther upriver, Pond began to lose business, so he decided to head for uncharted territory. Earlier explorers had heard of Lake Athabasca (located in the region that is now northern Alberta and Saskatchewan) but had failed to find it. In 1787 Pond canoed up the Churchill River to Île-à-la-Crosse Lake and then headed northwest to Methye Lake. From there he made a difficult 13-mile portage to the Clearwater River. This river led to the Athabasca River, which flows into Lake Athabasca.

Pond built a post on the Athabasca River and spent the next 10 years trading there. During that time, he studied the territory to the north and west of the river. After gathering all the information available about northwest Canada, he made a map of the area in 1785. He gave copies of the map to the governor of Canada and to the U.S. Congress, hoping to obtain funds for an expedition to find a route to the Pacific Ocean. Although his requests were denied, the map was eventually seen by Thomas Jefferson. It helped spark Jefferson's interest in further exploration of northwestern North America, which led in turn to the expedition of MERIWETHER LEWIS and WILLIAM CLARK.

A Suspicious Ending

In 1787 Pond probably traveled as far north as the Great Slave Lake and may have reached what is now called the Mackenzie River. But around that time, one of Pond's rivals died mysteriously. Pond left his post on the Athabasca River and the fur trade altogether. Little is known of his later life. He is said to have died in poverty in Boston.

Pond had believed that the river he had explored flowed into the Pacific Ocean, but he never had a chance to test his theory. His replacement at the Athabasca post was Alexander Mackenzie, who journeyed down the river and learned that it empties into the Arctic Ocean, not the Pacific.

SUGGESTED READING Lawrence J. Burpee, *Two Western Adventurers: Alexander Henry and Peter Pond* (Ryerson Press, 1928); Harold Adams Innis, *Peter Pond, Fur Trader and Adventurer* (Irwin and Gordon, 1930).

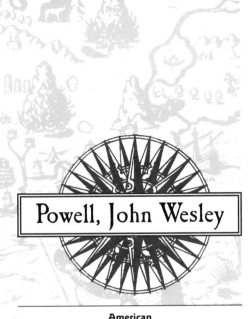

Powell, John Wesley

American
b March 24, 1834; Mount Morris, New York
d September 23, 1902; Brooklin, Maine
Explored Colorado River and Grand Canyon

specimen sample of a plant, animal, or mineral, usually collected for scientific study or display

fossil trace left in rocks by a plant or animal that lived long ago

John Wesley Powell was a gifted naturalist and scientist whose expeditions on the Colorado River helped the United States to develop the West.

During the summer of 1869, Major John Wesley Powell led nine men in small wooden boats on a 1,000-mile expedition. On this historic voyage down the Green and Colorado Rivers, these men became the first to journey through the Grand Canyon by boat. Powell's accomplishment earned him a place in the history of the American West. He also contributed to the development of that region through his work as a scientist and as a government official.

The Young Scientist

John Wesley Powell was born in 1834 to a family of English immigrants. His father, Joseph, was a preacher. Since Joseph was always in search of good farmland and opportunities to minister, the Powells moved frequently. Each time they relocated—always farther west—Joseph would settle his family on their new farm and then leave them to run it, while he traveled and preached for weeks. John Wesley spent his childhood moving from farm to farm in Ohio and Wisconsin. He became fascinated with natural science and spent his free time collecting **specimens** of rocks, **fossils,** animals, and plants. He received little formal education.

Just before he turned 16 years old, Powell left home because his father would not let him attend school to study science. Powell went to a one-room school for a year, working on a nearby farm to pay the tuition. During the next 10 years, he supported himself by teaching in other one-room schools while continuing his own research. Each summer he took long trips to collect specimens along the banks of the Mississippi River. Powell later studied at several universities, but he discovered that he already knew more than most of his professors.

Early in 1860, Powell joined the Union Army. He quickly became familiar with military engineering in order to qualify as an officer. During the Civil War, at the Battle of Shiloh, Powell was wounded in the right arm. Two days later, doctors had to cut off his arm above the elbow in order to save his life.

Into the Rockies

When the war ended, Powell moved to Illinois, where he became a university professor. A few years later, he was named director of the new Illinois State Natural History Museum. In 1867 the museum sponsored Powell's first organized scientific expedition to the Rocky Mountains and the Colorado River region. Powell brought along his wife, Emma, and a party of 15 scientists and students. They collected specimens as they made their way through the lands west of Denver, Colorado. The party also made a difficult climb to the top of Pikes Peak. Emma Powell was the first woman ever to achieve this feat.

John Wesley Powell became one of the first men to journey through the Grand Canyon by boat, despite having lost an arm during the Civil War.

anthropology the scientific study of human societies

longitude distance east or west of an imaginary line on the earth's surface; in 1884 most nations agreed to draw the line through Greenwich, England

latitude distance north or south of the equator

Since this first expedition was successful, John Powell had no trouble getting financial backing for a second trip to the West. He returned in the summer of 1868 with a much larger party of scientific experts. After spending the summer exploring in northern Colorado, Powell and some members of his group set up camp on the White River. This area was the winter home of a large tribe of Ute Indians. Powell conducted surveys of the courses of the White, Yampa, and Grand Rivers. He spent the winter studying the Ute language and customs. Through this experience, Powell developed an interest in **anthropology.**

Trial by Water

On May 24, 1869, Powell and nine others left Wyoming and headed down the Green River. Powell, the only scientist in the group, had chosen the hardiest mountain and river men he could find to accompany him on this voyage. They traveled in four wooden boats with long oars. Powell directed the small fleet from a chair that was strapped to the deck of the lead boat. As they proceeded along the Green River and down the Colorado River, Powell made scientific observations. He took compass readings and calculated altitudes, distances, **longitudes,** and **latitudes.** He also measured the rate and volume of the river's flow, as well as the temperature of the water.

portage transport of boats and supplies overland between waterways

anthropologist scientist who studies human societies

The party was forced to run dangerous rapids and to **portage** around waterfalls. Early in the journey, one boat was lost. Unfortunately, it had held nearly half of the expedition's food, equipment, and other supplies. One member of the group quit after only a few days. By the middle of the trip, the food supply had been reduced to one bag of dried apples, some coffee, one bag of old flour, and some rotting bacon. There were few animals to hunt at the bottom of the deep canyon.

Never knowing what lay around the next bend in the uncharted river, the men were risking their lives at nearly every moment. Powell wrote in his journal: "We are three quarters of a mile in the depths of the earth, and the great river . . . dashes its angry waves against the walls and cliffs that rise to the world above." At night the party often had to make camp on narrow ledges or sandbars. Describing their discomfort, Powell wrote: "It is raining hard and we have no shelter, but kindle a fire and have supper. We sit on the rocks all night, wrapped in our ponchos." All three boats were leaking badly from constant battering against rocks.

Three more members left the expedition near the lower end of the Grand Canyon. Although they successfully climbed to the canyon rim, they were killed by Indians as they tried to hike out of the wilderness. Finally, on August 30, Powell and his remaining companions arrived at the mouth of the Virgin River in Arizona, nearly drowned and half starved.

Powell had originally planned to take between six and nine months to complete the journey down the Colorado River. But after most of the food and equipment had been lost, he had been forced to make the trip in less than half the time. He did not have enough time to complete his scientific research, and most of his notes and specimens were lost in the river when the boats turned over.

To Tackle the River Again

Powell immediately began making plans for a larger, better-supported expedition. After he received funding from Congress, Powell spent most of 1870 seeking supply routes to the river and storing supplies at locations along these paths. He also spent time with the Indian tribes of the region, studying their languages and cultures and collecting specimens. Powell shipped many of these samples back to Washington, D.C.

On May 22, 1871, Powell set off again down the Colorado River. During the next 4½ months, his party covered about half the river's length and then stopped at the foot of Glen Canyon (now the site of Lake Powell). They returned in August 1872 and continued the survey, ending up at the mouth of the Kanab River.

Powell gained national fame from his public lectures and his written accounts of his adventures on the Colorado. His observations of the Grand Canyon won him admiration from the scientific community. Moreover, his mapping of the Colorado River region for the U.S. government was the first accurate survey of that part of the country. In 1877 he published *Introduction to the Study of Indian Languages,* a report which confirmed his reputation as an **anthropologist.**

A Lifelong Interest in the West

Powell continued to study the Colorado River region. In 1878 he published his *Report on the Lands of the Arid Region of the United States,* in which he criticized the government's land policy in the West. The following year, he helped to persuade Congress to create the U.S. Geological Survey. Powell became the first director of the survey's Bureau of Ethnology, a department devoted to gathering information on Indian tribes. Powell held this post for the rest of his life. From 1881 to 1894, he was also the director of the U.S. Geological Society. He died at his summer home in Maine in September 1902.

SUGGESTED READING Ann Gaines, *John Wesley Powell and the Great Surveys of the American West* (Chelsea House, 1991); John Wesley Powell, *The Exploration of the Colorado River and Its Canyons* (Doubleday, 1961); Wallace E. Stegner, *Beyond the Hundredth Meridian: John Wesley Powell and the Second Opening of the West* (University of Nebraska Press, 1982); John Upton Terrell, *The Man Who Rediscovered America: A Biography of John Wesley Powell* (Weybright and Talley, 1969).

Przhevalski, Nikolai Mikhaylovich

Russian
b April 6, 1839; Smolensk, Russia
d November 1, 1888; Karakol, Kirgiziya
(now Przheval'sk, Kyrgyzstan)
Explored central Asia;
attempted to reach Lhasa, Tibet

caravan large group of people traveling together, often with pack animals, across a desert or other dangerous region

In the late 1800s, the Russian explorer Nikolai Mikhaylovich Przhevalski devoted 18 years to what has been called "the race for the holy city of Lhasa." Lhasa, the capital of Tibet, was the residence of the Dalai Lama, the spiritual leader of Tibetan Buddhism. Tibetans were determined to keep foreign explorers out of the holy city, and Przhevalski's four attempts to reach Lhasa were all unsuccessful. Nevertheless, his expeditions greatly added to the small amount of information Europeans had about eastern central Asia's geography and its plant and animal life. He even discovered two animals previously unknown to Europeans—a wild camel and a wild horse that is now called Przhevalski's horse.

A Reputation for Toughness

In 1869 Przhevalski made his way to Irkutsk, a city on the shores of Lake Baikal in eastern Siberia. The next year, he and three companions set out toward Lhasa. They traveled southeast through Mongolia and the Gobi Desert to Kalgan (now Zhangjiakou), about 100 miles from Beijing, China. During the journey, he and his men fought off a group of about 100 bandits. When several members of his **caravan** refused to continue, Przhevalski threatened to shoot them. He escaped so many plots against his life that the local people began to think that he was a saint on the way to see the Dalai Lama. The party was forced to turn back by the harsh winter weather, but Przhevalski earned a reputation for courage and endurance.

Przhevalski tried to reach Lhasa again in 1876. Departing from Kuldja (now called Yining), on the western border of what is now Xinjiang, he headed directly for the holy city but again failed to reach it. By the time of his third expedition, three years later, Przhevalski had become one of the most skilled scientific explorers of his day. Setting out from Russian Turkistan, he journeyed across the mountains called the Altun Shan. He then passed around the eastern edge of the swamps and valleys of the Tsaidam depression and was met by Tibetan officials 170 miles from Lhasa. Suspecting that he was the leader of a Russian plot to capture the Dalai Lama, the Tibetans forced Przhevalski to turn back.

Scientific Observations

Although Przhevalski did not reach his goal, he returned with many detailed scientific descriptions and plant samples. He reported that northern Tibet had no trees, only three types of bushes, and several kinds of grass. But this poor plant life was still enough to feed huge herds of yak, antelope, and donkey. Przhevalski also described the salt marshes and clay flats at Tsaidam. These areas were often swept by strong winds. Przhevalski wrote about the loneliness that he felt while traveling through such barren lands.

By 1883 Przhevalski had become a major general in the Russian army. He then began his fourth and final Tibetan expedition. This time he tried to reach Lhasa by way of the rugged mountain regions that lie between Mongolia and Tibet. Along the way, he visited Issyk-Kul, one of the world's largest mountain lakes. He died there from drinking contaminated water. A town near the site of his death was named after him to honor his achievements as an explorer.

SUGGESTED READING Donald Rayfield, *The Dream of Lhasa: The Life of Nikolay Przhevalsky (1839–88), Explorer of Central Asia* (Ohio University Press, 1976).

In his quest to reach Lhasa, Nikolai Przhevalski traveled more than 20,000 miles through the wilds of central Asia.

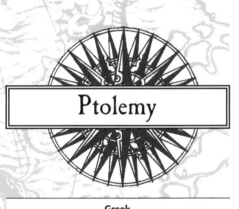

Ptolemy

Greek
b A.D. 90; Alexandria, Egypt
d A.D. 168; ?
Developed world map; improved grid system used on maps

longitude distance east or west of an imaginary line on the earth's surface; in 1884 most nations agreed to draw the line through Greenwich, England

latitude distance north or south of the equator

Ptolemy, also known as Claudius Ptolemaeus, was an influential Greek astronomer, geographer, and mathematician. His ideas, though often incorrect, were generally accepted by European and Arab scientists for over 1,000 years. Ptolemy's most dramatic error was his claim that the earth was the center of the universe. Not until 1543 was this theory replaced by the Polish astronomer Nicolaus Copernicus's realization that the earth revolves around the sun. Ptolemy's writings also misled geographers and explorers, who relied on his calculations of the circumference of the earth and the size of Asia. Despite these errors, his world map, which showed vast areas of uncharted land, was a great contribution to the field of exploration.

Mapping the Earth

Ptolemy's breakthroughs in geography were based on the earlier work of ERATOSTHENES and HIPPARCHUS. Ptolemy wrote an eight-volume *Guide to Geography,* which became a standard reference for hundreds of years. In his guide, Ptolemy improved upon the grid system that had been developed by Hipparchus. This system had divided the sphere of the earth into 360 segments that later evolved into the degrees of **longitude** used in modern geography. Ptolemy divided each degree into 60 minutes and each minute into 60 seconds. His improved grid system is still the basis for all modern mapmaking, and his work brought the terms *longitude* and **latitude** into common usage. He even listed the longitude and latitude of over 8,000 locations in Europe, Africa, and Asia.

This woodcut from 1513 illustrates Ptolemy's concept of the universe. Earth is at the center, surrounded by spheres containing water, air, fire, the moon, the sun, the planets, and the stars.

Ptolemy also introduced the custom of arranging maps with north at the top. He made that decision because at the time, the areas of the world best known to him were to the north of the areas that were less well known. Among his other innovations was a projection, a way to present a part of the spherical earth on a flat surface such as paper. The main problem with Ptolemy's maps and geographical descriptions is that he lacked accurate facts. He mentioned nothing about the climate, natural resources, or people of the areas he described.

Changing the Course of History

Ptolemy's lack of data caused him to make a serious mistake. More than 300 years earlier, the Greek astronomer Eratosthenes had calculated the circumference of the earth. He had estimated that each degree of longitude at the equator was equal to between 70 and 80 miles on the surface of the earth. The correct figure is 69, so Eratosthenes came quite close to an accurate measurement of the earth's circumference. But Ptolemy argued that each of the 360 degrees of longitude covered only 50 miles, so that the circumference of the earth equaled 18,000 miles—much less than the real circumference of about 25,000 miles.

Ptolemy's maps also showed the continent of Asia as stretching over 180 degrees of longitude rather than the 130 degrees it actually covers. As a result, his map presented distances on the earth incorrectly. According to Ptolemy, the distance from the eastern end of Asia to the western end of Europe was relatively small. This theory may have been one of the reasons why the Italian explorer Christopher COLUMBUS thought that he could reach Asia easily by traveling west from Europe. Neither Ptolemy nor Columbus knew that two continents and two oceans lie between Asia and Europe.

Ptolemy also suggested that the southern end of Africa was connected by a large landmass to Asia, and he therefore depicted the Indian Ocean as an inland sea. Many later explorers searched for a southern continent, which became known as *Terra Australis Incognita.* In 1775 Captain James COOK finally proved that such a landmass does not exist.

Ptolemy's Universe

The Greek astronomer's belief in an unmoving earth at the center of the universe was one of his most important ideas. People believed it for many centuries, perhaps because they were attracted to the notion of a universe in which people occupied the center. Ptolemy did provide supporting evidence for his theory. He reasoned that since all falling objects drop toward the center of the earth, the earth must be at the center of the universe. The true cause of this phenomenon is the force of gravity, which was not discovered until the late 1600s by Sir Isaac Newton.

SUGGESTED READING Claudius Ptolemy, *The Geography*, translated and edited by Edward Luther Stevenson (Dover, 1991).

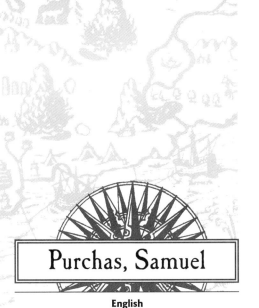

Purchas, Samuel

English
b 1577?; Thaxted, England
d 1626; London, England
Collected writings on early English exploration

Many voyages of discovery were inspired by Samuel Purchas's early efforts to write a history of exploration.

A clergyman by profession, Samuel Purchas showed a lifelong interest in the discoveries then being made around the world. Instead of navigating the seas or trekking overland himself, he gathered the stories of those who had done so.

In 1613 Purchas published his first collection of travel writings. It was titled *Purchas his Pilgrimage: Relations of the World and the Religions Observed in All Ages and Places Discovered*. This work showed Purchas's passion for exploration as well as for religion. It remained popular for many years.

His second collection of writings, published in 1625, was called *Hakluytus Posthumus or Purchas his Pilgrimes; Contayning a History of the World, in Sea Voyages and Lande Travells, by Englishmen and Others*. It was well received throughout England, and it challenged the English to face the dangers of exploring distant lands.

Purchas was not the first to write a travel encyclopedia. He followed in the footsteps of Richard HAKLUYT, a well-known English writer whose letters and books had encouraged the English to continue the exploration and colonization of North America. Hakluyt and Purchas probably knew each other; Purchas's second collection even contains some of Hakluyt's previously unpublished writings. Purchas's volumes are the only reliable source of information on some aspects of early English exploration and geographical history.

SUGGESTED READING Samuel Purchas, *Purchas his Pilgrimes*, 20 volumes, (James MacLehose and Company, 1905-1907).

Pytheas

Greek
b ?; Massilia (present-day Marseilles, France)
d 300s B.C.; ?
Sailed from Mediterranean Sea to northern Europe

cosmography the scientific study of the structure of the universe

In the 300s B.C., the Greek mariner Pytheas made a remarkable sea voyage from the warm Mediterranean Sea to the icy waters of northern Europe. Although other merchants and adventurers of ancient Greece may have visited northwestern Europe, Pytheas is the earliest one whose name and history are known today. He was also a scientist who had a great influence on Greek geography and **cosmography.**

Beyond a Blockade

The ancient Greeks and Romans lived near the Mediterranean Sea, but their world was not limited to its shores. Travelers such as HERODOTUS, HANNO, NEARCHUS, and ALEXANDER the Great journeyed to distant lands in all directions. The stories they brought back gave

PYTHEVS.
Apud F. Vrsinum in nomismate æres

One of the earliest known explorers, Pytheas astounded the ancient Greeks with the strange tales he brought back from northern Europe.

the people of the Mediterranean region some early knowledge of the earth's geography.

The Greeks were master mariners who traveled the Mediterranean Sea and established many colonies on its shores. Pytheas lived in Massilia, a Greek settlement on the southern coast of what is now France. Historians know little about him except that he was skilled in astronomy and mathematics.

In Pytheas's time, another Mediterranean power competed with Greece and Rome. The Phoenicians had expanded from their homeland (in what is now Lebanon) and, like the Greeks, had planted settlements around the Mediterranean Sea. Some Phoenician merchants had even ventured into the Atlantic Ocean in order to trade Mediterranean goods for tin and silver from mines in western Europe and the British Isles. To control the trade in these metals, the Phoenicians tried to keep the location of the mines a secret. They set up a blockade by posting ships in the Strait of Gibraltar, the narrow waterway that connects the Mediterranean Sea with the Atlantic Ocean. The Phoenician ships refused to allow mariners from other nations to enter the ocean.

Despite the blockade, Pytheas left Massilia around 325 B.C. and made his way into the northern Atlantic. Most historians believe that he sneaked past the Phoenicians and sailed through the Strait of Gibraltar. Others have suggested, however, that he traveled overland through France and boarded a ship near the English Channel.

Metal, Amber, and Thick Water

On the west coast of what later became England and Wales, Pytheas visited tin mines and learned about the tin industry. He then sailed all the way around the British Isles, landing in many places to investigate local conditions. He reported that the country was very cold and that its inhabitants, though friendly, lived hard and uncomfortable lives.

Historians disagree about Pytheas's route from that point. He later wrote of "the island of Thule," which could be reached by sailing north from the British Isles for six days. He said that at Thule, in the middle of summer, the sun remained in the sky for 24 hours a day. This clue and other descriptions have led historians to believe that Thule was either Iceland or part of Norway. But they are not certain whether Pytheas visited this place himself or merely learned about it while in Britain. He also said that beyond Thule the sea water began to thicken, so that ships could not sail through it. That report baffled and amazed his doubtful fellow Greeks, but modern scholars believe that it is the first known description of ice forming in the frigid northern waters.

In his account of his voyage, Pytheas went on to describe the northern coast of Europe. In one passage, he wrote about an island where the sea washed ashore valuable chunks of amber. This reference may be to the coasts of Germany or Sweden, on the Baltic Sea. He also mentioned reaching the mouth of a river in that region, which may have been the Vistula River (now in Poland).

Author, Astronomer, Geographer

After returning to Massilia, Pytheas wrote an account of his journey. Unfortunately, no copies of *On the Ocean* exist today. Pytheas's story is known only from the work of other ancient writers who quoted from his account or mentioned it. Many of them were scornful and called Pytheas a liar because his tales seemed so incredible. Few people could believe that there were places where the sun shone all night or where the sea was too thick to sail through. But in the following centuries, other travelers discovered such places again.

Despite the doubts about his work as an explorer, Pytheas had a successful career as a mathematician. He used geometry to show that the length of a day in a given location is related to the location's **latitude,** and he accurately measured the latitude of Massilia. He also studied tides, which he suggested were caused by the moon, and made accurate observations of the position of the Pole Star, which was used by sailors to find north and to determine latitude. Some historians have proposed that Pytheas made his voyage partly to make observations to test his theories.

SUGGESTED READING Felix Barker and others, *The Glorious Age of Exploration* (Doubleday and Company, 1973); Ann Gaines, *Herodotus and the Explorers of the Classical Age* (Chelsea House, 1994).

latitude distance north or south of the equator

Qian, Zhang. See *Zhang Qian.*

Quadra, Juan Francisco de la Bodega y. See *Bodega y Quadra, Juan Francisco de la.*

Quesada, Gonzalo Jiménez de. See *Jiménez de Quesada, Gonzalo.*

Quirós, Pedro Fernandez de

Portuguese
b 1565; Evarol, Portugal
d 1614; Panama
Discovered Vanuatu;
explored Marquesas and Santa Cruz Islands

Pedro Fernandez de Quirós was a Portuguese navigator who was known for his religious zeal. During a voyage to seek *Terra Australis Incognita* on behalf of Spain, he discovered an island that is now part of Vanuatu. However, his attempts to build a city there were unsuccessful, and in just 20 years, he went from hero to outcast. His death marked the end of ocean exploration by Spain for nearly 200 years.

Rising to the Occasion

Quirós was born in the Portuguese province of Evarol, but he spent most of his life in the service of Spain. When he was about 30 years old, he was appointed chief pilot for a voyage commanded by Alvaro de MENDAÑA DE NEHRA. It was Mendaña's second attempt

Pedro Fernandez de Quirós hoped to build a perfect Christian society on a Pacific island, but Spanish officials did not share his vision.

to establish a Roman Catholic colony in the Pacific Ocean. After Mendaña died in the Santa Cruz Islands, the islanders became hostile toward the Europeans. Quirós led the would-be settlers on a three-month voyage in rotting boats through uncharted seas. When they safely reached the Philippine Islands, Quirós was considered a hero.

Quirós next went to Peru and then to Spain. From there he traveled to Rome with a new vision. He believed that he had been divinely chosen to discover *Terra Australis Incognita,* the continent said to lie in the southern Pacific Ocean. Quirós also felt that God wanted him to establish there a European settlement, where all would live in Christian brotherhood. Quirós even received the blessing of Pope Clement VIII for his quest. Although religious conversion was often a goal of Spanish expeditions, Quirós was especially passionate about his mission. In the front of each of his ships, he placed a statue of Saint Peter, the founder of the church.

A Mysterious Decision

Quirós left Peru on December 21, 1605, with three ships. Less than five months later, he sighted a large, mountainous landmass. It was an island in a group of islands now known as Vanuatu. He named the island Austrialia del Espíritu Santo. It is still known as Espíritu Santo today.

Quirós often conducted lengthy religious ceremonies, and he strictly regulated the behavior of his crewmen. His emphasis on religion made him unpopular with the men, and his efforts to build a city on Espíritu Santo angered the people native to the island. Perhaps because of the tension among his crew and the unrest among the islanders, Quirós left his expedition and sailed for Peru after only three weeks on the island. He did not even tell his second-in-command, Luis Vaez de TORRES, why he was leaving. His reasons are still unknown.

Quirós reached Acapulco on November 23, 1606, and seven months later, Torres led the rest of the expedition from Espíritu Santo to the Philippines. The Spanish authorities disapproved of Quirós's actions. Although they had once praised him for his insight, they now regarded him as a fraud and a nuisance. They refused to grant his requests for funds for a new expedition. Quirós became very poor and spent his time writing papers in an effort to clear his name.

Finally, in October 1614, Spanish officials in Madrid gave Quirós a letter that authorized a new expedition. At the same time, they told officials in Peru to ignore the letter and not to provide the explorer with ships. Quirós never learned of their deception, for he died in Panama on his way to Peru.

SUGGESTED READING Sir Clements Markham, *The Voyages of Pedro Fernandez de Quirós* (Hakluyt Society, 1904).

Radisson, Pierre Esprit

French
b 1636; Paris, France?
d 1710; England
Opened up Hudson Bay to fur trade

New France French colony that included the St. Lawrence River valley, the Great Lakes region, and until 1713, Acadia (now called Nova Scotia)

The shifting loyalties of the French fur trader Pierre Esprit Radisson affected the histories of the French and British Empires in North America.

While hunting for beaver furs, Pierre Esprit Radisson and his brother-in-law, Médard Chouart des GROSEILLIERS, recognized an opportunity to start a profitable fur trading business near Hudson Bay. When France rejected the opportunity to support their venture, Radisson and Groseilliers sought and won the backing of England. The fur traders eventually formed England's Hudson's Bay Company. By declining to back them, France weakened its chances for lasting power in North America.

The Perfect Partner

Radisson arrived in **New France** in about 1651. Within the year, he was captured by Iroquois Indians while he was hunting near Trois-Rivières, Québec. The Iroquois adopted Radisson, who was only 15 years old at the time. He eventually escaped and traveled to Fort Orange (present-day Albany, New York), where he served as an interpreter until he was able to return to Trois-Rivières.

In 1653 his widowed half sister married Groseilliers, who was the perfect partner for Radisson. Groseilliers was a careful organizer, while Radisson was adventurous and outgoing. Groseilliers went on a fur-trading journey west of Québec from 1654 to 1656, but it is not clear whether Radisson went with him. The pair did journey west together in 1659 and may have reached the upper Mississippi River. While on this expedition, they made contact with some midwestern Indians. Until that time, the Huron and other eastern Indian tribes had acted as middlemen in the fur trade, keeping their midwestern rivals away from the Europeans.

Radisson and Groseilliers spent long winter nights with Indians around campfires north of Lake Superior. The Cree, Sioux, and Huron tribes spoke of ponds full of beaver between Lake Superior and Hudson Bay. Radisson and Groseilliers knew that carrying furs to Québec by an overland route was slow and difficult. They quickly realized that it would be much easier to ship their beaver pelts to market by sea from Hudson Bay.

The partners returned to Québec with a rich supply of valuable furs. Since they also came equipped with information on the location of additional furs and had a plan for transporting them out of the wilderness more easily, Radisson and Groseilliers expected a hero's welcome. Instead their furs were seized, and the traders were fined because they had left Québec without a license from the governor to trade. The French officials sold the partners' furs to help support the colony. Angered by their unfair treatment, Radisson and Groseilliers decided to take their business and their ideas elsewhere.

The Hudson's Bay Company Is Born

For several years, the two partners traded in New England and what is now eastern Canada. While in Boston in 1664, they met Colonel George Cartwright, an officer for King Charles II of England. The fur traders presented Cartwright with a proposal for a journey to Hudson Bay to develop the British fur trade there. Cartwright took them to London, where they explained their plan to the king himself. Charles II was always interested in schemes that would make money for his court. He promised them a ship to make a trading voyage to Hudson Bay.

Sponsored and supplied by England's Prince Rupert and a group of English merchants, the expedition left in June 1668, with Radisson sailing on one ship and Groseilliers traveling on another. But a violent storm forced Radisson's ship to turn back, and he spent the next two years waiting in London while Groseilliers completed the voyage and set to work in Canada.

The partners were reunited when Groseilliers returned to London. His successful trading expedition had proved their theory that a profitable fur-trading business could be operated out of Hudson Bay. Charles II was pleased to grant a royal charter establishing the existence of the Hudson's Bay Company. He gave the company the right to trade in the waters and lands of the Hudson Bay region.

Back to the French

Radisson made several voyages to Hudson Bay on behalf of the newly formed company. But by 1674, he and Groseilliers had decided that the English did not appreciate their efforts. They switched their loyalties back to France and tried to ruin England's business in the Hudson Bay region. On one occasion in 1683, Radisson tricked a group of inexperienced English traders and managed to return to Québec not only with his own furs but with theirs as well. But once again the French failed to reward Radisson for his accomplishments. Instead they charged a tax of 25 percent on the furs. Enraged, Radisson went back to the English.

Although Radisson remained loyal to England from then on, he was not well treated by the company that he and Groseilliers had helped to create. As time passed, he gradually lost his influence in the company, and he was eventually forced to beg for a job at its London warehouse. According to official records, the Hudson's Bay Company paid a very small sum for Radisson's funeral expenses when he died in 1710.

Radisson left behind a written account of his adventures. The work, titled *Voyages,* is full of descriptive details that are vivid but not always accurate. His greatest contribution to exploration was the creation of the Hudson's Bay Company, which still exists today.

SUGGESTED READING Arthur T. Adams, editor, *The Exploration of Pierre Esprit Radisson* (Ross and Haines, 1961); Grace Lee Nute, *Caesars of the Wilderness: Médard Chouart, Sieur des Groseilliers and Pierre Esprit Radisson, 1618–1710* (reprint, Minnesota Historical Society, 1978); Pierre Esprit Radisson, *Voyages of Pierre Esprit Radisson* (Burt Franklin, 1967).

Rae, John

Scottish
b September 30, 1813; Orkney Islands, Scotland
d July 22, 1893; London, England
Explored Arctic coast of Canada

Inuit people of the Canadian Arctic, sometimes known as the Eskimo

Northwest Passage water route connecting the Atlantic Ocean and Pacific Ocean through the Arctic islands of northern Canada

scurvy disease caused by a lack of vitamin C and once a major cause of death among sailors; symptoms include internal bleeding, loosened teeth, and extreme fatigue

John Rae of Scotland did not achieve great fame as an Arctic explorer, but his skills and accomplishments were extraordinary.

The Arctic explorer John Rae was the man who finally solved the mystery of Sir John FRANKLIN's missing expedition. In 1848 the British navy and Franklin's wife, Lady Jane Franklin, launched one of the biggest rescue missions in history. Rae, who was conducting a survey of the Canadian Arctic, was invited to join the search for Franklin. Using survival skills adopted from the **Inuit,** Rae and four men from the Hudson's Bay Company succeeded in their mission. On the same trip, Rae found the strait that separates King William Island from Boothia Peninsula (now called Rae Strait). This waterway was the last link in the discovery of the **Northwest Passage.**

From Surgeon to Explorer

Rae began working in the Arctic region in 1833, when he joined the Hudson's Bay Company. He was hired as ship's surgeon and eventually became the company's resident surgeon at Moose Factory, south of James Bay. While in the polar region, Rae developed skills as a hunter and mastered the Inuit methods of travel by snowshoe, dogsled, and canoe. He learned how to build igloos and how to ward off **scurvy** by eating berries and freshly killed animals. Rae undertook his first journey of exploration in 1846, charting 700 miles of coastline from Melville Peninsula to Boothia Peninsula.

Proof of a Tragedy

In 1848 the British navy invited Rae to join Sir John Richardson in an overland search for Sir John Franklin along the north coast of the Canadian mainland, between the Mackenzie River and the Coppermine River. Although the expedition failed to find the missing explorer, Rae impressed his supervisors with his skills, and he was put in charge of another search party. This second expedition surveyed the southern coast of Victoria Island and then headed north through Victoria Strait. Rae then made a survey of Boothia Peninsula and discovered the strait that separates it from King William Island. While in that area, he heard accounts of Franklin's fate from some Pelly Bay Inuit, who sold him silver spoons and other objects that had belonged to Franklin and his men. With this hard evidence in his possession, Rae reported the tragic news to Britain in 1854.

After the Boothia survey, Rae led an active life of exploring and pursued his scientific interests. He charted hundreds of miles of coastline and is said to have walked more than 23,000 miles through the Arctic, often at record-breaking paces. Although Rae was never celebrated as a great Arctic explorer, his travel techniques and survival skills rank him with Roald AMUNDSEN.

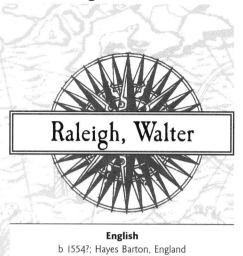

Raleigh, Walter

English
b 1554?; Hayes Barton, England
d October 29, 1618; London, England
Organized first English settlement in North America; explored Orinoco River

El Dorado mythical ruler, city, or area of South America believed to possess much gold

privateer privately owned ship hired by a government to attack enemy ships

SUGGESTED READING E. E. Rich and Alice M. Johnson, editors, *John Rae's Correspondence with the Hudson's Bay Company on Arctic Exploration, 1844-1855* (Hudson's Bay Record Society, 1953); R. L. Richards, *Dr. John Rae* (Caedmon of Whitby, 1985).

Sir Walter Raleigh is perhaps best known as the loyal knight who spread his cloak over a mud puddle so that Queen Elizabeth I would not get her shoes wet. However, Raleigh achieved much more in his lifetime than such simple noble acts. He established two early English settlements at Roanoke, in what is now North Carolina. The Roanoke colony did not last long, but it was England's first organized attempt to settle North America. Later, Raleigh explored the Orinoco River in South America in search of the fabled land of **El Dorado.**

A Man of Vision

Raleigh was the younger half brother of Sir Humphrey GILBERT. Like Gilbert, he was persuasive, insightful, and a favorite of Queen Elizabeth I. When Gilbert was lost at sea on a return voyage from North America, Raleigh took over his brother's plans to start an English colony there. A well-organized leader, Raleigh first sent out an expedition to explore the North American coast and select a site for settlement. Led by Philip Amadas and Arthur Barlowe, the party left Plymouth, England, in April 1584. They landed on an island near what is now Nags Head, North Carolina, and claimed it for England. After a peaceful encounter with the Roanoke Indians, they headed home, arriving in September.

Queen Elizabeth knighted Raleigh for this successful mission. Raleigh named the new territory Virginia after Elizabeth, who was called the Virgin Queen because she was not married. The name Virginia was applied at that time to all of England's possessions along the Atlantic coast of North America south of Cape Breton, which is now part of Nova Scotia.

Raleigh spent the winter of 1584 to 1585 preparing a colonizing expedition for the next spring. Although he did some **privateering** to finance the journey, he did not raise enough money. The queen agreed to grant him funds on the condition that he stay at home. She did not want to lose Raleigh as she had lost Gilbert.

Raleigh appointed Sir Richard Grenville commander of the voyage and chose Ralph Lane to become the governor of the colony once it was established. Raleigh also began a long tradition in English exploration by naming a scientist to make maps and to study the new land and its peoples. Raleigh even sent an artist to make drawings of Indians, animals, and plants. In just seven months, he organized an expedition that involved 500 people.

Scared Away

The ships set sail on April 9, 1585, with about 250 sailors and 108 colonists aboard. The remaining crew members were soldiers, specialists, and others who were not expected to stay in the colony. On July 3, the fleet arrived at Roanoke Island. While most of the crew stayed on board, Grenville led a group on an exploration of

Sir Walter Raleigh dreamed of colonizing both North and South America with English settlers.

Pamlico Sound. This body of water separates the eastern shore of what is now North Carolina from a group of narrow barrier islands.

The Indians of Roanoke Island invited the English to establish a colony there. However, the other local Indians did not welcome the strangers to the area. After a while, relations between the colonists and the Indians became very unfriendly. The English began to fear attacks, and there was a great deal of tension among the settlers. They were also worried about how long their supplies would last. When Sir Francis DRAKE visited the colony in June 1586, the surviving colonists suddenly decided to go back to England with him. They were so eager to escape that they left behind three men who were out exploring.

The Lost Colony

Raleigh was surprised when the first group of colonists returned home, but he immediately made plans to send another group. In the spring of 1587, a party of 117 settlers arrived in Roanoke. The 14 families and 78 unmarried men were led by John White, who had participated in the first expedition. Their plan was to start a new settlement on Chesapeake Bay, possibly near the mouth of the James River. For reasons that are not clear today, however, the ship's captain refused to go farther than Roanoke.

Remembering the failures of the first group of colonists, the Englishmen tried to improve relations with the local Indians. For a time, everything seemed to be going well. On August 18, 1587, Governor White's daughter gave birth to Virginia Dare, the first English child born in North America. As the ships prepared to sail back to England later that month, the colonists asked White to return to their homeland. They wanted him to keep Raleigh interested in the colony and to request more supplies.

White accepted the mission, but it was three years before he was able to return to Roanoke. In 1588 the fleet known as the Spanish Armada attacked England. This crisis required all of England's attention and resources. When White finally managed to sail back to Roanoke in 1590, he found no trace of the colonists. He did find one word carved on a tree: "Croatoan." This word was the name the Indians used for what is now called Hatteras Island. White believed that the colonists had moved there. Croatoan was a fairly safe island where the Indians were friendly. But when White tried to reach it, bad weather drove his ship farther and farther into the Atlantic Ocean, and he decided to return to England.

None of the Roanoke colonists was ever seen again. However, a legend has survived among the Lumbee Indians of present-day Robeson County, North Carolina. According to this oral tradition, the colonists married and lived among members of the tribe. If the tales are true, then some of the Lumbee are descendants of the lost colonists of Roanoke.

Time in the Tower

Raleigh had failed to establish a permanent colony in North America, but he soon had greater worries. In 1588 he married, keeping this fact a secret because he knew that Queen Elizabeth would be displeased by his attachment to another woman. Four years later, his wife gave birth to a son, and Raleigh's deception was revealed. The queen imprisoned Raleigh and his wife in the Tower of London. Although Raleigh was eventually set free, he was no longer welcome in the royal court. As a result, he had much more freedom to pursue his own adventures.

In 1595 he set off for South America in search of the legendary kingdom of El Dorado. Dropping anchor off the island of Trinidad, Raleigh entered the swamps and rain forest of the Orinoco River (in present-day Venezuela). The expedition failed to find gold, but Raleigh returned to England with tall tales about headless men whose eyes were in their shoulders and whose mouths were in the middle of their chests.

Several years later, Queen Elizabeth died, and James I became the king. Raleigh did not find favor with the new ruler. James was a Catholic and wanted to make peace with Spain, a mostly Catholic nation. Since Raleigh was openly opposed to Spain, he was again imprisoned in the Tower of London. Charged with plotting against the king, Raleigh remained in prison for 13 years under a death sentence. In 1616 he tried to obtain his freedom by proposing another expedition to South America. He promised to bring back gold without raiding any Spanish mines. James released him from the tower, but the king warned Raleigh that he would be put to death if he engaged in piracy.

Raleigh again traveled up the Orinoco River. But the only gold to be found was in the mines that were controlled by the Spaniards. Raleigh's son was killed in a fight at one of these mines. When Raleigh returned to England without riches, the king used the incident at the mine as an excuse for ordering the death sentence. Raleigh was executed in 1618.

SUGGESTED READING Henrietta Buckmaster, *Walter Raleigh: Man of Two Worlds* (Random House, 1964); Robert Lacey, *Sir Walter Raleigh* (Atheneum, 1973); Willard M. Wallace, *Sir Walter Raleigh* (Princeton University Press, 1959); H. Ross Williamson, *Sir Walter Raleigh* (reprint, Greenwood, 1978).

Rapôso de Tavares, Antonio

Portuguese
b 1598?; Alentejo, Portugal
d ?; ?

*Explored South America from east coast of
Brazil to Andes Mountains in Peru*

Antonio Rapôso de Tavares is honored by Brazilians as an explorer, pioneer, and patriot. In 1627 he organized and led the first **bandeira** in what later became Argentina and southern Brazil. Rapôso de Tavares later headed several other raids into what are now Paraguay, Bolivia, Uruguay, and Peru. On one of these journeys, he crossed South America from the Atlantic coast of Brazil to the Andes in Peru and then traveled down the Amazon River. These bandeiras increased Portugal's power in South America and brought new slave labor and wealth to Brazil's economy.

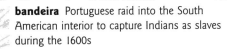

bandeira Portuguese raid into the South American interior to capture Indians as slaves during the 1600s

Jesuit member of the Society of Jesus, a Roman Catholic order founded by Ignatius of Loyola in 1534

bandeirante member of a Portuguese raid into Brazil during the 1600s

Treaty of Tordesillas agreement between Spain and Portugal dividing the rights to discovered lands along a north-south line

tributary stream or river that flows into a larger stream or river

Village Raids

Antonio Rapôso de Tavares was born in about 1598 in Portugal. He arrived in São Vicente (in what is now Brazil) with his father in 1618 and moved to São Paulo four years later. In 1627 Rapôso de Tavares led the first major bandeira. Traveling south into the Paraná River valley (in present-day Argentina), he raided villages of Indians who had been converted to Christianity by **Jesuit** missionaries. He then pushed into the Guaira region in southern Brazil, where he defeated the occupying Spaniards, enslaved the Indians, and claimed the land for Portugal.

While the Spanish focused their attention on the riches of Peru, Rapôso de Tavares and other **bandeirantes** crossed the boundary that had been agreed upon by the Spanish and Portuguese in the **Treaty of Tordesillas.** The bandeirantes claimed the lands they explored for Portugal. From 1636 to 1638, Rapôso de Tavares raided the territory of the Itati Indians along the Taquari River in what is now western Brazil.

An Expanded Mission

The Portuguese monarchy was restored in 1641, after years of Spanish rule. As a result, the bandeira movement became involved more in politics than in the capture of slaves. In May 1648, Rapôso de Tavares set out on what would be called "the greatest bandeira by the greatest bandeirante." His main goal was to gather geographical information to help Portugal establish boundaries with Spanish territory. The Portuguese also hoped to open a route to Peru and to search for silver or gold deposits.

Rapôso de Tavares left São Paulo with 200 Portuguese and more than 1,000 Indians. He traveled downstream on the Tietê River to the Paraná River; then he journeyed westward overland to Corumbá, where he waited until the end of the rainy season. In April or May 1649, the bandeirantes crossed the swampy regions of the upper Paraguay River. When they reached the Chaco region of Paraguay, the journey became very difficult. The men fought off starvation, fever, and Indian attacks.

From Paraguay the expedition went around the eastern slopes of the Andes to Potosí. After exploring several little-known rivers in what is now Bolivia, the Portuguese navigated the Río Grande, where their journey became easier. Following the Grande to the Mamoré and Madeira Rivers, Rapôso de Tavares approached the Amazon River. Although his exact route from this point is uncertain, he eventually arrived in Quito (in what is now Ecuador). According to legend, he waded into the Pacific Ocean holding his sword high in triumph. However, there is no historical proof that he reached the Pacific. From Quito the bandeirantes traveled down the **tributaries** of the upper Amazon and into the Amazon River itself. They took a detour to explore the Río Negro and then continued down the Amazon to the east coast of Brazil.

The Mystery Man

Rapôso de Tavares returned to São Paulo in 1652. He was so scarred and battered from his difficult journey that his family and friends did not recognize him. The bandeiras of Rapôso de Tavares are well recorded in historical documents, but the man himself remains a mystery. The date and place of his death are still unknown. Nevertheless, his great bandeira, covering over 7,000 miles through vast and unexplored areas, made him a legendary hero of Brazil.

SUGGESTED READING John Hemming, *Red Gold: The Conquest of the Brazilian Indians* (Harvard University Press, 1978); Richard M. Morse, editor, *The Bandeirantes: The Historical Role of the Brazilian Pathfinders* (Alfred A. Knopf, 1965).

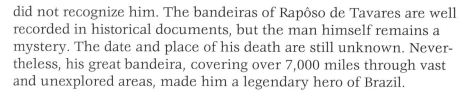

Rasmussen, Knud Johan Victor

Danish
b June 7, 1879; Jakobshavn, Greenland
d December 21, 1933; Gentofte, Denmark
*Explored Greenland and Canadian Arctic;
studied Inuit cultures*

Inuit people of the Canadian Arctic, sometimes known as the Eskimo

Knud Rasmussen's ability to speak the difficult Inuit language aided his investigation of their culture.

Driven by curiosity about his **Inuit** heritage, Knud Johan Victor Rasmussen traveled across the Arctic Ocean from eastern Greenland to the Bering Strait. Although earlier explorers had already discovered all of the major sites in the polar region, Rasmussen made some useful corrections to Robert PEARY's flawed map of northern Greenland. Rasmussen also made important contributions to the modern understanding of Inuit culture. From a trading station on the northwest coast of Greenland, he led a series of seven scientific missions, known as the Thule Expeditions. Rasmussen began with a study of the Polar Inuit and their environment but then expanded his research to include all of the Inuit peoples.

Child of Two Worlds

Rasmussen was born in a small settlement on the shores of Disko Bay in western Greenland, where his Danish father was a missionary to the Inuit. Knud's mother was part Inuit, and the boy grew up learning the customs and languages of both the Danish and the Inuit cultures. Although his studies at Copenhagen University provided him with insight into European culture, Rasmussen longed to understand his mother's Inuit heritage. As a young boy, he had heard a great deal about the Polar Inuit, a tribe that had maintained most of its own traditions. The Polar Inuit were said to live "with the North Wind himself." When he was 12 years old, Rasmussen decided that he would visit them someday.

In 1900 he went to Iceland as a reporter for the *Christian Daily* newspaper. The following year, he traveled to Swedish Lapland to collect materials for his book about the Lapps, the people native to the far northern regions of Scandinavia. When he was 23 years old, he finally reached the far north of Greenland as part of a Danish expedition. Rasmussen felt that he was being called by his ancestors, and he returned to Greenland's Cape York district many times to visit the Polar Inuit. In time, he was accepted into the tribe, as he put it, "as one of their own, as a friend and fellow-hunter."

In 1910 Rasmussen set up a trading station that he called Thule, on Wolstenholme Fjord north of Cape York. The station was also established as a base for exploration and research in northern Greenland. Working with Peter Freuchen, Rasmussen began to introduce modern practices and European culture to the local people. Peary had already changed the region's economy by bringing guns and raw materials such as steel and lumber to the region. Rasmussen wanted to continue this process without destroying the

Inuit's traditions. He hoped to create a similar balance between Inuit and European ways in his own life.

The Thule Expeditions

In 1912 Rasmussen led the first Thule Expedition on a mission to find a missing group led by Einar Mikkelsen. Accompanied by Freuchen, two Inuit, and 54 dogs, Rasmussen crossed the Greenland ice sheet from Clements Markham Glacier on the west coast to Denmark Fjord on the northeast coast. After covering this 504-mile stretch, the party traveled 72 miles from the base of the **fjord** to the Greenland Sea. Along the way, Rasmussen made discoveries in the Denmark Fjord region and proved that what Peary had called a channel was not a fjord but a lowland.

The next three Thule expeditions continued research on Greenland. The explorers studied its ice cap, the geography of the north coast, and the mythology of the Polar Inuit. Rasmussen led the Second Thule Expedition in 1917 on an investigation of the major inlets of the north coast of Greenland. He was not part of the third expedition of 1919, which left food supplies for Roald AMUNDSEN at Cape Columbia. But Rasmussen resumed his explorations the following year on an expedition to the east coast. There he collected Inuit stories in the settlement of Angmagssalik.

Tracing the Past

The Fifth Thule Expedition, from 1921 to 1924, was a large undertaking with several different stages and kinds of activities. Its main purpose was to gain an understanding of the migration of Inuit culture across North America. In the beginning stages, two Danish **anthropologists** studied the region around Danish Island in Canada's Hudson Bay. Their work showed that the culture of the modern Inuit differed from that of the Dorset culture that had flourished in the region over 1,000 years earlier. Other members of the expedition took valuable film footage of the Inuit.

For his own part, Rasmussen made an extensive 17-month survey of the Arctic coast of North America. Traveling with only two Inuit companions, he left Danish Island on March 11, 1923, and arrived at Kotzebue, Alaska, on August 21, 1924. He studied all of the Inuit peoples that he encountered along the way. Rasmussen had thoroughly mastered Inuit techniques of hunting and **sledge** travel. His party lived off the land and used the same dog team for the entire journey of more than 1,800 miles. No one else had ever attempted such a feat.

Rasmussen's accomplishment proved how easily the Inuit's ancestors could have come to North America from Asia. He collected proof that all of the modern Inuit peoples were descended from one great migration of people, which he called the Thule culture. Since then, other anthropologists and archaeologists have confirmed his findings. They have shown that the Thule Inuit culture replaced the earlier Dorset culture around A.D. 1000.

On the next two Thule expeditions, Rasmussen continued his work in southeastern Greenland. On his last journey, he came down with a case of food poisoning, followed by influenza and then

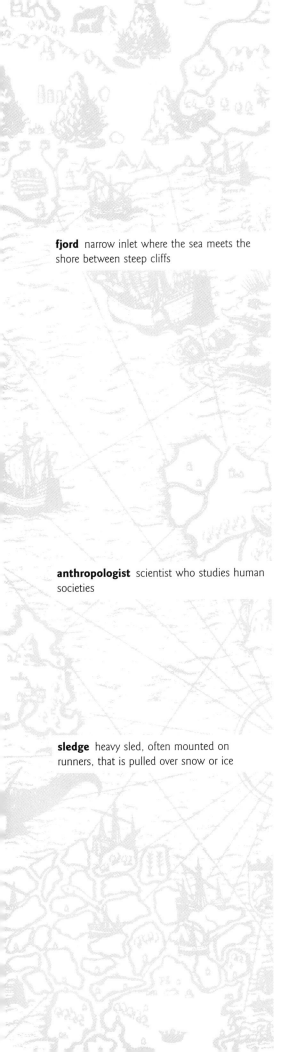

fjord narrow inlet where the sea meets the shore between steep cliffs

anthropologist scientist who studies human societies

sledge heavy sled, often mounted on runners, that is pulled over snow or ice

pneumonia. Rasmussen died on the way back to Copenhagen. His published works include *Greenland by the Polar Sea* (1919) and *Across Arctic America* (1928).

SUGGESTED READING Peter Freuchen, *I Sailed with Rasmussen* (Viking, 1961).

Ricci, Matteo

Italian
b October 6, 1552; Macerata, Italy
d May 11, 1610; Beijing, China
Traveled and lived in China; created world map

Jesuit member of the Society of Jesus, a Roman Catholic order founded by Ignatius of Loyola in 1534

mission settlement founded by priests in a land where they hoped to convert people to Christianity

Matteo Ricci was one of the first people to succeed in crossing the cultural barrier between China and Europe.

Matteo Ricci was a **Jesuit** missionary and scholar who was able to live and work in China at a time when it was closed to most outsiders. The emperor Wan-li called him to the royal city of Beijing and allowed him to spend the last nine years of his life there. While Ricci's intelligence certainly contributed to his success, the key factor was probably his efforts to adapt to Chinese culture. He mastered the Chinese language so well that he could memorize a list of 400 written Chinese characters after reading it once. He learned a great deal about China's land and people, and his maps of China were sought worldwide. Ricci's work provided China and Europe with a way to learn about each other.

Ricci's Mission

Matteo Ricci was the son of an Italian pharmacist. His father sent him to Rome to study law, but within several years, Ricci joined the Society of Jesus. After studying mathematics for a short time, Ricci volunteered to work at Jesuit **missions** in Asia. He was sent to Goa, a Portuguese settlement on the west coast of India, where he spent four years teaching rhetoric, the art of communication. He was then selected to become a missionary to China.

For 30 years, several different groups had been trying to establish a lasting Christian settlement in China. The Jesuits developed a new strategy. Rather than try to force European customs on the Chinese, they would adapt to Chinese ways. When Ricci went to the island of Macao to study the language, his superiors ordered that none of his other tasks be allowed to interfere with his language study.

Ricci's disciplined studies were assisted by a stroke of good luck. In 1583 a new governor came to power in Zhaoqing, which was then the capital of Guangdong province. He gave Ricci and a fellow Jesuit permission to settle in the city. The two Jesuits built a small mission house there, and they converted part of it into a museum of European culture. They furnished it with glass prisms, chiming clocks, and books showing maps of European towns and drawings of European architecture. The Jesuits hoped to introduce the culture of Europe to the Chinese who visited the museum.

Changing the World

An oval-shaped world map was hung on the wall in the visiting room of the mission house. This map startled the Chinese people who saw it. Ricci later wrote that the Chinese knew almost nothing of the outside world. In the

late 1500s, Chinese maps of the world showed the 15 existing Chinese provinces surrounded by sea and a few small foreign lands. The sea and the foreign lands together were smaller than one Chinese province.

The powerful officials of the empire asked Ricci to make a Chinese version of his world map for them. Ricci agreed, but he revised the map so that the officials would not be offended. He placed China in the center and used a method of mapmaking that exaggerated the size of the map's central regions. The result was a huge success among the Chinese. Ricci received so many requests for copies that he decided to redesign the map. He drew a new, larger map that included the most recent discoveries by explorers as well as information from Chinese sources.

More than a Mapmaker

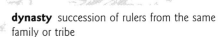

cartography the science of mapmaking

Ricci's new map has been called a breakthrough in **cartography.** It measured 6 feet by 12 feet and was printed on fine paper and silk. The map was accompanied by lengthy geographical notes and references. Its widespread influence is demonstrated by the records of the Ming **dynasty,** which show that a hand-painted copy of the map reached the emperor himself. Copies of the Ricci map were also sent to Europe, introducing European nations to the geography of China.

dynasty succession of rulers from the same family or tribe

Ricci's work was not limited to geography. High-ranking Chinese officials also asked him to teach them mathematics, and they sought his opinion on such other topics as the manufacture of clocks. Ricci's place in Chinese society gave him the freedom to make great advances in his missionary work. In 1601 the emperor Wan-li invited Ricci to the imperial city of Beijing. Ricci remained there until he died in 1610.

SUGGESTED READING Matteo Ricci, *China in the Sixteenth Century, in the Journals of Matteo Ricci, 1583–1610,* translated by Louis J. Gallagher and S. J. Gallagher (Random House, 1953).

Richthofen, Ferdinand Paul Wilhelm von

German
b May 5, 1833; Karlsruhe, near Brieg, Prussia (now Brzeg, Poland)
d October 6, 1905; Poland
Explored China and wrote about its geography

geologist scientist who studies the earth's natural history

geology the scientific study of the earth's natural history

Ferdinand Paul Wilhelm von Richthofen used his skills as both a geographer and a **geologist** to make great improvements in maps of China. He went on a long series of journeys in that country and presented the geographical data he gathered in a five-volume work. Some of his other writings dealt with the tasks, methods, and goals of geography in the 1800s.

Richthofen's early work focused on the **geology** of Transylvania (in what is now Romania) and of the Alps in northern Italy. His accomplishments led to an invitation to serve as the geologist on an 1860 German mission to Asia. He visited Ceylon (now Sri Lanka), Japan, Formosa (now Taiwan), the Celebes, Java (in present-day Indonesia), and the Philippines. He also crossed the Malay Peninsula from Bangkok to Moulmein, Burma (now Myanmar). In 1863 Richthofen began to study the geology of California. Some of his work led to the discovery of new goldfields there.

Richthofen then returned to Asia and led a series of seven expeditions that covered almost every region of China. On the first trip, he followed the course of the Chang Jiang (also known as the Yangtze River) and explored the area to its south. He later traveled the entire eastern coast of China from the Liaodong Peninsula southwest to Guangzhou (also known as Canton). Richthofen also explored China's interior. He traveled over land between Beijing and Guangzhou and explored the provinces of Shanxi, Shaanxi, and Sichuan, a few years after Francis GARNIER was there.

SUGGESTED READING Ettinger, Nathalie, and others, *Exploring Africa and Asia* (Doubleday, 1973).

Ride, Sally Kristen

American
b May 26, 1951; Encino, California
living
First American woman in space

---

astronaut American term for a person who travels into space; literally, "traveler to the stars"

Sally Ride almost became a professional athlete, but she chose science instead and became the United States's first woman astronaut.

Sally Kristen Ride was the United States's first woman **astronaut.** Her achievement came 20 years after Russia's Valentina TERESHKOVA became the first woman in space. Ride's entry into the U.S. space program and her two missions on the **space shuttle** were the result of important changes in space exploration: a greater emphasis on scientific missions and a new desire to train a more diverse astronaut corps.

Science in School

Throughout her childhood in California, Sally Ride was an outstanding athlete, and her skill in tennis earned her a partial scholarship to a private high school. Ride soon discovered that she was interested in physics, but she dropped out of Swarthmore College to become a professional tennis player. Before long, however, she decided that science would make a better career. Ride enrolled at Stanford University in California, earned undergraduate degrees in physics and English, and went on to earn her Ph.D. in physics.

In 1977, while looking for a job as a research physicist, Ride learned that **NASA** wanted young scientists to fly on future space missions. Though she had never before considered becoming an astronaut, she decided to apply.

Science in Space

America's first astronauts had all been test pilots in the military. All of them were men because there were no women test pilots. By the 1970s, however, NASA was moving away from the sort of missions that had required only experienced test pilots—such as the early flights into **orbit** and to the moon. NASA trained scientists to work on the **space station** *Skylab,* but again, only men were chosen.

By 1980, NASA had readied a vehicle for a new phase of the space program: the reusable space shuttle. Pilots would still fly the shuttle, but the missions included much scientific work that would be best performed by expert scientists and engineers. At the same time, women in the United States were succeeding in many jobs that had once been closed to them, and the number of women scientists

space shuttle reusable spacecraft designed to transport people and cargo between the earth and space

NASA National Aeronautics and Space Administration, the U.S. space agency

orbit stable, circular route; one trip around; to revolve around

space station spacecraft that circles the earth for months or years with a human crew

Rivera, Juan Maria de

Spanish
b 1700s; ?
d 1700s; ?
Explored American Southwest

New Spain region of Spanish colonial empire that included the areas now occupied by Mexico, Florida, Texas, New Mexico, Arizona, California, and various Caribbean islands

Jesuit member of the Society of Jesus, a Roman Catholic order founded by Ignatius of Loyola in 1534

was increasing. The U.S. government insisted that NASA include qualified women among the newest astronauts.

Sally Ride was one of the first six women chosen. In 1982, NASA selected Ride to fly on *Challenger* on its seventh shuttle mission. About to be the first American woman in space, Ride became an overnight celebrity. Although she did not care for publicity, she knew that she had become a role model and that it was important for her to succeed. As she said, "People were going to be watching what I did really closely." Her duties aboard the shuttle *Challenger* included assisting the pilot during launch and landing as well as testing the shuttle's mechanical robot arm. The six-day mission, in June 1983, went smoothly, and upon landing she reported: "I'm sure that it was the most fun that I'll ever have in my life."

Ride made a second flight on *Challenger* in 1984. Two years later, the shuttle exploded, and Ride served on the committee that investigated the disaster. Eager to return to research, she left NASA in 1987 and became a physics professor at Stanford University and the University of California at San Diego.

SUGGESTED READING Carolyn Blacknall, *Sally Ride: America's First Woman in Space* (Dillon Press, 1984); Barbara Kramer, *Sally Ride: A Space Biography* (Enslow, 1998); Karen O'Connor, *Sally Ride and the New Astronauts: Scientists in Space* (Franklin Watts, 1983).

Juan Maria de Rivera was an experienced soldier on the northern frontier of **New Spain.** He made the first recorded journeys into the mountain regions that are now parts of Colorado and Utah. Between 1761 and 1765, Rivera led three expeditions north from Taos to the southern Rocky Mountains. While on a mission to the lands of the Ute Indians, Rivera navigated the Gunnison River in southwestern Colorado and reached southeastern Utah by way of the Colorado River.

A Moment in the Spotlight

There is no information on Rivera's life before he gained attention fighting for Spain in a war against the Ute Indians, who had attacked settlements along the northern frontier of New Spain. After the war, Rivera explored for gold, silver, and gemstones. He also guided **Jesuit** missionaries to what became the southwestern United States.

In 1761, on the first of three expeditions, Rivera headed northwest from Taos and followed the San Juan Piedra River into what is now Colorado. There he discovered silver ore and named the surrounding mountains the La Plata Mountains, which in Spanish means Silver Mountains.

Rivera took a group of soldiers, traders, and missionaries along the same route on his second journey. Passing just west of the La Plata Mountains, the party then followed the Dolores River to where it meets the San Miguel River. After crossing the San Miguel, the group climbed to the highland of the Uncompahgre Plateau.

The Lost Journals

In 1765 Rivera was sent by Governor Cachupín of the Spanish province of New Mexico on a trading mission into the lands of the

Ute. Rounding the San Juan Mountains, he traveled through the Uncompahgre River valley until he reached the junction of the Uncompahgre and Gunnison Rivers. There he carved a cross, his name, and the year on a tree. He traded with the Indians in the Gunnison River area and returned to New Mexico. Although his journal of the journey is now lost, most historians agree that on the return trip, he traveled down the Gunnison River to the Colorado River in southeastern Utah and then down the Dolores River. Nothing is known about his life after this mission.

Juan Maria de Rivera opened several important trade routes from New Spain into what became the southwestern United States. His journals provided Father Silvestre Vélez de ESCALANTE with important geographical information for an expedition 10 years later. Data gathered by Rivera also helped Alexander von HUMBOLDT to make his famous map in 1811.

SUGGESTED READING Frederic J. Athearn, *A Forgotten Kingdom: The Spanish Frontier in Colorado and New Mexico, 1540–1821* (Bureau of Land Management, Colorado State Office, 1992); Phil Carson, *Across the Northern Frontier: Spanish Explorations in Colorado* (Johnson Books, 1998).

Roggeveen, Jacob

Dutch
b February 1, 1659; Middelburg, the Netherlands
d 1729; ?
Discovered and named Easter Island

From 1721 to 1722, Jacob Roggeveen led the last great Dutch voyage of discovery into the Pacific Ocean. This journey marked the end of the Dutch search for *Terra Australis Incognita,* the unknown southern continent. Roggeveen discovered Easter Island and what is now Samoa.

An Inherited Opportunity

The son of a successful businessman, Roggeveen worked for the Dutch East India Company. He rose through the ranks and became a member of the Council of Justice in Batavia (now Jakarta, Indonesia). In 1696 Roggeveen's father proposed to the rival Dutch West India Company an expedition to find the southern continent. The elder Roggeveen died before starting the project, but in his will, he left his son the rights to the expedition.

By 1721 Jacob Roggeveen had retired from the Dutch East India Company with a large fortune. At the age of 62, he went to the Dutch West India Company and renewed his father's application for the voyage to seek *Terra Australis Incognita.* Captain Edward Davis claimed to have found a "low, sandy island" that was close to the legendary continent. Anxious to find these lands, the company approved Roggeveen's request and supplied him with three ships.

Roggeveen and his crew sailed south from the Netherlands on August 21, 1721. They fought off an attack by five pirate ships near the Canary Islands. After crossing the Atlantic Ocean, the fleet rounded South America's Cape Horn. During their three-week passage to the Pacific Ocean, the Dutch encountered cold, stormy weather, which led Roggeveen to believe that a large landmass existed in the polar region. Unaware of the existence of Antarctica, he thought that he was nearing *Terra Australis Incognita.*

Roggeveen was enchanted with his next landing place, the Juan Fernández Islands off the coast of Chile. He made plans to establish

Jacob Roggeveen of the Netherlands (second from left) commanded the last major Dutch voyage of discovery in the Pacific Ocean.

latitude distance north or south of the equator

anthropologist scientist who studies human societies

scurvy disease caused by a lack of vitamin C and once a major cause of death among sailors; symptoms include internal bleeding, loosened teeth, and extreme fatigue

a settlement there on his return voyage. From these islands, he proceeded west at a **latitude** of about 28° south in search of the land that Davis had reportedly found.

The Stone Statues of Easter Island

On Easter Sunday of 1722, Roggeveen reached a fertile, inhabited island, which he named Easter Island. He quickly established friendly relations with the islanders, even though they tried to take whatever they wanted from the Dutch—including the hats from the sailors' heads. The Dutch marveled at these people, who wore very little clothing and were covered with tattoos. The islanders' earlobes were pierced and stretched by ornaments, some of which were three inches long. Roggeveen wrote in his log that if the islanders' earlobes got in their way, they simply looped them over the tops of their ears.

When Roggeveen and his men went ashore, one of the islanders tried to grab a Dutchman's gun. In the brief fight that followed, 10 islanders were killed, but the rest remained friendly. They brought Roggeveen and his crew bananas, potatoes, sugarcane, and poultry.

Roggeveen and his men were further amazed to see the islanders worshiping 30-foot-high stone figures. The statues were made to look like human beings; some appeared to wear robes and carry great baskets on their heads. **Anthropologists** today still debate the meaning and origin of the stone figures.

Justice Prevails in Court

Easter Island was neither low nor sandy, so after a week, Roggeveen sailed on. In mid-May, he reached the outer islands of the northern Tuamotus. He stayed at what is now Takapoto, Makatéa. While they were there, members of Roggeveen's crew fired on a crowd of islanders who were standing on the beach. Although the Dutch tried to make peace after the incident, the islanders took revenge the next day. Ten Dutch sailors were stoned to death. In addition to these losses, one of Roggeveen's ships was wrecked on the dangerous reefs surrounding the islands.

After a month, Roggeveen held a meeting with his crew. They were discouraged by their inability to find *Terra Australis Incognita* and worried that their wages would not be paid. Instead of returning east to the Juan Fernández Islands, Roggeveen decided to continue west, toward Dutch outposts at Java (in present-day Indonesia). He sailed past Bora-Bora and other islands; then he headed for Samoa. By then, **scurvy** among the crew was so severe that Roggeveen did not dare to stop.

When Roggeveen reached Batavia, the Dutch East India Company seized his ships and sent him and his crew back to the Netherlands. After a legal battle in court, Roggeveen and his crew were finally paid for their hard work, but the Dutch West India Company did not consider Roggeveen's voyage a success. Today, however, a cape at the eastern tip of Easter Island bears Roggeveen's name in honor of his discovery.

Rohlfs, Friedrich Gerhard

German
b April 14, 1831; Vegesack, Prussia (now in Germany)
d June 2, 1896; Rüngsdorf, Germany
Explored North Africa

sultan ruler of a Muslim nation

mosque Muslim house of prayer and worship

Friedrich Rohlfs gave up a promising career as a soldier, doctor, and diplomat in order to explore North Africa.

SUGGESTED READING Jacob Roggeveen, *The Journal of Jacob Roggeveen*, edited by A. Sharp, (Clarendon University Press, 1970).

Friedrich Gerhard Rohlfs was the first European to cross Africa from the Mediterranean Sea to the Gulf of Guinea. His expeditions took him to many areas that had never before been visited by a European—most notably the Oases of Kufra in what is now Libya. Though Rohlfs did not have the technical training needed to conduct scientific research, his detailed sketches and accounts of his experiences proved valuable. His work helped to explain some of the mysteries of North Africa's lands and cultures.

Restless for Adventure

Rohlfs was a restless youth who quit both medical school and the Austrian army. He then joined the French Foreign Legion and was sent to Africa. He spent five years in Algeria, learning the local customs and language. When he was discharged in 1861, Rohlfs traveled to Morocco. Since he spoke Arabic and had medical training, he was appointed physician general to the army of the **sultan** of Morocco. His high rank was unusual in a land where foreigners were not often trusted. But Rohlfs soon became bored and left the post in 1862. Disguising himself as an Arab, he set out for the African interior. He headed south across Morocco's Atlas Mountains and continued to the Oases of Tafilalt. There he was attacked and almost killed by a band of robbers.

Despite this dangerous incident, Rohlfs pressed on, determined to learn what lay farther inland. The possibility of danger made the journey even more appealing to him. He first traveled east to Ghadames, though he was unable to reach Timbuktu. Then he journeyed south from Tripoli through the Sahara, successfully crossing the African continent from the Mediterranean to the Gulf of Guinea.

After accomplishing that feat, Rohlfs went back to Tripoli. From there he intended to head southeast, toward the Libyan Desert, but the German Colonial Office in Berlin had other plans for him. Impressed by his work in Africa, the office chose him for a diplomatic mission to Bornu (in present-day Nigeria). Rohlfs was to visit the sultan Omar on behalf of King William I of Prussia. However, Rohlfs was not interested in this commission. When he furiously protested his assignment, the office agreed to relieve him of the duty and asked him to find a substitute. Rohlfs persuaded the physician and explorer Gustav NACHTIGAL to take the post.

Desert Dreams

Rohlfs's goal was to become the first foreigner to travel southeast to Kufra. This town was home to the Senussi, a group of Muslims known for their aggression and hostility toward Christians. Rohlfs undertook three difficult expeditions through hundreds of miles of arid desert, and in 1879, after 10 years, he finally reached his destination. The seemingly endless desert led to the lakes, **mosques,** and castles of the Oases of Kufra. Rohlfs's visit was brief because the local people were so unfriendly. He later wrote that the 10-year

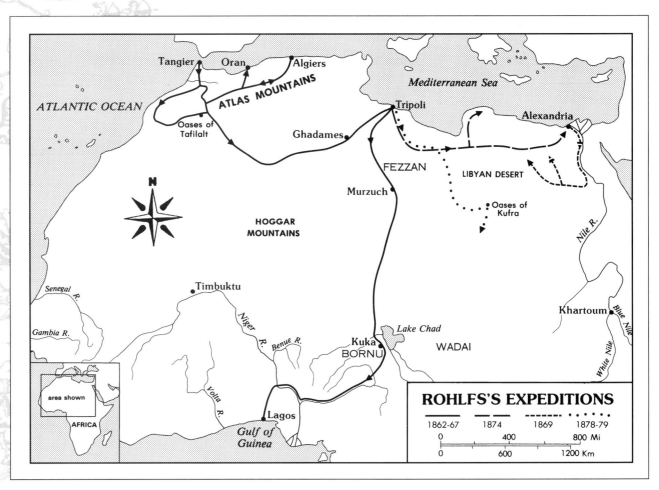

ROHLFS'S EXPEDITIONS			
1862-67	1874	1869	1878-79
0	400		800 Mi
0	600		1200 Km

Rohlfs spent nearly 20 years traveling in Africa. He greatly influenced Europe's understanding of the continent.

mission had aged him greatly but had been worthwhile. No other European visited Kufra for the next 40 years.

From Kufra, Rohlfs headed south on an expedition to Wadai (in modern Chad) on behalf of the German government. But at the beginning of the journey, he was attacked by Suaya Arabs. Since all of his equipment was stolen, he was forced to give up the project. Rohlfs's remaining days in Africa were spent peacefully as the German representative in Zanzibar. He later returned to Germany.

SUGGESTED READING Christopher Hibbert, *Africa Explored* (W. W. Norton, 1983).

Rondón, Cândido Mariano da Silva

Brazilian
b May 5, 1865; Cuiabá, Brazil
d January 19, 1958; Rio de Janeiro, Brazil
Explored northwest Brazil; discovered and explored River of Doubt

Between 1906 and 1909, Brigadier General Cândido Mariano da Silva Rondón explored 193,000 square miles of northwestern Brazil. He also charted the courses of 15 rivers and discovered the River of Doubt, known as the Rio da Dúvida in Portuguese. In 1913 he mapped the River of Doubt during a famous scientific expedition with former U.S. President Theodore ROOSEVELT.

Penetrating the Rain Forest
Rondón was born on May 5, 1865, in Cuiabá, Mato Grosso, Brazil. Orphaned at the age of one, he was raised by his uncle. When

Rondón was a young man, he enlisted in the army; he graduated from military school in 1890. Rondón taught mathematics at the school for a short time and then served with the army corps of engineers. In 1906 the Brazilian government selected him to map a river system in a remote region of the state of Mato Grosso. He was also to supervise the construction of telegraph lines in the area.

During the next four years, Rondón led expeditions deep into the Brazilian rain forest. He mapped the courses of several rivers, including the Sepotuba and Juruena. On May 3, 1909, he departed on a journey that took him down the Jiparaná River and into the Madeira River. When he and his party finally reached the Madeira, they were greatly weakened by starvation, illness, and overexposure to the sun. But Rondón was not easily discouraged. He pressed onward and discovered a previously unknown river running northwest between the Jiparaná and Juruena Rivers. He named it the River of Doubt, since it was still unexplored.

An Explorer and a Peacemaker

As a result of his travels, Rondón became an expert on the plant life, animals, and Indians of the Brazilian interior. He also became very familiar with its physical geography. Rondón's work led to an expedition to map the River of Doubt with former U.S. president Theodore Roosevelt, an adventurer in his own right. The Roosevelt-Rondón Scientific Expedition started in late 1913. After months of hardships, the party finally reached the mouth of the river on April 26, 1914, and discovered that it was a branch of the Aripuanã River.

Rondón directed Brazil's National Service for the Protection of Indians until 1940. He also worked to establish peace among nations in the Americas, and his efforts were recognized with a nomination for the Nobel Peace Prize in 1952. To honor Rondón's achievements, the Brazilian government changed the name of the territory of Guaporé to Rondônia in 1956.

SUGGESTED READING John A. Zahm, *Through South America's Southland* (D. Appleton and Company, 1916).

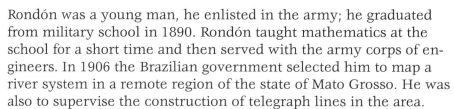

Roosevelt, Theodore

American
b October 27, 1858; New York, New York
d January 6, 1919; Oyster Bay, New York
Explored River of Doubt in Brazil

Theodore Roosevelt was a man of many interests and achievements. He served as governor of New York and was the 26th president of the United States. For his role in ending a war between Russia and Japan, the Russo-Japanese War, he received the 1906 Nobel Peace Prize. Roosevelt was a great promoter of ethics in politics, a respected historian and author, and a devoted conservationist. But he was also an experienced outdoorsman, having lived in the wilderness of the Dakota Territory in the 1880s and hunted in Africa in 1910. In 1913 Roosevelt joined Cândido RONDÓN to map the 400-mile-long River of Doubt in western Brazil.

The River's Challenge

Born in New York City on October 27, 1858, Roosevelt showed an early interest in natural history. After graduating with honors from Harvard University in 1880, he became a historian and a writer and

Theodore Roosevelt went from the presidency of the United States to co-command of a nearly fatal expedition on the River of Doubt in Brazil.

dysentery disease that causes severe diarrhea

specimen sample of a plant, animal, or mineral, usually collected for scientific study or display

eventually entered politics. As a child, he had overcome asthma and poor eyesight by teaching himself to ride, shoot, and box. However, by the time of the Brazilian expedition, Roosevelt was blind in one eye, the result of a boxing injury.

Roosevelt served as U.S. president from 1901 to 1909. Four years later, he went on a lecture tour to Argentina and Brazil. The tour planners organized an expedition to map the River of Doubt, and the Brazilian government arranged for Cândido Rondón to join the group. Rondón had discovered the river several years earlier.

The Roosevelt-Rondón Scientific Expedition set out in late 1913. The party traveled through western Brazil by canoe, van, and mule, as well as on foot, and began the trip down the River of Doubt on February 27, 1914. Along the way, they had to cope with fire ants, flies, termites, illness, rainstorms, sweltering heat, and dangerous rapids. It took them two months to reach the mouth of the river. During the journey, two members of the group were killed in a whirlpool. Roosevelt and his son, Kermit, almost drowned. Roosevelt also suffered from fever, **dysentery,** an infected leg, and heart problems, but he always kept his spirits up.

The mapping expedition was a great success. Rondón renamed the river Rio Roosevelt to honor the achievement. In addition, the party collected over 2,500 **specimens** of birds and about 500

species type of plant or animal

specimens of mammals, including many **species** previously unknown to science.

SUGGESTED READING Theodore Roosevelt, *Through the Brazilian Wilderness* (Scribners, 1914).

Ross, James Clark

English
b April 15, 1800; London, England
d April 3, 1862; Aylesbury, England
***Discovered North Magnetic Pole and parts of
Antarctica; explored Canadian Arctic***

Northwest Passage water route connecting the Atlantic Ocean and Pacific Ocean through the Arctic islands of northern Canada

Inuit people of the Canadian Arctic, sometimes known as the Eskimo

boat-sledge boat mounted on sled runners to allow travel on both ice and water

Rear Admiral Sir James Clark Ross was one of the best polar explorers in the British navy. He learned many of his Arctic survival skills while serving on expeditions under William Edward PARRY and his uncle, John Ross. An even-tempered commander with sound judgment, Ross proved his leadership ability on his great mission to Antarctica from 1839 to 1843. During that journey, he discovered and named Victoria Land, the Ross Sea, the Ross Barrier (now called the Ross Ice Shelf), and two volcanoes. He also collected much valuable scientific data in the polar region.

Learning the Ropes

As a young man, James Ross gained an understanding of navigation from his uncle, John Ross, who was an experienced Arctic explorer. James joined the navy in 1812 and served under his uncle for five years, sailing in northern waters from the North Sea to the White Sea. In 1818 the young Ross, his uncle, and Parry participated in the mission that rediscovered Baffin Bay but failed in its goal of finding the **Northwest Passage.** The following year, James Ross served under Parry aboard the *Hecla* on the first of the many Arctic expeditions they would undertake together.

From 1821 to 1823, Ross participated in Parry's exploration of the Melville Peninsula. While aboard the *Fury,* Ross witnessed the first attempt by Europeans to learn the **Inuit** art of dogsledding, a technique which he later mastered. In 1824 he again served on the *Fury* and was on board when it was wrecked in Prince Regent Inlet. Two years after he returned home, Ross joined Parry on the failed mission to reach the North Pole from Spitsbergen, an island group north of Norway, by **boat-sledge.**

After this exhausting mission, Ross was promoted to commander in the fall of 1827. By then he was an accomplished navigator of icy waters. He was also an expert on magnetism, a successful whaler, and a student of natural history. Ross agreed to join his uncle on another expedition to search for the Northwest Passage. John Ross wanted to resume the quest at Prince Regent Inlet, where ice had forced Parry to turn back four years earlier.

Family Business

John Ross was not able to interest the British navy in the project, but Arctic exploration was widely popular at that time. The elder Ross financed the expedition with money from private sources, including a large donation from Sir Felix Booth. Although John Ross again missed the strait (later named Bellot Strait) that would have led him to the Northwest Passage, the journey satisfied the public's desire for adventure. James Ross also accomplished some significant scientific research.

The Ross expedition, from 1829 to 1833, set a record for Arctic survival by Europeans. The explorers were trapped in ice at Lord Mayor Bay, at the base of Boothia Peninsula, for three years in an old steam **packet** named the *Victory.* Then they spent another year in a rickety shelter on Somerset Island.

At the beginning, the mission seemed promising. In the summer of 1829, the *Victory* traveled farther than Parry had gone in two summers. It passed southward through Prince Regent Inlet into the Gulf of Boothia. However, the warm weather that allowed the ship to sail so quickly also allowed it to sail so far into the gulf that it became trapped in the ice.

John Ross was not as good as Parry at entertaining his men, but James passed the time by making long trips by **sledge.** During these journeys, he made magnetic and celestial observations and collected **specimens.** His most important accomplishment was his communication with some Inuit who approached the ship in January 1830. Ross used his knowledge of their language and customs to build good relations. This friendship was the key factor in the party's survival. The Inuit offered the Europeans meat, as well as clothing that was suitable for Arctic winters. They also drew a map of the southern part of the Gulf of Boothia, correctly showing that there was no local water route that could be part of the Northwest Passage.

A veteran of many Arctic expeditions, Sir James Clark Ross turned down an important mission in the 1840s in order to spend time with his new wife.

packet small, fast ship used during the 1800s to carry mail, cargo, and passengers

sledge heavy sled, often mounted on runners, that is pulled over snow or ice

specimen sample of a plant, animal, or mineral, usually collected for scientific study or display

Ross the Scientist

In the spring of 1830, James Ross began exploring by dogsled with the help of the Inuit. He made several trips around Boothia Peninsula with Inuit guides. That May he crossed to the west coast and traveled across the strait that was later named after him. He then explored the region west of the strait, which he called King William Land (now King William Island). He followed its coast north to Cape Felix and then southwest to Victory Point. A shortage of supplies prevented him from going any farther. At Cape Felix, Ross observed an enormous ice mass that was moving toward the southeast.

During these travels, Ross made careful magnetic observations. He calculated the position of the North Magnetic Pole and reached the exact site the following year—on May 31, 1831. This discovery fulfilled his dreams and was actually more important to science than the Northwest Passage. Ross felt that his accomplishments had made the expedition worthwhile.

Despite its hopeful start, the *Victory* was still imprisoned in the ice by 1832. The men abandoned the ship and returned by sledge to Parry's old camp at Fury Point. From there they traveled by boat to Baffin Bay but were stopped again by ice, which forced them to winter at Fury Point. Thin and exhausted, the men finally rowed out of Prince Regent Inlet in the summer of 1833. They were picked up by the whaler *Isabella.* Back in England, where they had been presumed dead, the Rosses received a hero's welcome. James was made a post captain, and John was knighted.

Rushing to the South Pole

In 1836 James Ross returned to the Arctic on a mission to save some whalers who were trapped by ice in Davis Strait. Three years later, he was chosen to command an expedition to the South Magnetic Pole. The *Erebus* and the *Terror* set out from England in September 1839. Two other expeditions were also trying to reach the pole. One was led by the Frenchman Jules DUMONT D'URVILLE, and the other was commanded by the American Charles WILKES. In order to beat these competitors to the pole, Ross headed straight through the ring of ice that surrounds Antarctica. His ships were badly damaged and barely survived the difficult voyage through the ice pack. On January 10, 1841, Ross discovered and named Victoria Land. Soon after that, he found the Ross Sea and the Ross Barrier (now called the Ross Ice Shelf) and two great volcanoes that he named after his ships.

On this voyage, Ross successfully navigated the *Erebus* and the *Terror* through dangerous conditions. He also kept his crew healthy for four years by spending the winters either in Van Diemen's Land (now Tasmania) or in Australia. Ross maintained a strict program of scientific observations. He measured magnetism, water temperatures, and water depths. Among his many important discoveries, Ross proved that life exists even on the deepest ocean floor.

Ross returned to England in September 1843. He was knighted and received many other honors. That year he married and settled in Aylesbury, Buckinghamshire. He returned to the sea only once. In 1848 he commanded a rescue expedition to search for his friend Sir John FRANKLIN's missing party. After conducting a search of Somerset Island, he found no sign of Franklin. Ross returned to England and spent the rest of his days on land. He died peacefully at the age of 62.

SUGGESTED READING Ernest Dodge, *The Polar Rosses: John and James Clark Ross and Their Explorations* (Faber and Faber, 1973); Maurice James Ross, *Polar Pioneers: John Ross and James Clark Ross* (McGill-Queen's University Press, 1994).

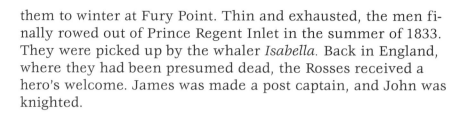

Rubruck, William of. See *William of Rubruck.*

Saint Brendan. See *Brendan.*

Saint Francis Xavier. See *Xavier, Francis.*

German
b 1380; near Lohhof, Bavaria (now in Germany)
d 1440?; ?
Traveled throughout Asia as captive of
Turks and Mongols

sultan ruler of a Muslim nation

khan title of an Asian ruler

Johann Schiltberger was a young German nobleman who spent 32 years traveling through Asia as a captive of the Turks and the Mongols. After he had escaped and returned to Bavaria, he wrote an account of his experiences, titled the *Reisebuch* (Travel Book). It was one of the first German contributions to the growing field of geography.

Prisoner of War

Schiltberger was just 15 years old when he fought against the Turks in the army of King Sigismund of Hungary. On September 28, 1396, during the battle of Nicopolis (now Nikopol, Bulgaria), Schiltberger's cavalry unit was defeated and captured by the Turks. The next day, the Ottoman **sultan** Bajazet ordered his men to behead every German prisoner over the age of 20—about 10,000 in all. The younger Germans, including Schiltberger, were taken as slaves to Constantinople (now Istanbul, Turkey).

As a prisoner of Bajazet, Schiltberger later wrote that he "was obliged to run on my feet with the others, wherever he went, it being the custom that lords have people to run before them." After several years, Schiltberger was allowed to ride with the sultan. During the 12 years he spent with the Turks, Schiltberger gained a detailed knowledge of Asia Minor (the peninsula now occupied by Turkey) and Egypt, and he made one unsuccessful attempt to escape.

Serving Other Masters

On July 20, 1402, the Turks were defeated by the Mongols at Ankara. Schiltberger became a prisoner of the Mongol **khan** Timur (also known as Tamerlane), who was famous for his bloodthirsty ruthlessness. Schiltberger's book describes an incident in which a conquered town revolted against Timur's rule. The khan ordered the execution of all of the men and most of the children, then burned the village. He treated Schiltberger well, however, and took him to Samarkand (now part of Uzbekistan). Schiltberger traveled widely throughout Armenia, Georgia, the middle Volga River region, and southeastern Russia, but he was not allowed to go home.

After Timur died in 1405, Schiltberger was sent to Khorasan (now in northeastern Iran) to live with the khan's son, Shah Rokh. Later, a young Tartar prince who was staying at the khan's court was called back to rule his home region in Siberia. Instructed to go with the prince, Schiltberger traveled to the cities of Tobolsk and Tomsk. He later visited Mecca (in present-day Saudi Arabia) and wrote a remarkably accurate account of the Muslim religion and the life of the prophet Muhammad. On the return trip from Mecca, Schiltberger and four other German prisoners escaped. They boarded a European ship headed for Constantinople and then returned to Munich by crossing through east central Europe.

Schiltberger's book provided Europeans with a rare account of Asian politics and geography in the Middle Ages. It was also unique because he saw those lands from a slave's point of view, unlike some other explorers, who were often the honored guests of Asian rulers. Read widely in Europe, the *Reisebuch* was filled with information on the eastern lands that would soon be visited during the Age of Exploration.

SUGGESTED READING Johannes Schiltberger, *The Bondage and Travels of Johann Schiltberger, a Native of Bavaria, in Europe, Asia, and Africa, 1396–1427,* translated by John Buchan Telfer (reprint, B. Franklin, 1970).

Schnitzer, Eduard

German
b 1840; Oppeln, Prussia (now Opole, Poland)
d October 1892;
Kinema, Congo (now the Democratic Republic of Congo)
Explored East Africa

specimen sample of a plant, animal, or mineral, usually collected for scientific study or display

Eduard Schnitzer, also known as Emin Pasha, originally traveled to Africa as a doctor. But he remained on the continent for more than 10 years as governor of the Egyptian province of Equatoria (now a province of Sudan). While in Equatoria, Schnitzer helped to develop the area and improved the standard of living in the region.

The Faithful One
As a youth, Schnitzer was fascinated by natural history, but he chose to study medicine. After graduating, he left Berlin and went to Turkey, where he worked as a tutor. He later traveled in Europe for several years before going to Egypt in 1874. There he practiced medicine to raise money for a trip to Khartoum (in present-day Sudan). Schnitzer arrived in the city in 1875 and found that his medical skills were needed on a military expedition to Equatoria. At this time, Schnitzer took the name Emin, meaning "faithful one," as well as the title of Pasha.

Schnitzer met the expedition's leader, British colonel Charles Gordon, at the town of Lado. Gordon intended to explore the region, limit the spread of disease there, and protect its inhabitants from Egyptian slave traders. By late 1875, the British troops had restored some order, and Gordon left. Schnitzer stayed in Equatoria to serve as surgeon general.

Governor of Equatoria
At his new post, Schnitzer explored extensively, visited local tribal rulers, and collected **specimens** that he sent back to Europe. After two governors of Equatoria had resigned from their positions due to illness, Gordon returned to the province in 1878 and appointed Schnitzer governor. The local people respected the German leader. He developed towns, roads, and farms in the region and worked to eliminate the local slave trade. However, he met resistance from Egyptians living in the province, many of whom were government workers who had been sent there as a punishment for dishonesty. An Arab named Mahdi, who claimed to be a messiah, later led a revolt that forced Schnitzer out of power. When Mahdi attacked Lado in 1883, Schnitzer retreated south. Unfortunately, Europe did not become aware of his troubles until three years later.

Pushed into action by a public outcry, both Germany and Britain sent rescue expeditions to Africa. In 1888 the British explorer Henry Morton STANLEY located Schnitzer at Lake Albert (in present-day Uganda), but Schnitzer wanted help defending the province, not escaping from it. After a year, he finally agreed to go to Africa's east coast with Stanley, who resented his ingratitude. Schnitzer also angered the British public by refusing to travel to England and then by accepting a commission to return to Africa in 1890 to claim land for Germany. At the village of Kinema near the Congo River, he was beheaded by Arab soldiers, who were acting on the orders of a local ruler.

SUGGESTED READING Olivia Manning, *The Remarkable Expedition* (Doubleday, 1985); Iain R. Smith, *The Emin Pasha Relief Expedition* (Clarendon, 1972).

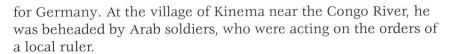

Schomburgk, Robert Hermann

English
b 1804; Freiburg, Prussia (now in Germany)
d 1865; Berlin, Prussia (now in Germany)
Explored interior of British Guiana

botany the scientific study of plants
specimen sample of a plant, animal, or mineral, usually collected for scientific study or display

Robert Schomburgk was the first European to see the mountain of Roraima in southern British Guiana.

Sir Robert Hermann Schomburgk once wrote: "My love for **botany** and natural history, and an ardent desire to travel, led me, in 1830, to the West Indies." In 1831 he surveyed the coast of Anegada, one of the British Virgin Islands, to help navigators avoid its dangerous reefs and sandbars. Four years later, Britain's Royal Geographical Society appointed him to explore British Guiana and to collect **specimens** there.

Beginning in 1836, he tried to navigate the Essequibo and Courantyne Rivers, but both times he was forced to turn back because of large waterfalls that blocked his progress. On the Berbice River, he encountered stampeding hogs, swarms of attacking ants, and a lack of fresh food. Nevertheless, he completed his survey of Guiana in 1838 and returned to England the following year.

In England, he recommended that the government make a greater effort to develop its territory in British Guiana. However, Guiana's boundaries were disputed by Brazil and Venezuela. Schomburgk was appointed by Britain to the position of boundary commissioner.

In 1841 Schomburgk returned to South America to determine Guiana's boundaries with Brazil and Venezuela. Among the rivers he surveyed were the Rio Branco, the Orinoco, the Waini, and the Barima. The boundary that he determined was accepted by all three countries and became known as the Schomburgk Line. After completing his survey of Guiana, Schomburgk was knighted, and he later served as the British representative to the Dominican Republic in 1848 and to Siam (now Thailand) from 1857 to 1864. He died in Berlin at the age of 61.

SUGGESTED READING Paul Russell Cutright, *The Great Naturalists Explore South America* (Macmillan, 1940).

Schouten, Willem Corneliszoon

Dutch
b 1567?; Hoorn, the Netherlands
d 1625; ?
Discovered Le Maire Strait; explored southern Pacific Ocean

In 1615 the Dutch navigator Willem Corneliszoon Schouten went on a mission to find trading lands that were not already under the control of the Dutch East India Company. On this expedition, he sailed south of the Strait of Magellan and charted a new route into the Pacific Ocean. Schouten also found and named several islands in the Pacific.

Challenging the Authorities
Schouten had already made three voyages to southeastern Asia when a businessman named Isaac Le Maire proposed a private

voyage to discover new lands in the Pacific Ocean. He chose Schouten to pilot the *Eendracht,* captained by Le Maire's son, Jacob. The *Eendracht* was joined by the *Hoorn,* under the command of Schouten's brother, Jan.

The Dutch East India Company, in order to protect its dominance of Dutch trade in Southeast Asia, hoped to defeat Le Maire's plan. The company forbade Le Maire's ships to enter the Pacific either by rounding Africa's Cape of Good Hope or by sailing through the Strait of Magellan at the southern tip of South America. Nevertheless, the ships left the Netherlands in May 1615 and reached Patagonia in December. The *Hoorn* was destroyed by fire while anchored in Patagonia, but the *Eendracht* continued the voyage in January. South of the Strait of Magellan, Schouten discovered a new passage—which he named Le Maire Strait—leading to the Pacific Ocean. By sailing through the strait, he avoided rounding the cape he named Hoorn (now Cape Horn) after his birthplace in Holland.

Island to Island

Schouten traveled west through what are now called Fiji, Samoa, and the Tuamotu Islands. He found and named Alofi, Futuna, and the Hoorn Islands. Jacob Le Maire suggested that they sail farther west to look for *Terra Australis Incognita,* the unknown southern continent. But Schouten declined to enter such mysterious and dangerous waters. Instead they headed northwest and charted the north coast of New Guinea. They also discovered and named the Schouten Islands off New Guinea's northwest coast.

When the explorers reached Java, officials of the Dutch East India Company arrested them. The officials did not believe that Schouten had found a new route to the Pacific Ocean. Schouten and Le Maire were sent back to Holland, but Le Maire died on the way. Schouten lived to tell the tale of their discoveries and published an account of the voyage in 1619.

SUGGESTED READING Oliver E. Allen, *The Pacific Navigators* (Time-Life Books, 1980).

Schweinfurth, Georg August

German
b December 29, 1836; Riga, Latvia
d September 19, 1925; Berlin, Germany
Explored East Africa and Central Africa

geology the scientific study of the earth's natural history

botany the scientific study of plants

specimen sample of a plant, animal, or mineral, usually collected for scientific study or display

Georg August Schweinfurth was a trained scientist who studied the **geology, botany,** and natural history of East Africa. He created maps that helped locate the region's bodies of water and that included valuable information about little-known tribes of the interior. While exploring the upper Nile River region, Schweinfurth found the Uele River. His work added greatly to Europe's understanding of the lands and peoples of Africa.

Pondering Plant Life and Cannibals

Schweinfurth studied botany at several German universities. While learning about the plant life of Africa, he became interested in traveling to that continent. In 1862 he completed his studies and departed for Egypt. For three years, he traveled up the Nile River, visiting Khartoum (in present-day Sudan) and exploring the coast of the Red Sea. The plant **specimens** that he brought back to Germany earned him a grant to conduct further studies in East Africa.

watershed ridge of high ground forming the boundary between regions where the water of each region flows into a different river system

tributary stream or river that flows into a larger stream or river

In 1869 Schweinfurth returned to Khartoum. He sailed up the White Nile River and then journeyed across the **watershed** of the Nile and Congo Rivers until he came to an unknown river, in March 1870. At first he thought it was a **tributary** of the Niger River, which actually lay far to the northwest. But it proved to be a tributary of the Ubangi River to the south. Schweinfurth determined that this newly discovered river, the Uele, flowed in the opposite direction from the waters of the Nile. His findings helped geographers to establish the western limits of the Nile River system.

During this two-year expedition, Schweinfurth conducted a thorough study of the botany and geology of the Sudan. He also investigated several tribes of whom Europeans knew little at that time. These peoples included the Bongo, the Mangbetu, the Pygmies, and the Naim-Naim. The Naim-Naim were reportedly cannibals who sharpened their teeth into points. Schweinfurth's description of the Pygmies, who were first found by the explorer Paul Belloni Du Chaillu in 1863, was the first detailed report on that tribe.

A Passion for Africa

Schweinfurth returned to Germany in 1871 and published *The Heart of Africa,* an informative book that presented data about his discoveries. Two years later, he set out again for the African continent with the explorer Friedrich Gerhard Rohlfs, who was married to Schweinfurth's niece. Rohlfs wanted to visit the Oases of Kufra, a trip that required crossing unexplored areas of the Libyan Desert. Some of this barren terrain had not had rainfall in 10 years. After their camels had gone two weeks without water, the two men were forced to turn back.

In 1875 Schweinfurth settled in Cairo, Egypt, where he lived for more than 10 years. He undertook two minor desert expeditions, but he concentrated on scientific studies of Egypt. He also served as a consultant to the Egyptian government and helped to found the country's geographical society. In 1885 he was offered the opportunity to lead Britain's expedition to Mount Kilimanjaro, but he declined for health reasons. However, he lived for another 40 years, finally retiring to Germany in 1888. There he continued to write, and he remained involved in African studies until his death in 1925 at the age of 89.

Georg Schweinfurth's expeditions into the African interior uncovered valuable information about little-known African tribes, including the Pygmies.

SUGGESTED READING Georg August Schweinfurth, *The Heart of Africa: Three Years' Travels and Adventures in the Unexplored Regions of Central Africa from 1868 to 1871* (Gregg, 1969).

Scoresby, William

English
b October 5, 1789; Cropton, England
d March 21, 1857; Torquay, England
Explored Norwegian Arctic and eastern Greenland

William Scoresby was a British whaling captain whose interests ranged from marine biology to religion. In 1817 he noticed an unusual warming of the Arctic Ocean off the coast of Greenland. He contacted Sir Joseph Banks, the president of the Royal Geographical Society, about this possible change in the area's climate. Scoresby's observation led to efforts by the British navy to locate the **Northwest Passage.** Many of Scoresby's insights on the polar region were published in 1820 in a volume titled, *An Account of the Arctic Regions and Northern Whale Fishery.* The book impressed the

Northwest Passage water route connecting the Atlantic Ocean and Pacific Ocean through the Arctic islands of northern Canada

mate assistant to the commander of a ship

latitude distance north or south of the equator

William Scoresby, a British whaling captain, impressed scientists and novelists alike with his insightful observations of the Arctic region.

American author Herman Melville, who referred to it frequently in his novel *Moby-Dick*.

The Right Skills

Scoresby was the son of a wealthy whaler, who began teaching him about the whaling industry when William was only 11 years old. By the time he was 17, Scoresby was chief **mate** on a ship, piloted by his father, that reached a record-high **latitude** of 81°30' north. The following year, he began to study philosophy and chemistry at the University of Edinburgh, but he left school to join the navy. After he had served in battle and then returned to school for a short time, his father put him in charge of a whaling ship. This combination of study and practical experience enabled him to make valuable observations of the Arctic Ocean.

A Focus on Faith

After writing his first book, Scoresby led three profitable whaling voyages. In 1822 he and his father explored over 800 miles of the eastern Greenland coast in two ships. But when his wife died the following year, Scoresby decided to study for the ministry. He received an advanced degree from the University of Cambridge and became a minister in the Church of England. He continued to write about navigation and the Arctic Ocean until his death in 1857.

SUGGESTED READING William Scoresby, *The Polar Ice* (reprint, Caedmon of Whitby, 1980) and *An Account of the Arctic Regions* (reprint, A. M. Kelley, 1969); Tom Stamp and Cordelia Stamp, *Scoresby, Arctic Scientist* (Caedmon of Whitby, 1976).

Scott, Robert Falcon

English
b June 6, 1868; Devonport, England
d March 29?, 1912; Ross Ice Shelf, Antarctica
Explored Antarctica;
led second expedition to South Pole

Captain Robert Falcon Scott led a successful three-year scientific expedition to Antarctica between 1901 and 1904. Five years later, he joined the race to become the first person to reach the South Pole. When he and his team arrived at their destination in January 1912, they discovered that the Norwegian explorer Roald AMUNDSEN had beaten them to the pole by one month. Devastated, Scott and his party began the journey back to their base camp, only to die of cold and starvation on the way. Despite his failure and tragic death, Scott's heroism and the drama of the journey captured the imagination and sympathy of the world, especially among his fellow Britons.

The Making of a Young Hero

Scott joined the British navy as a young man. At the age of 18, as a midshipman, he won a sailing race and gained the attention of Sir Clements Markham, president of the Royal Geographical Society. Markham had dinner with Scott after the race and was impressed, he wrote, by his "intelligence, information, and the charm of his manner." He envisioned Scott as commander of a future expedition to Antarctica. Although Scott had no experience in polar exploration, Markham believed that the personal qualities of a British officer would equip him for any type of task. Markham also realized

Robert Falcon Scott perished in Antarctica, but the diary he had kept carried his last words to the British public.

geologist scientist who studies the earth's natural history

glacier large, slowly moving mass of ice

sledge heavy sled, often mounted on runners, that is pulled over snow or ice

depot place where supplies are stored

scurvy disease caused by a lack of vitamin C and once a major cause of death among sailors; symptoms include internal bleeding, loosened teeth, and extreme fatigue

plateau high, flat area of land

that the handsome, well-spoken Scott would capture the hearts of the British public.

In 1900 Scott was chosen to lead the first British expedition to explore the interior of Antarctica. Long ago the continent was covered with abundant plant life, but now it lies beneath an ice sheet that is 8,800 feet thick at the South Pole. Antarctica's frigid climate is the most severe in the world. At the time of Scott's expedition, very little was known of the region's interior. There were many important scientific questions to be answered. The scientists of the Royal Geographical Society wanted the famous **geologist** J. W. Gregory to lead the expedition, rather than the inexperienced and relatively uneducated Scott. However, Markham insisted that the Royal Navy be in charge. Professor Gregory resigned, and Scott was appointed commander.

Starvation and Snow Blindness

On August 6, 1901, Scott set sail from England on the *Discovery.* By January the ship had reached the edge of the floating **glacier** known as the Ross Ice Shelf. After using a hot-air balloon to survey the area, Scott set up a base on James Ross Island. In the spring, he sent out **sledge** parties in three directions. Accompanied by Dr. Edward Wilson and Ernest SHACKLETON, Scott journeyed 380 miles over the ice shelf toward the pole. After 59 days of exploration, the team began a nightmarish return trip. Although the men had established supply **depots** along the way, many of their dogs starved and had to be killed and fed to the surviving dogs. Wilson suffered from snow blindness, and Shackleton and Scott fell ill with **scurvy.** On December 21, the men were still 300 miles from their base, and Scott wrote in his diary: "Misfortunes never come singly." They reached camp on February 3, but Shackleton was so ill that he had to be sent back to England early. Scott's parties continued to have problems with scurvy, even though by that time, most Arctic explorers had eliminated the disease through careful management of their diet.

Scott set out again the next spring on a 360-mile trip to the polar **plateau,** about 9,000 feet above sea level. His team covered about 14½ miles a day without using dogs. Each member of the party pulled a sled attached by a harness. Although Scott could have used more modern methods of travel, he treasured the experience. He wrote:

> *To my mind no journey ever made with dogs can approach the height of the fine conception which is realized when a party of men go forth to face hardships, dangers, and difficulties with their own unaided efforts . . . Surely in this case the conquest is more nobly and splendidly won.*

By this time, Scott's accomplishments were truly impressive. He had endured conditions much worse than other explorers had faced in the Arctic Ocean, and he had become the first person to see the

Scott and his party took this photograph at the South Pole. Their morale was shattered when they found a flag already planted by Roald Amundsen.

Inuit people of the Canadian Arctic, sometimes known as the Eskimo

Northwest Passage water route connecting the Atlantic Ocean and Pacific Ocean through the Arctic islands of northern Canada

South Polar ice cap. The *Discovery* left Antarctica in February 1904 and returned to England in triumph on November 7.

Old-Fashioned Technique

Despite Scott's successful efforts in the polar region, he had used outdated techniques that were considered inadequate for exploration in that climate. He rejected the advice of the experienced Arctic explorer Fridtjof NANSEN, who had suggested that he learn a version of the **Inuit** method of driving Greenland dogs. Scott's decision to use Siberian dogs was a terrible failure. Markham later claimed that Scott had rejected Nansen's method because it was inhumane. Nansen's approach required the explorers to kill some dogs as a sledge's load became lighter and to feed them to the remaining dogs. But Scott's method may actually have been less merciful, since he usually allowed his dogs and ponies to starve before killing them.

Race to the South Pole

From 1904 to 1909, Scott served in the Royal Navy. In 1909 he decided to try to reach the South Pole. After spending two years raising funds, Scott left England aboard the *Terra Nova* in June 1910. On the way to Antarctica, he stopped in Australia, where he learned that Roald Amundsen was also attempting to reach the pole. In successfully navigating the **Northwest Passage** several years earlier, the Norwegian explorer and a small crew had accomplished what

For a map of Scott's route, see the profile of Roald AMUNDSEN in Volume 1.

the entire British navy had failed to do in several centuries of trying. Now he was challenging his British rivals once again.

Scott reached James Ross Island on January 22, 1911, and hurried to make preparations. Using the same unwise sledging techniques as before, he set out for the pole in late September with extensive support parties, transported by dogs, ponies, and motorized sledges. He soon made a serious mistake. When he left his last supply party at the Beardmore Glacier on January 4, 1912, he suddenly decided to add Lieutenant H. R. Bowers to the small team that would make the final push to the pole. However, the party had no additional supplies or skis for Bowers. The lieutenant was also a short man, and it was difficult for him to trudge through the snow. Already exhausted from struggling through blizzard conditions, the team was further slowed by Bowers. When they reached the pole on January 16, the British explorers discovered the flag of Norway and a small tent—Amundsen had already been there. Scott wrote in his diary: "Great God this is an awful place and terrible enough for us to have labored to it without the reward of priority."

Discouraged and demoralized, Scott and his men then began the 800-mile journey back to their base. One member of the party died on February 16, and a second died a month later, after wandering alone into a blizzard. When they were just 11 miles away from a depot and only 150 miles from base, the last three survivors encountered another snowstorm. Freezing and starving to death, Scott remained in his tent and wrote in his diary. His last words were: "We shall stick it out to the end, but we are getting weaker, of course, and the end cannot be far. It seems a pity, but I do not think I can write any more."

SUGGESTED READING Roland Huntford, *Scott and Amundsen* (Atheneum, 1984); Robert Falcon Scott, *The Voyage of the* Discovery, 2 volumes (Greenwood, 1969); Edward Wilson, *Diary of the* Discovery *Expedition to the Antarctic Regions, 1901–1904*, edited by Ann Savours (Batsford, 1967) and *Diary of the "Terra Nova" Expedition to the Antarctic: 1910–1912*, edited by H. R. King (Humanities, 1972).

Sequeira, Diogo Lopes de. See *Lopes de Sequeira, Diogo.*

Serra, Junípero

Spanish
b November 24, 1713; Petra, Spain
d August 28, 1784; Carmel, California
Explored and settled California

mission settlement founded by priests in a land where they hoped to convert people to Christianity

New Spain region of Spanish colonial empire that included the areas now occupied by Mexico, Florida, Texas, New Mexico, Arizona, California, and various Caribbean islands

Father Junípero Serra was a Franciscan priest who established the first **mission** in what is now California. He eventually founded a total of nine Spanish settlements between San Diego and San Francisco, giving Spain a strong presence in Alta (Upper) California. Serra was also an active supporter of the Indians to whom he ministered.

Missionary Work

Serra was baptized with the name Miguel José, but took the name Junípero in 1731 when he became a Franciscan priest. In 1749 he requested permission to join other Franciscans who were going to **New Spain** to do missionary work. He spent nine years among the Indians of Sierra Gorda as well as several more years in Mexico City. In 1767 he was appointed president of the Franciscan missions in Baja California.

Father Junípero Serra established a chain of Spanish missionary settlements throughout California.

scurvy disease caused by a lack of vitamin C and once a major cause of death among sailors; symptoms include internal bleeding, loosened teeth, and extreme fatigue

José de Gálvez, a Spanish official who was visiting New Spain, became determined to enlarge Spain's empire in the Americas. He was concerned about rumors that Russia was expanding its territory eastward from the Aleutian Islands, which lie west of Alaska. To counter possible foreign advances into the Pacific Northwest, Gálvez decided to set up a series of missions in California. These settlements would be separated from each other by a distance of one day's ride and would extend from Baja California to Monterey. Gálvez believed that the missions would eventually grow into colonies, discouraging other countries from settling California. Father Serra was chosen to head this project.

Establishing the Missions

In 1769 a total of four expeditions set out for Upper California—two by land and two by sea. Serra was a member of the second and larger overland journey, commanded by Gaspar de Portola. Their difficult trek across the dry terrain of Baja California was particularly difficult for Serra, who suffered from severe pains in one of his legs. This condition had bothered him ever since his arrival in New Spain, but now his leg had become so swollen that he could barely walk on it. When Portola threatened to send him back, Serra asked a mule driver how he would treat an animal with a similar problem. The man made a mixture of herbs and animal fat to put on the leg, and within a few days, the swelling went down. However, Portola left Serra behind at San Diego with a group of sailors who were suffering from **scurvy.** Portola himself continued north to look for Monterey Bay. On July 16, 1769, Serra founded San Diego de Alcala, the first mission in California.

A ship arrived at San Diego the next spring, and Serra sailed on it to Monterey. There, on June 3, he established the mission of Carmel. This settlement served as his headquarters for the rest of his life. During the next 14 years, Serra worked to develop the mission system of California. He founded San Antonio, San Gabriel, San Luis Obispo, San Francisco, San Juan Capistrano, Santa Clara, and San Buenaventura (present-day Ventura). Despite his poor health, he visited the missions frequently. He was always welcomed with great affection, both by his fellow Franciscans and by the local Indians.

A Champion of Justice

Serra strongly opposed prejudice and supported fair treatment by the Spanish of the Indians whom he served. During his time in California, some 6,000 Indians were converted to Christianity. Serra cared not only for their spiritual needs but for their material needs as well. By the end of his ministry, nearly 30,000 farm animals had been brought to Upper California, and the missions produced about 30,000 bushels of grain and vegetables annually. Serra and the other priests also taught the Indians crafts, such as sewing and blacksmithing. The missions produced many of the goods needed by the other Spanish settlements in California.

A strong-willed man, Serra often came into conflict with the Spanish civil authorities with whom he shared power in California. Nevertheless, no one ever questioned his loyalty to Spain. His hard work was essential in establishing a strong Spanish presence in Upper California. To Serra, however, his dedication to the souls he served was more important. The people he met honored, respected, and loved the frail but determined Franciscan.

SUGGESTED READING Katherine Ainsworth and Edward M. Ainsworth, *In the Shade of the Juniper Tree* (Doubleday, 1970); Maynard Geiger, *The Life and Times of Fray Junípero Serra*, 2 volumes (Academy of American Franciscan History, 1959); Antonine Tibesar, *Writings of Junípero Serra*, 4 volumes (Academy of American Franciscan History, 1955); Winifred E. Wise, *Fray Junípero Serra and the California Conquest* (Scribners, 1967).

Shackleton, Ernest Henry

Anglo-Irish
b February 15, 1874; Kilkee, Ireland
d January 5, 1922; South Georgia, Scotia Sea
Explored Antarctica

sledge heavy sled, often mounted on runners, that is pulled over snow or ice

scurvy disease caused by a lack of vitamin C and once a major cause of death among sailors; symptoms include internal bleeding, loosened teeth, and extreme fatigue

Ernest Henry Shackleton took part in some of the most dangerous journeys of the exploration of Antarctica. His wisdom, courage, and leadership earned him the nickname "the Boss" from the members of his expeditions. Despite the life-threatening challenges they faced, no member of his teams was ever killed or injured. His decision in 1909 to turn back just 97 miles from the South Pole was the kind of action that won him both a loyal following and a knighthood.

A Craving for Adventure

Shackleton was never a good student, though he did attend college in England before joining the merchant marine. He served on a ship that carried soldiers to the Boer War in South Africa and later coauthored a book about his experiences. But this large and energetic man craved adventure. After enlisting in the Royal Naval Reserve in 1901, he volunteered for Robert Falcon SCOTT's first expedition to Antarctica.

The trip proved to be a humiliating disappointment for Shackleton. He was chosen to accompany Scott on a long **sledge** journey over the Ross Ice Shelf, but Shackleton fell ill with a serious case of **scurvy.** Since he became a burden to the party's progress, he had to be sent home early on a relief ship. The public felt that Shackleton had behaved heroically, but Scott's popular book about the trip told a less flattering story. Shackleton was angry when Scott wrote that, "at the end of each march he is panting, dizzy, and exhausted."

Nevertheless, Shackleton's charm, imagination, and musical Irish accent soon made him a sought-after public speaker. He became secretary of the Royal Scottish Geographical Society in 1904 and created a stir with his energetic leadership. Convinced of his popularity, he decided to run for a seat in Parliament in 1906, as the representative for Dundee, Scotland. Although he won the vote of working-class districts in the city, he lost the election. However, his efforts were noticed by William Beardmore, a businessman from Glasgow, Scotland, who offered the former politician a job. Shackleton soon persuaded him to sponsor an expedition to Antarctica.

Sir Ernest Shackleton (left) led some of the most dangerous Antarctic journeys without loss of life or even injury to his crews.

depot place where supplies are stored

glacier large, slowly moving mass of ice

plateau high, flat area of land

Exercising Wisdom

Shackleton hoped to reach both the magnetic and geographic poles from the base that Scott had set up on James Ross Island in 1902. But Scott planned to return to Antarctica himself, and he asked Shackleton to establish his own base. In August 1907, Shackleton sailed on the *Nimrod* and headed for a point east of the island. When he reached the Ross Ice Shelf, however, ice conditions forced him to follow his original plan to use Scott's base.

One party, led by T. W. Edgeworth David, made a remarkable journey to the South Magnetic Pole, the spot to which magnetic compasses point in the southern hemisphere. Meanwhile, Shackleton set up a series of supply **depots** across the Ross Ice Shelf. Heading out in the Antarctic spring of 1908, Shackleton hoped to reach the geographic South Pole—a round trip of 1,730 miles. Although he had had the wisdom to bring an automobile to move supplies across frozen McMurdo Sound, he had not obtained Greenland dogs to pull his sledges. The ponies he employed were not able to travel very far, so the men in his party had to haul the sledges themselves.

The team crossed the ice shelf and came to the great **glacier** that cuts through the Queen Maud Mountains to the polar **plateau.** Shackleton named the glacier after Beardmore. It was slick, steep, and full of deep canyons. The party lost their last pony when it stepped through a snowdrift and fell into a canyon. By Christmas, Shackleton and his companions had reached the 9,000-foot-high polar plateau, and on January 9, 1909, they arrived at the South Magnetic Pole. At that point, they were only 97 miles from the geographic pole, but Shackleton decided to turn back. The men had overcome tremendous obstacles to reach the magnetic pole, and Shackleton knew that to risk going farther would probably be disastrous.

An Amazing Rescue Mission

Shackleton was preparing for another Antarctic mission when World War I broke out. He offered the British government the use of his two ships, the *Endurance* and the *Aurora,* but he was ordered to proceed with his expedition. He planned to explore the Weddell Sea and then cross Antarctica to Victoria Land. A group led by A. E. Mackintosh sailed to the Ross Sea in the *Aurora* to lay supply depots for the team that would travel across the continent. In January 1915, Shackleton and the *Endurance* reached Coats Land on the Antarctic shore of the Weddell Sea. But the *Endurance* became trapped in ice, drifted for nine months, and was finally crushed, 1,000 miles from any source of help. Shackleton led his party by sledge and boat to Elephant Island. With five of his men, he then navigated a 22-foot boat 800 miles across the rough southern Atlantic Ocean to the English island of South Georgia, where he found help. He led four attempts to rescue the other survivors on Elephant Island and finally succeeded. Shackleton told the dramatic story of this rescue mission in his book titled *South.*

In this photograph, Antarctic ice surrounds one of Shackleton's ships. He overcame such hazards with leadership and perseverance.

After several other missions and business ventures, Shackleton returned to South Georgia Island in 1921, intending to explore Enderby Land in Antarctica. However, his heart failed before he could begin. At his memorial service in 1922, the British nation mourned his death.

SUGGESTED READING Sir Ernest Shackleton, *South: The Story of Shackleton's Last Expedition, 1914–1917* (William Heinemann, 1919).

Sharif al-Idrisi, ash-. See *Idrisi, al-*.

Sheldon, May French

American
b May 10, 1847; Pittsburgh, Pennsylvania
d 1936; London, England
Explored East Africa

At a time when women explorers who traveled alone were rare, May French Sheldon led an expedition to study the tribes of East Africa. Most journeys of exploration in that day were military missions led by men. But in 1891 Sheldon succeeded in proving that African tribes would accept white people who approached them in friendship. In recognition of her accomplishment, she was one of the first women to be elected a Fellow of Britain's Royal Geographical Society.

"Lady Boss"
Born and raised in America, Sheldon married an American banker and publisher who lived in London, where she owned a publishing company. She was an enthusiastic admirer of the English explorer Henry Morton STANLEY and was inspired by his adventures in Africa. Stanley and others, however, advised her against going to the African rain forest, which they felt was no place for a woman.

May French Sheldon approached Africa's people with friendship and respect, but her toughness earned her the nickname "Lady Boss."

sultan ruler of a Muslim nation

circumnavigate to travel around

Undaunted, Sheldon asked the **sultan** of Zanzibar for help, and he supplied her with aides; he also provided letters that ordered the tribes she met to give her safe passage.

Sheldon's party included over 100 guides and servants. Her assistants carried a wicker couch, enclosed in curtains mounted on poles, that was large enough for her to sleep and ride on. Sheldon wore expensive tailored outfits and brought an elaborate silk dress to wear whenever she met a chief. Despite her sophisticated clothing, she quickly earned a reputation as a tough leader. On one occasion, when her party refused to continue because they felt that she did not know the way, she aimed her gun at a vulture flying overhead and killed it with one shot. She then threatened to shoot anyone who did not follow her. Her strong determination in such situations led her companions to call her "Bebe Bwana," which in Swahili means Lady Boss.

The Joy of Life

While traveling through what is now Tanzania, Sheldon viewed Africa's highest mountain. She later wrote: "I saw more than I can ever hope to recount of the grandeur of Kilimanjaro." She visited 35 different tribes, of most of whom she said: "They live to enjoy, and enjoy to live, and are as idyllic in their native ways as any people I ever encountered." Sheldon also visited Lake Chala, **circumnavigating** it in a flat-bottomed copper boat left behind by a previous visitor. She wanted to explore the land of the Masai, a fierce warrior tribe, but her guides and carriers refused to enter Masai territory. This time, faced with the possibility that her party really would abandon her, she turned back.

Sheldon's expedition proved that woman explorers could succeed in the most challenging areas of Africa. She was one of the first white travelers to approach African peoples and their cultures in a sympathetic manner. After she returned to London, she wrote a book about her experiences titled *Sultan to Sultan*.

SUGGESTED READING Marion Tinling, *Women Into the Unknown: A Sourcebook on Women Explorers and Travelers* (Greenwood Press, 1989).

Shepard, Alan Bartlett, Jr.

American
b November 18, 1923; East Derry, New Hampshire
d July 21, 1998; Pebble Beach, California
First American in space; landed on moon

Alan Shepard was part of the American space exploration program from its beginning. He was the second person—and the first American—to fly into space. Ten years later, he stepped onto the surface of the moon.

Dangerous Work

Shepard grew up in New England, where his elementary school was a one-room country schoolhouse. After high school, Shepard attended the U.S. Naval Academy at Annapolis, Maryland. He served in the Pacific Ocean during the final months of World War II and later trained to be a fighter pilot.

In 1950 Shepard became a Navy test pilot, with the dangerous job of flying new and experimental military aircraft. He logged thousands of flight hours and instructed other test pilots. He was about

Soviet Union nation that existed from 1922 to 1991, made up of Russia and 14 other republics in eastern Europe and northern Asia

NASA National Aeronautics and Space Administration, the U.S. space agency

astronaut American term for a person who travels into space; literally, "traveler to the stars"

cosmonaut Russian term for a person who travels into space; literally, "traveler to the universe"

capsule small early spacecraft designed to carry a person around the earth

orbit stable, circular route; one trip around; to revolve around

Test pilot Alan Shepard was the only astronaut to serve on space missions in both the Mercury and Apollo programs.

Simpson, Thomas

Scottish
b July 2, 1808; Dingwall, Scotland
d June 14, 1840; near Red River of the North in Manitoba, Canada
Charted Arctic coast of Canada

Northwest Passage water route connecting the Atlantic Ocean and Pacific Ocean through the Arctic islands of northern Canada

to take a command position in the Atlantic Ocean fleet when he received a more interesting offer.

The United States was developing a space program, motivated in part by competition with the **Soviet Union. NASA** invited 110 test pilots to volunteer to become **astronauts,** and Shepard was among the seven selected in 1959.

Flying Higher

America's first astronauts underwent a tough two-year training program of physical tests and scientific study. However, NASA lost the race to send a man into space. The Soviet **cosmonaut** Yuri GAGARIN orbited the earth in April 1961. Soon afterward NASA announced that Shepard would make the first American spaceflight, called Mercury 3. On May 5, in a small **capsule** named *Freedom 7,* he was launched into space from Cape Canaveral, Florida.

Shepard was in space and experienced weightlessness for 5 minutes, but he did not **orbit** the earth as Gagarin had done. During the 15-minute flight, Shepard flew the capsule manually before splashing down safely in the Atlantic Ocean, 302 miles from the launch pad. The flight was a great boost to American self-confidence and pride.

Shepard participated in two other Mercury missions as a controller on the ground. In 1963 he developed a problem with fluid in his ear, and NASA told him that he could no longer fly. He spent the next few years as the administrator of NASA's Astronaut Office. Unwilling to give up flying, he underwent an operation in 1969 that solved his ear problem, and he returned to flight duty.

By then NASA was deeply involved in the Apollo missions to the moon. On January 31, 1971, Shepard made his second and final space flight as commander of the Apollo 14 mission, the third mission to land on the moon. With Edward Mitchell, he spent 33½ hours collecting rock samples. Shepard also found time to hit two golf balls on the lunar surface. The astronauts returned to earth and splashed down in the Pacific Ocean on February 9. Three years later, Shepard retired from the Navy. He pursued a career as a businessman in Houston, Texas, until his death in 1998.

SUGGESTED READING Gregory P. Kennedy, *The First Men in Space* (Chelsea House, 1991); Douglas MacKinnon and Joseph Baldanza, *Footprints* (Acropolis Books, 1989); Paul Westman, *Alan Shepard: The First American in Space* (Dillon Press, 1980).

From 1837 to 1839, Thomas Simpson charted the last unknown stretches of the Arctic shore of North America, from what is now Point Barrow, Alaska, to Boothia Peninsula. By completing the survey of the Canadian coast begun by Sir John FRANKLIN in 1819, Simpson renewed the quest for the **Northwest Passage.** He also located the mouth of the Great Fish River (now called the Back River), which the English explorer Sir George BACK had navigated several years earlier.

A Historical Survey

Simpson, a highly energetic and ambitious man, was a distinguished graduate of the University of Aberdeen. He was introduced to the field of exploration by his uncle, Sir George Simpson, the governor in

A gunshot cut short Thomas Simpson's ambitions as an explorer of Canada, but questions remain about who pulled the trigger.

chief of the Hudson's Bay Company. The company appointed Simpson and Peter Warren Dease to map the north coast of Canada.

Setting out from the Mackenzie River, the pair traveled west on foot, reaching Point Barrow on Alaska's northern coast on August 4, 1837. They spent the winter at Great Bear Lake. The following June, they journeyed east down the Coppermine River to Turnagain Point, where their progress was halted by bad weather. This site was the easternmost point reached by Franklin during his survey of the coast some 15 years earlier. After another winter at Great Bear Lake, Simpson and Dease traveled through the strait south of King William Island, which would later be named after Simpson. While in that region, they discovered a supply of goods that had been left in Chantrey Inlet by Back. Heading north, they then arrived at Boothia Peninsula.

Sudden Death

Simpson did not have time to explore the area thoroughly, but he was convinced that he was close to finding an ice-free water route to the Gulf of Boothia—the key to the Northwest Passage. Finding the passage had been one of the original missions of the Hudson's Bay Company when it was founded, more than 150 years earlier.

The British government heard of Simpson's achievement and approved his future plans for exploration of the Arctic coast. However, before he could carry out his mission, Simpson died of gunshot wounds to the head while traveling through Sioux territory on his way to New York. His companions claimed that he had gone mad and shot himself and two others, but the truth of the matter remains uncertain.

SUGGESTED READING Alexander Simpson, *The Life and Travels of Thomas Simpson, the Arctic Discoverer* (reprint, Baxter, 1963).

Singh, Kishen

Indian
b 1850?; Milam?, India
d 1921?; Itarsi?, India
Explored Tibet and western China

surveyor one who makes precise measurements of a location's geography

Kishen Singh was one of the pundits, Indian men who explored central Asia on behalf of the British government of India. Like his cousin Nain SINGH and KINTUP, Kishen Singh went on secret and dangerous missions in the late 1800s to explore and map regions where Europeans could not travel. Of all the pundits' treks, Kishen Singh's was the longest, and the chairman of Britain's Royal Geographical Society called it a "marvelous journey."

The Spies of India

British administrators in India began training the pundits in the mid-1860s. Travel into the Himalaya mountain ranges north of India had become too dangerous for British **surveyors** and mapmakers. Himalayan kingdoms, such as Ladakh and Nepal, were suspicious of—and often hostile to—foreigners, and Tibet had closed its borders to all outsiders. Greater knowledge of central Asia would help the British to compete with Russia and China for influence in the region.

The solution was to use surveyors who were native to India or central Asia. Such men could travel more safely than Europeans in disguise. The British trained these geographical spies to use

In a single journey through the mountain kingdoms of central Asia, Kishen Singh traveled more than 2,800 miles in 4½ years.

plateau high, flat area of land

caravan large group of people traveling together, often with pack animals, across a desert or other dangerous region

surveying equipment and provided them with money, false identities, and other aids such as clothing with secret pockets.

The Early Journeys of A.K.

Sometime in the late 1860s, Kishen Singh left his hometown of Milam, in the mountainous northern region of Kumaon, and traveled west to Dehra Dun. There he began his training under Nain Singh and officials of the British Survey of India, who gave him the code names "A.K." and "Krishna." In 1871 he made his first expedition into Tibet, accompanied by four assistants disguised as animal drivers and servants. Their goal was Koko Nor (also known as Qinghai), a large lake in northern Tibet. They entered Tibet safely, but as they approached the Jang Thang—Tibet's high central **plateau**— they were attacked by robbers. Stripped of their supplies, the spies returned to India to report the failure of their mission.

Kishen Singh headed north again in 1873, when he and Nain Singh accompanied British diplomats to the city of Yarkant (now in the Chinese region of Xinjiang Uygur). The following year, he explored the area south of Yarkant and ventured into the rugged Pamir Mountains of Afghanistan. His greatest achievement, however, was yet to come.

Merchants, Servants, and Spies

In May 1878, Kishen Singh set out with two assistants from Darjeeling, in northeastern India, on an ambitious mission. Their assignment was to cross Tibet from south to north, explore the fringes of Mongolia's Gobi Desert, and return home by a different route through Tibet.

Singh disguised himself as a merchant, and the three explorers went first to Lhasa, where they stayed for more than a year, waiting to join a **caravan** bound for Mongolia. Singh spent his time studying the city, its people, and its lively social, religious, and economic life.

Finally Singh and his companions joined a group of Tibetans and Mongolians headed north. Following a seldom-used route in hopes of avoiding bandits, the caravan passed through a mountain range and entered the Jang Thang. Soon Singh was in territory that had never been visited by a pundit or any other British agent.

The caravan crossed the mountains of the Kunlun Shan on the northern edge of the Jang Thang—and then bandits struck. Singh was left with no money or possessions other than his hidden surveying instruments. This time, however, he did not turn back. He and his servants pressed on, crossing a corner of the Tsaidam, a vast salt marsh. They also passed Koko Nor, the goal of Singh's earlier trip. To earn money during the winter of 1879 to 1880, they worked as camel herders for a Tibetan priest. In the spring, one of Singh's servants deserted him, taking nearly all of the group's meager supplies, so Singh and his remaining assistant, Chumbel, again worked as animal tenders. By January 1881, they were moving north again, toward the city of Dunhuang on the edge of the Gobi Desert.

Few outsiders had visited Dunhuang since Marco POLO had crossed Asia in the 1200s. Singh made many careful notes about the city. He compared its climate with that of Yarkand and described the local cotton and silk industries. Most of the people in Dunhuang were Chinese, and there was a Chinese army fort nearby. Singh noted that girls' feet were bound with cloth to limit their growth and transform their shape, in keeping with Chinese tradition.

Singh and Chumbel soon left Dunhuang, but they were forced to return by the town's governor, who suspected them of being spies or thieves. He forbade them to leave for several months, during which the two men tried to earn a living as fruit vendors. At last a **lama** persuaded the governor to release Singh and Chumbel. The lama then journeyed southward, with the two explorers as his servants.

The Homeward Route

Across the Tsaidam and the Jang Thang, Singh and Chumbel served the lama. They parted from him near Chhergundo, a trade center east of Tibet, and joined a caravan headed for Tatsienlu (present-day Kangding, China). The two agents were still many hundreds of miles from home.

French missionaries in Tatsienlu, who knew the men's real identities, gave them a little money. Singh and Chumbel left Tatsienlu in February 1882. The rest of the trip brought many delays and perils, but Singh continued his surveying.

The two travelers painstakingly worked their way westward until they were near Lhasa. Then they turned south and struggled back toward Darjeeling, which they reached in November 1882—out of money, exhausted, and near starvation. Kishen Singh's notebooks had survived his long journey, and British officials in India highly valued the information they contained. The pundit retired and lived out his life in northern India, treasuring his books, maps, and the medals he had received from the geographical societies of Europe.

SUGGESTED READING Peter Hopkirk, *Trespassers on the Roof of the World: The Race for Lhasa* (John Murray, 1982); Derek Waller, *The Pundits: British Exploration of Tibet and Central Asia* (University of Kentucky Press, 1990).

lama Buddhist priest or monk of high rank in Tibet and Mongolia

Singh, Nain

Indian
b 1830?; Milam?, India
d 1882?; Moradabad, India
Explored Tibet

surveyor one who makes precise measurements of a location's geography

Nain Singh was among the first in a group of brave and resourceful Indian men called pundits, who were trained as explorers by British colonial officers in the 1800s. Singh acted as a secret agent, traveling several times through Tibet, which Europeans were forbidden to enter. His journeys greatly increased Europeans' knowledge of that mysterious land high in the mountains of central Asia.

Deadly Competition

In the 1800s, India was Britain's largest and most important colony. British army officers and **surveyors** began to probe beyond India's northern border, where the land rises in a series of immense, forbidding mountain ranges called the Himalaya. Many of the kingdoms in those mountains refused to allow foreigners to map their lands. Tibet was especially strict in enforcing this policy. Despite the danger, Britain was eager for knowledge of—and influence in—central Asia. Similar advances by Russia and China only added to Britain's sense of urgency. British spies attempted to enter Tibet in disguise, but by the mid-1800s, several had been killed, and colonial officials in India sought an alternative way to explore Central Asia.

T. C. Montgomerie, a British surveyor in India, won support for an unusual idea. He planned to train Indians in surveying and map-making and then secretly send them into regions that were closed to Europeans. In 1863 Montgomerie selected the first two candidates for his program, cousins named Nain Singh and Mani Singh.

Training the Pundit

Nain Singh, whose father had helped a British explorer 40 years earlier, was the schoolmaster of Milam, a village in the mountainous northern region called Kumaon. He was known as a learned man— a *pandit,* in his language. The British pronounced this word "pundit" and used it as Nain Singh's code name. They later applied the term to all of their undercover Indian explorers.

At Dehra Dun, a city west of Milam, British officials trained the Singhs for two years. The cousins learned how to use navigational tools to determine a place's **latitude, longitude,** and height above sea level. Their clothes and luggage had secret compartments to hide the tools. They also learned to walk in steps of exactly equal length, so that by counting their paces, they could measure the distance they traveled. The spies also developed false identities and memorized codes in which to take notes.

Spy Inside the City

In 1865 the Singhs went on their first mission into Tibet. They were turned back at the border, but Nain Singh later managed to enter the country alone. He spent three months in Lhasa, the capital, observing the city's layout, markets, and diverse peoples. Risking death if he were to be caught, he used a **sextant** to measure the positions of the sun and stars over Lhasa. On one memorable day, Singh was part of a group that visited the Dalai Lama, the spiritual leader of Tibet, in his palace. Though greatly worried that guards would discover his mapmaking tools, Singh managed to measure and map the palace.

By the time he returned to Dehra Dun, in late 1866, he had traveled more than 1,200 miles. He had mapped several important trade routes and part of the course of the Zangbo River, which flows through Tibet. Geographers used his astronomical readings to place Lhasa accurately on maps for the first time. Montgomerie wrote to the Royal Geographical Society in London, praising Singh's accomplishments highly. The society awarded Singh a gold watch, the first of many honors he would receive.

The Risk of Exposure

In May 1867, the pundit set off with several companions—including his brother, Kalian Singh—on another mission. His goal was Thogjalung, a region of western Tibet where gold was said to be mined. He had to bribe suspicious border guards, trek through blizzards, and climb through a mountain pass that was 18,570 feet high. The gold mines did exist, and Nain Singh made a detailed report on their operation when he returned to India in late 1867. The following year, Kalian Singh carried out a mission of his own in western Tibet.

Nain Singh's final and most ambitious assignment was to travel west from Ladakh (now part of Kashmir in northern India), all the

latitude distance north or south of the equator

longitude distance east or west of an imaginary line on the earth's surface; in 1884 most nations agreed to draw the line through Greenwich, England

sextant optical instrument used since the 1750s to determine distance north or south of the equator

Nain Singh, an explorer and spy, was one of several Indian secret agents who inspired the British writer Rudyard Kipling's famous novel *Kim.*

plateau high, flat area of land

way across Tibet and China. Disguised as Buddhist monks, Singh and four companions left Leh, the capital of Ladakh, in the summer of 1874. As they crossed the high central **plateau** of Tibet, they mapped several lakes that were unknown to European geographers. The explorers also studied more gold mines, dodging robbers along the way.

Exhausted after a four-month trek, the party reached Lhasa—only to learn that the messenger who was supposed to meet them with money had not arrived. To make matters worse, Singh heard that Chinese officials in the area were on the lookout for a British spy. When he accidentally met a merchant from Ladakh who knew his true identity, Singh decided to leave Lhasa without delay. Without additional funds, he could not hope to make the long journey to Beijing in eastern China. Instead he sent two of his companions back to Ladakh and led the other two south across the Himalaya, back to India—the end of a 1,400-mile journey.

The Pundit Returns to Teaching

Nain Singh was awarded the gold medal of the Royal Geographical Society, but with his eyesight failing, he had to retire from active exploration. He helped the British to train other pundits for secret missions and then retired to his home on land that was given to him as a reward. Nain Singh's successful missions inspired the work of other pundits, such as his cousin Kishen SINGH and KINTUP. The pundits solved many of the geographical mysteries of the Himalaya region, known as the "Roof of the World." In 1876, a British official said of Nain Singh: "His observations have added a larger amount of important knowledge to the map of Asia than those of any other living man."

SUGGESTED READING Peter Hopkirk, *Trespassers on the Roof of the World: The Race for Lhasa* (John Murray, 1982); John MacGregor, *Tibet: A Chronicle of Exploration* (Routledge and Kegan Paul, 1970); Derek Waller, *The Pundits: British Exploration of Tibet and Central Asia* (University of Kentucky Press, 1990).

Sintra, Pedro de

Portuguese
b 1445?; Portugal
d ?; ?
Explored West Africa

caravel small ship with three masts and both square and triangular sails

Pedro de Sintra was one of the last explorers to be commissioned by Prince Henry the Navigator of Portugal. For over 40 years, Prince Henry sent his most able mariners to map the unknown coast of West Africa. Sintra's two expeditions greatly advanced the Portuguese effort.

Thundering Mountains on the Coast

In 1460 Henry chose Sintra, a young attendant in his service, to sail a **caravel** as far down the African coast as possible. On his first trip, Sintra reached what is now Guinea. Henry was pleased enough to equip him for a second expedition, but the prince soon died. Though his successor, King Alfonso V, did not share Henry's enthusiasm for exploration, he allowed Sintra's mission to proceed as planned.

Sintra led two caravels past the Gambia River and landed on the Bissagos Islands, off the coast of Guinea. He explored the islands' interiors but failed to communicate with the people who lived there. From that point on, the coast was uncharted territory. Sintra sailed for about 250 miles before reaching a high land protruding out to sea. He named it Cape Sagres after the town where Henry had established a training center for navigators. Continuing south, Sintra came upon a massive mountain range on the coast. Thunder echoing through the mountains made a roaring sound, so he named them the Sierra Leona, which means Mountains of the Lioness in Portuguese.

A Guest at Court

Sintra sailed on and named the Rio Roxo, meaning Red River, because soil in the water gave it a reddish color. The Portuguese soon celebrated the feast of Saint Anne by discovering and naming the Cape of Saint Anne. Sixty miles farther along the coast, they found a river with palm trees on its bank, and Sintra named it Rio das Palmes.

After the explorers had charted about 600 miles of coastline, Africans approached them in canoes. Sintra returned to Portugal with an African man and presented him to the court. However, the Portuguese were unable to communicate with their guest. They gave him new clothes and gifts and later returned him to West Africa.

SUGGESTED READING G. R. Crone, *The Voyages of Cadamosto and Other Documents on Western Africa in the Second Half of the Fifteenth Century* (reprint, Kraus Reprint, 1967).

Siqueira, Diogo Lopes de. See *Lopes de Sequeira, Diogo.*

Smith, Jedediah Strong

American
b June 24, 1798; Bainbridge, New York
d May 27, 1831; near Cimarron River
*Led first American overland
expedition to California*

Jedediah Strong Smith was one of the most famous Mountain Men and the first American to make an overland journey to California. In a rowdy, lawless environment, Smith was known as a man who drank little, did not use tobacco, and carried a Bible at all times. Unfortunately, much of his knowledge of the West went unrecorded when he died violently at age 32.

The Dangers of Being a Mountain Man

Jed Smith was born in upstate New York, and at the age of 13, he took a job as a clerk on a Lake Erie cargo vessel. He was fascinated by the stories told by traders returning from the West, so he moved to St. Louis. In 1822 he joined William Henry ASHLEY's Rocky Mountain Fur Company and was soon considered an experienced mountain man. In the fall of 1823, he was chosen to lead an expedition to the West.

One startling incident on this journey demonstrated Smith's physical and mental toughness. He was traveling through South Dakota's Black Hills when a grizzly bear sprung from a thicket and took Smith's head in its mouth, ripping open the scalp from Smith's left eye to his right ear. His skull was exposed, one of his ears was hanging loose, and he was bleeding badly. Smith remained conscious and instructed his men to sew up his wounds and reattach his ear with a needle and thread. After taking only 10 days to recover, he continued to lead his men west.

In early 1824, the party came upon South Pass, a 20-mile-wide gap in the Rocky Mountains. Smith's group was the first to find the pass since its discovery 12 years earlier by Robert STUART. It later became the gateway through which thousands of settlers migrated to Oregon and California.

A determined and religious man, Jed Smith survived attacks by bears and Indians to lead overland journeys to California.

The Country of Starvation

In 1826 Smith and two others bought Ashley's company. Smith's partners traded in the Rocky Mountains while he took a party southwest to look for new trapping territory. In August, Smith left the area of the Great Salt Lake with 15 men and wandered south for a month over the Wasatch Mountains. They were near the eastern rim of Nevada's Great Basin, traveling farther into what Smith called a "country of starvation." The landscape of reddish soil and clumps of brush was obviously not beaver country. Nevertheless, they crossed the Colorado River and followed it into the Black Mountains of what is now Arizona.

By then, however, the party was dangerously low on food and water. Luckily they came upon a fertile valley where they met friendly Mojave Indians. The Mojave gave them supplies and told them of a trail that led to the ocean. Smith did not expect to find beaver ahead, but he was unwilling to go back the way he had come. So he and his men headed west across the Mojave Desert, following a river that often disappeared underground for miles at a time. After 15 days in the desert's blazing heat, they arrived at Mission San Gabriel, near the site of present-day Los Angeles. However, the Americans had entered Mexican territory without permission. They were held by local officials, who suspected them of being spies rather than fur traders. Three American sea captains who were in the area persuaded the authorities to free Smith, as long as he and his men left immediately the way they had come.

Across the Great Basin

Smith immediately disregarded the agreement and spent the winter in the San Joaquin Valley, trapping beaver. Leaving most of the party behind at a sheltered spot, he and two others made a dangerous eight-day crossing of the Sierra Nevada. On the other side, the men were faced with the Great Basin, a barren plain that stretched ahead for hundreds of miles.

Rather than go back across the mountains to rejoin their party, Smith and his two companions pushed ahead. On June 25, one of the men, Robert Evans, collapsed from exhaustion. The other two had no choice but to leave him. Fortunately, they found water three miles ahead, and Smith carried some back to revive Evans. On July 3, the three travelers reached Bear Lake, the site of the 1827 rendezvous, an annual meeting of Mountain Men, trappers, and traders. However, Smith's journey was not yet over—11 men were still waiting for him in California.

History Repeats Itself

After 10 days at the rendezvous, Smith gathered a party of 18 men and 2 women for a return trip to California. Avoiding the Great Basin, Smith followed the same route west that he had taken the year before—and experienced many of the same hardships. Meanwhile, the Mojave had turned hostile, possibly because they had been attacked by trappers during the previous year. While Smith's group was attempting to ferry across the Colorado River, the Indians struck, killing 10 men and capturing the women, whose fate is still unknown. Smith and 8 other men were on a raft in the middle of the river and escaped unharmed. However, they had few supplies and little ammunition, and they still had to cross the Mojave Desert. Another difficult journey across the desert was again followed by imprisonment in California. As before, a sea captain helped Smith win his freedom on the condition that he leave immediately. Smith again broke that promise.

Gathering the remaining members of his two expeditions, Smith wintered in the Sacramento River valley. In the summer of 1828, the group headed to the north, looking for an eastward route north of the Great Basin. After a hostile encounter with some Kelawatset Indians, Smith and 2 men went scouting on the Umpqua River. While they were gone, the Kelawatset retaliated, raiding the main camp and killing 15 of the 16 men who were there. The lone survivor joined Smith and the other 2 at Fort Vancouver on the Columbia River.

Before going east again, Smith noted the excellent possibilities for agricultural and commercial settlement in the Northwest. He later made a report to the U.S. secretary of war. Smith pointed out that settlers with wagons and even dairy cows could easily move westward through the South Pass, all the way to the Pacific Ocean.

Smith retired from fur trapping in 1830 and settled in St. Louis, intending to draw maps that would illustrate his accomplishments. Before doing so, he made one last trading journey to Santa Fe. While looking for water alone near the Cimarron River (near the present-day border of Oklahoma, Colorado, and Kansas), he was surprised and killed by a party of Comanche Indians.

SUGGESTED READING John L. Allen, *Jedediah Smith and the Mountain Men of the American West* (Chelsea House, 1991); Harrison C. Dale, *The Explorations of William H. Ashley and Jedediah Smith, 1822–1829* (University of Nebraska Press, 1991); Dale L. Morgan, *Jedediah Smith and the Opening of the West* (Bobbs-Merrill, 1953).

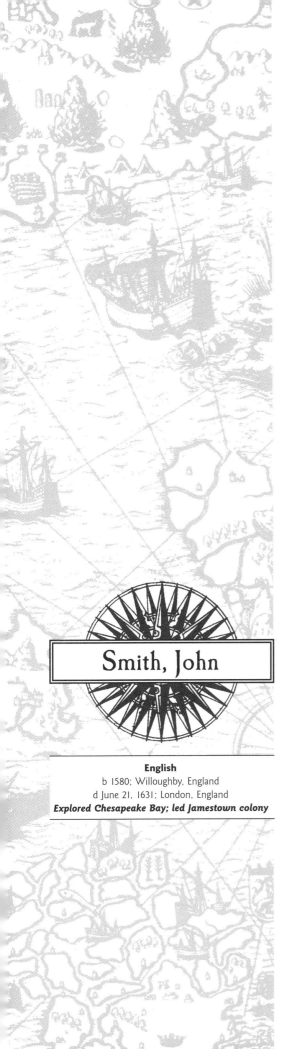

Smith, John

English
b 1580; Willoughby, England
d June 21, 1631; London, England
Explored Chesapeake Bay; led Jamestown colony

From 1607 to 1609, John Smith almost singlehandedly saved Jamestown, England's first permanent settlement in America, from starvation. During that time, he explored and mapped Chesapeake Bay. He later charted the coast of New England and gave the region its name.

The Bored Adventurer

As a young man, Smith spent several years as a soldier and adventurer in Europe. He later became known for telling stories about his escapades, such as the time he was taken prisoner by Turks. He was sent to Constantinople (now Istanbul, Turkey) as a servant to the wife of a powerful ruler. The noblewoman, Smith claimed, then fell in love with him and sent him to her brother, a prince, whom Smith allegedly killed in order to escape. He eventually made his way back to England in 1604, but he found domestic life dull in comparison to such adventures.

Smith signed on with the Virginia Company of London and helped to plan and organize the company's Jamestown colony. He accompanied the first settlers there in 1607 and soon found that many of them were reluctant to do the hard work that was necessary to build

John Smith became an American legend for his leadership of the Jamestown colony—as well as for his imaginative storytelling.

the colony. Realizing that food was Jamestown's most pressing need, Smith took on the task of trading for corn with the area's Indians. Despite their reluctance, he was usually able to persuade or pressure them to supply food to the colony.

On one trading mission, he was taken prisoner by Opechancanough, chief of the Pamunkey tribe. Using his limited knowledge of the Algonquin language, Smith escaped death by showing the chief a compass and entertaining him with tales of the sun and stars. Opechancanough turned Smith over to his brother, Chief Powhatan, who debated with his counselors and then decided to kill the prisoner. As Smith later told the story, the chief's favorite daughter, 12-year-old Pocahontas, placed her head on top of Smith's to prevent the warriors from clubbing him to death. He was returned unharmed to Jamestown, but the colony's relations with Powhatan remained uneasy.

Mapping Chesapeake Bay

Shortly after the arrival of new settlers in January 1608, a fire caused by carelessness burned down much of Jamestown. Smith oversaw the rebuilding of the village and the planting of crops. He then decided to go exploring, perhaps to escape the burden of managing a colony filled with lazy and scheming settlers. He made two separate trips around Chesapeake Bay in the summer of 1608. On the first, he encountered friendly Indians on the bay's eastern shore. He then traveled up the Potomac and Rappahannock Rivers, where the Indians were more suspicious and hostile. His second trip took him to the head of the bay, and there he discovered the mouth of the Susquehanna River. He also met the Susquehanna Iroquois, who offered to trade goods that they had bought from French traders to the north. Smith prepared a map of the bay that was considered valuable by sailors and colonists for the next 100 years.

When he returned to Jamestown, he found that he had been chosen to be the new leader of the colony. For the next year, he continued to solve the colony's problems. He pressured the Indians to provide food, but they grew more wary as more settlers kept arriving. In August 1609, a ship brought 300 new colonists, and Smith was overwhelmed by the prospect of feeding them all. A new governor was expected from England soon, but Smith was relieved of duty even earlier. A supply of gunpowder accidentally exploded in his canoe, and his injuries required him to return to England in October 1609.

Names for New England

Smith returned to America five years later at the request of a group of London merchants. They wanted him to map the coast of the area then called North Virginia (present-day New England). He passed the summer on Monhegan Island (off the coast of present-day Maine), and from there he charted the shore as far south as Cape Cod. His map included a harbor with the Indian name of Patuxet. Prince Charles of England insisted on renaming it Plymouth, because he felt that settlers would be more attracted to a place with an English name.

Smith returned to England, and in 1616 he published a book titled *A Description of New England.* This book gave the region its current name and proclaimed it a desirable area for settlement. The Pilgrims who sailed on the *Mayflower* in 1620 relied on Smith's map and book in choosing the harbor at Plymouth for their colony.

Smith spent the later years of his life writing several books. The last of these was titled *Advertisements for the Unexperienced Planters of New England, or Anywhere.* It contains valuable and sometimes amusing advice based on his personal experiences in North America.

John Smith was a daring and courageous explorer as well as a knowledgeable, responsible, and resourceful leader. The Jamestown colony would probably not have survived its first two years without him. Moreover, without his map and book, the Pilgrims would have had an even more difficult time settling in America than they did. John Smith therefore deserves much of the credit for the establishment and survival of the first two permanent English colonies in America.

SUGGESTED READING Philip L. Barbour, *The Three Worlds of Captain John Smith* (Houghton Mifflin, 1964); Alden T. Vaughan, *American Genesis: Captain John Smith and the Founding of Virginia* (HarperCollins, 1990).

Smith, William

English
b 1800?; Blyth, England
d ?; ?
*Discovered South Shetland Islands
and tip of Antarctic Peninsula*

William Smith, a British sea captain, is sometimes credited with discovering continental Antarctica in 1820. This find would never have been made if not for a fortunate accident a year earlier. An English engineer had hired Smith to transport equipment from Chile to the Río de la Plata in Argentina. To do so, Smith had to sail his vessel, the *Williams,* around Cape Horn at the southern tip of South America.

The ship was driven almost 500 miles south of the cape by a severe storm, and on February 18, 1819, Smith found himself among a group of previously unknown islands, later named the South Shetlands. When he reported his discovery, few people believed him, but he returned in October and planted the British flag on the islands.

By that time, word of the discovery had spread, and the British navy planned a survey of the area. Smith commanded the *Williams* on an expedition led by Edward Bransfield. On January 30, 1820, the explorers sighted a mainland, which turned out to be Graham Land, the northern tip of the long Antarctic Peninsula. Although the region was rich in seals and fish, the British government did little to establish control over it. Other nations soon made rival claims, some of which are still unresolved today. The details of Smith's life after that expedition remain obscure.

SUGGESTED READING Colin Monteath, *Antarctica: Beyond the Southern Ocean* (HarperCollins, 1996).

Soto, Hernando de

Spanish
b between 1496 and 1501;
Jerez de los Caballeros, Spain
d May 21, 1542; Mississippi River
(near modern Natchez, Mississippi)
*Explored southeastern United States
and Mississippi River*

Hernando de Soto played a major role in the Spanish conquest of Nicaragua and Peru in the early 1500s. He is best known, however, for his exploration of what became the southeastern United States. On that difficult journey, he traveled through land that is now part of nine states. He was also the first European to cross the Appalachian Mountains and the Mississippi River.

Fame and Fortune in the Americas
Soto was born into a Spanish family of minor nobility sometime between 1496 and 1501. Nothing is known of his youth. He probably

Hernando de Soto's desire for greater wealth and power led him into conflicts and hardships on both American continents.

league unit of distance, usually used at sea, roughly equal to 3.5 miles

arrived in the Americas in 1514 with a governor of Panama, Pedro Arias de Ávila, also known as Pedrarias. Under Pedrarias's guidance, Soto developed his skills as a soldier. He distinguished himself during Francisco Fernández de Córdoba's conquest of Nicaragua in 1524 and became one of the leading citizens of the newly founded colony there.

Seeking more power and independence, Soto joined Francisco Pizarro's raid on the Inca Empire of Peru in 1531. In December of that year, he brought 100 men and 25 horses to Pizarro at Puná Island. Greatly outnumbered by the Inca, Pizarro welcomed these reinforcements, and Soto was a key figure in the campaign. On a scouting mission to locate passes through the Andes mountain range, Soto became the first Spaniard to see the Inca civilization. When he reached the village of Caxias, along the road known as the Inca highway, he saw signs of the empire's great wealth. He was also the first Spaniard to meet the Inca emperor Atahualpa. Reportedly, Soto opposed Pizarro's later decision to execute the emperor.

When Soto returned to Spain in 1536, he was a wealthy and admired man. Those who knew him described him as a gentleman—kind, generous, and charming. The king of Spain rewarded his successes in Peru with a knighthood and the noble title of Marquis. Soto then married one of Pedrarias's daughters, Isabella de Bobadilla.

Expedition to La Florida

Despite his new wealth and status, Soto still wanted greater independence and power, and he repeatedly asked the king to make him governor of a colony. In 1537 the king appointed him governor of Cuba and granted him the right to conquer and colonize the territory of La Florida. That region, which had been discovered in 1513 by Juan Ponce de León, was vaguely defined as including all land north of Cuba. Soto was told to select 200 **leagues** along the coast of La Florida to form a new colony, which he would then govern.

Soto had no trouble enlisting volunteers, partly because of his prestige and partly because of the potential for finding great riches, as Pizarro had done in Peru and Hernán Cortés had done in Mexico. On April 7, 1538, a group of 650 men and women, with 12 priests and about 250 horses, left Spain for Cuba. On May 30, they landed in La Florida in what is now called Tampa Bay.

The party traveled northwest, enduring blazing heat for several days before heavy rain slowed their movement. During an attack on hostile Indians, they found Juan Ortiz, a survivor of Pánfilo de Narváez's expedition. Ortiz, who had been stranded among the Indians of Florida for two years, joined Soto as a translator.

The Search for Indian Gold

Soto wintered in 1530 at the village of Apalachen, near the site of present-day Tallahassee. In his efforts to learn the locations of gold and silver, Soto treated the local Indians cruelly. He terrorized their villages, enslaved his prisoners, and sent vicious dogs to chase after those who escaped. To avoid such treatment, most Indians there and elsewhere tended to tell Soto what he wanted to hear: that a land of riches existed not far away. In early 1540, he heard of a

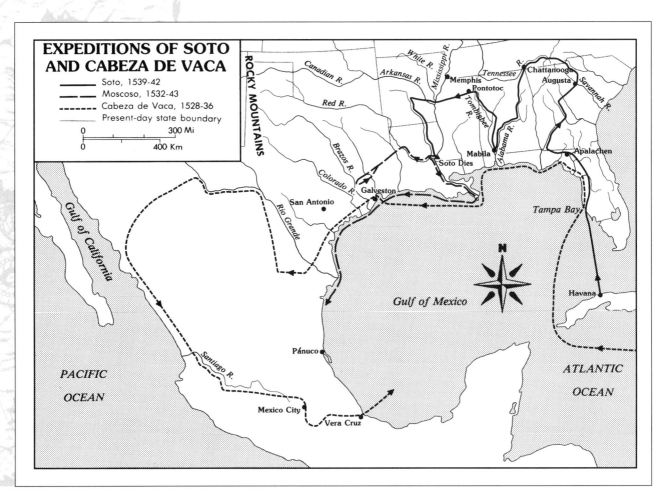

EXPEDITIONS OF SOTO AND CABEZA DE VACA

———— Soto, 1539-42
—— — Moscoso, 1532-43
- - - - - Cabeza de Vaca, 1528-36
———— Present-day state boundary

0   300 Mi
0   400 Km

Reports of the overland trek made by Álvar Núñez CABEZA DE VACA led directly to Hernando de Soto's exploration of what became the southeastern United States.

wealthy land called Cofitachequi. The Spanish broke camp on March 3 and headed east.

The explorers followed what are now called the Flint and Ocmulgee Rivers. Turning eastward, they arrived at Cofitachequi on April 30. An Indian queen, known to the Spanish as the Lady of Cofitachequi, sent canoes to ferry Soto and some of his men to the town. The only treasure she could offer him, however, was freshwater pearls.

Another report of gold then led Soto and his followers north toward the territory of the Chiaha Indians. The Spanish traveled between the Savannah and Saluda Rivers through what later became South Carolina and North Carolina. They then headed west and were the first Europeans to cross the Appalachian Mountains, reaching what is now the Tennessee River. Traveling downstream into what is now Tennessee, the explorers arrived on June 6 at the Chiaha settlement. The Indians had plenty of food but—to Soto's frustration—no gold.

The Expedition in Tatters

Soto then set out to meet a great Indian chief named Cosa who supposedly lived to the south. Following the Tennessee River, he led the Spaniards into what is now Alabama, over the Sand Mountains to the Coosa River. He met Chief Cosa, who took him to meet Chief Tuscaloosa of the Choctaw nation. After trading with the Indians, Soto entered the land of the Mobile Indians. A fierce battle broke out, and so much damage was done to the Spaniards' equipment and clothing that they were forced to dress in animal skins and make tools from natural materials.

After heading north again, the expedition made its winter camp near the site of present-day Pontotoc, Mississippi. The winter was uneventful until March 4, 1541, when a surprise attack by Chickasaw Indians took the lives of 12 Spaniards and 50 horses. The next month, the party left the camp and traveled west, hoping to find a route to the Pacific Ocean. On May 8, they discovered the Mississippi River and built four barges to cross it. No Europeans had seen the Mississippi since Alonso ALVAREZ DE PINEDA had noticed its outflow into the Gulf of Mexico in 1519.

For several months, the Spanish marched west across what is now Arkansas. They waded through swamps, climbed hills, and crossed the Arkansas River twice; all during a severe drought. The expedition finally settled in for a bitter, snowy winter at the Tula Indian village of Utiangue.

Death in the Mississippi

By the time Soto began traveling again, on March 6, 1542, he had only 300 people and 40 horses left. Rather than continue his hopeless westward course, he chose to move south along what is now the Ouachita River. He intended to reach the Mississippi River and search for an outlet to the Gulf of Mexico. After an unusual spring snowstorm forced them to stop for four days in what is now Louisiana, Soto fell ill with a serious fever. He died on May 21 near the site of present-day Natchez, Mississippi. His soldiers feared that Indians might learn of Soto's death and take the opportunity to attack, so the Spaniards secretly weighted their leader's body with sand and lowered it to the bottom of the Mississippi River.

Luis de Moscoso then took command of the expedition and tried to lead the survivors to **New Spain.** First he tried a westward land route into what is now Texas; he then gave up, turned back, and wintered not far from the place where Soto had died. The next spring, the Spaniards built seven boats, which they launched on the Mississippi River on July 2, 1543. They were the first Europeans ever to travel down the river. As they had hoped, the Mississippi carried them into the Gulf of Mexico. They followed the coastline to the west and straggled into Spanish settlements in September.

The expedition's accomplishments were not recognized at the time. It had obviously been a disaster, involving great suffering and loss of life, and no precious metals had been found to match the riches of Peru and Mexico. The Spanish authorities were not inclined to pay any further attention to the region that Soto had traveled.

In the history of exploration, however, Soto's journey was one of the most valuable ever made in North America. Soto covered over 4,000 miles in a large area that would one day become part of the United States. His expedition gathered a great deal of information about the land and provided the first descriptions of the Indian tribes who lived there. More than 450 years after Soto came ashore at Tampa Bay, citizens of Florida still honor him by reenacting his landing each year.

New Spain region of Spanish colonial empire that included the areas now occupied by Mexico, Florida, Texas, New Mexico, Arizona, California, and various Caribbean islands

SUGGESTED READING Miguel Albornoz, *Hernando de Soto, Knight of the Americas*, translated by Bruce Boeglin (Franklin Watts, 1986); Buckingham Smith, translator, *Narratives of de Soto in the Conquest of Florida, as told by a gentleman of Elvas* (Palmetto Books, 1968); John R. Swanton, *The United States DeSoto Expedition Final Report* (Smithsonian Institution Press, 1985); Garcilaso de la Vega, *The Florida of the Incas; A History of Adelantado, Hernando de Soto*, edited and translated by John Grier Varner and Jeanette Johnson Varner (University of Texas Press, 1951).

Speke, John Hanning

English
b May 4, 1827; Jordans, England
d September 15, 1864; Bath, England
***Explored central Africa;
discovered source of White Nile River***

---

tributary stream or river that flows into a larger stream or river

malaria disease that is spread by mosquitoes in tropical areas

For a map of Speke's routes, see the profile of Richard Francis BURTON in Volume 1.

Emerging from an expedition in central Africa, John Hanning Speke claimed to have traced the origin of the Nile, the longest river in the world, to what is now known as Lake Victoria. Although many of England's leading geographers and scientists were convinced that Speke had reliable evidence to support his discovery, others remained skeptical. The controversy over Speke's work continued for many years until later explorers, such as Henry Morton STANLEY, finally confirmed that Lake Victoria was indeed the source of the Nile.

Soldiers on a Mission

Born to a wealthy family, Speke left home at age 17 to join the British army in India. While there, he spent his free time exploring and hunting in the Himalaya mountain range. In 1854 he traveled to the east coast of Africa, where he met a fellow English soldier, Richard Francis BURTON. The pair set out on an expedition to explore Somaliland (present-day Somalia) and to locate the source of the Nile River. However, both men were wounded during an attack by Somali, and they were forced to end their mission. Undaunted by this incident, the soldiers returned to Africa the next year.

Speke and Burton began their second expedition together in December 1856, this time heading for the eastern interior of the continent. Burton had won the sponsorship of England's Royal Geographical Society and was appointed the leader of the expedition, with Speke as second-in-command. Their assignment was to search for the origin of the White Nile, the Nile River's largest **tributary.** They would begin by investigating an unexplored body of water known as the Sea of Ujiji.

The Controversial Claim

Departing from the island of Zanzibar, the party traveled west to Kazeh (now Tabora, Tanzania) and arrived at the Sea of Ujiji in early 1858. Burton fell severely ill with **malaria,** and Speke was temporarily blinded by a tropical eye disease. However, once Speke had partly recovered, he proceeded to investigate the Sea of Ujiji. He learned that it actually consisted of three large lakes. Lake Nyasa (also known as Lake Malawi) is the southernmost of the three. Farther north is the long and narrow Lake Tanganyika. To the northeast lies what was then called Lake Ukerewe, which Speke believed to be the source of the Nile River.

On July 30, Speke reached the southern shore of Lake Ukerewe and renamed it Victoria Nyanza in honor of Britain's queen. By this time, his vision had been largely restored, but he did not explore the lake. He spoke to local tribes and to German missionaries in the area, who said that a large river began on the lake's north side. Speke rejoined Burton and told him what he had learned, but

John Speke notified the Royal Geographical Society of his discovery by sending a telegram that read: "The Nile is settled."

Burton ridiculed Speke for believing these claims without evidence. Burton doubted that the Nile began at Lake Victoria. Speke, however, was convinced that there was a connection between the two bodies of water, and he set out to prove his theory.

Speke hurried back to Britain to present his discovery to the Royal Geographical Society. The society's officials did not completely accept his ideas, but they agreed to finance another trip to find the source of the Nile. Accompanied by a friend from the army, James Augustus Grant, Speke departed for East Africa in April 1860.

Speke returned to Kazeh and proceeded north around the western edge of Lake Victoria. On July 27, 1862, he reached the falls to the north of the lake, where the White Nile begins. He described the scene in his journal as "a sight that attracted one to it for hours—the roar of the waters, the thousands of passenger-fish, leaping at the falls with all their might." He was certain that the lake was "the great source of the holy river. . . ."

Jealousy and Doubt

Speke had hoped to sail the length of the Nile on his trip home, but hostile tribes in the region prevented him from making such a journey. Instead he rejoined Grant, who had been recuperating from an infected leg, just west of Lake Victoria. Traveling north by land, the pair followed the course of the river as closely as possible. By February 1863, they reached Gondokoro, in the Sudan, where they met fellow explorer Samuel White BAKER. From there Speke and Grant traveled to North Africa and then returned to Britain, where they were greeted as heroes.

Although many people believed that Speke had found the source of the Nile at Lake Victoria, others—especially Burton—were unconvinced. Burton insisted that since Speke had not followed the river's entire course to Gondokoro, he had not proved that the Nile emerged from Lake Victoria. Burton may have challenged Speke's claims because he was jealous that Speke had made such a long-sought discovery. The former partners made plans to debate the issue at a public meeting in Bath, England.

The debate attracted the attention of hundreds of Britain's leading scientists and geographers. But the day before the two men were scheduled to meet, Speke accidentally shot and killed himself during a hunting trip. False rumors spread that Speke had committed suicide because he was unprepared to debate Burton. Grant took Speke's place at the meeting, even though he had not actually been present when Speke found the Nile's source. Other expeditions soon confirmed Speke's discovery of the source of the Nile.

SUGGESTED READING William Harrison, *Burton and Speke* (W. H. Allen, 1984); Dorothy Kushler, *Deep Into Africa* (Aldus Books, 1968); Alexander Maitland, *Speke* (Victorian and Modern History Book Club, 1973); John Hanning Speke, *Journal of the Discovery of the Source of the Nile* (Dover Publications, 1996).

Stanley, Henry Morton

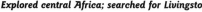

Welsh-American
b January 28, 1841; Denbigh, Wales
d May 10, 1904; London, England
Explored central Africa; searched for Livingstone

circumnavigate to travel around

dysentery disease that causes severe diarrhea

Henry Morton Stanley is considered by some historians to be the leading explorer and colonizer of Africa in the 1800s. He remains most famous for locating the missing Scottish missionary David Livingstone in central Africa. However, Stanley's other achievements are just as memorable. During almost 20 years of exploration, he **circumnavigated** Lake Tanganyika and Lake Victoria and settled lingering questions about the source of the Nile River. He helped both Belgium and Britain to develop African colonies. Stanley was also the first European to travel the length of the Congo River and to visit Mount Ruwenzori.

Stanley was a journalist who described his travels in dramatic books and news stories. Some critics accused him of stretching the truth to his advantage, and even his own autobiography was filled with deliberate lies. Scholars have speculated that as a result of his difficult childhood, Stanley felt the need to hide or misrepresent some facts about his life. Despite any insecurities he may have had, Stanley's work in Africa rightfully won him a prominent place in the history of exploration.

Poverty and Civil War

Stanley was born in Wales with the name John Rowlands. When he was 4 years old, his poor and unmarried mother left him at a reform school called the Saint Asaph Union Workhouse. The boy was a talented but stubborn student, and he ran away from the school when he was 15. After staying briefly with various relatives who were unable or unwilling to give him a home, he took a job on a ship sailing from Liverpool, England, to New Orleans, Louisiana.

Upon arriving in the United States, John Rowlands found both a job and a home with a cotton merchant named Henry Hope Stanley. The troubled youth took the name Henry Stanley as his own, but his rebellious nature did not change. He often argued with the elder Stanley, and he ran away several times before he was sent to live on a farm in Arkansas.

When the Civil War began in 1861, Stanley joined the Confederate Army, and he was captured the next year at the Battle of Shiloh in Tennessee. To stay out of prison, he enlisted in the Union Army, but he was soon discharged after falling ill with **dysentery.** Still determined to rejoin his family in Wales, Stanley returned in the summer of 1862 to see his mother. According to his later writings, she shut the door in his face. He went back to America and became a U.S. citizen.

The Opportunity of a Lifetime

Stanley enlisted in the U.S. Navy and then, dissatisfied, deserted after just a few weeks. He took a job as a reporter for the *New York Herald.* The work offered both travel and adventure, and Stanley knew that he had found an ideal profession at last. Thanks to his talent and dedication, he soon received assignments to report on highly significant events. He covered the U.S. Army's campaigns against the Indians of the American West as well as Britain's 1868 invasion of Abyssinia (modern-day Ethiopia)—the first time he traveled to Africa. In late 1869, Stanley was working in Spain when his publisher, James Gordon Bennett, called him to Paris. Bennett

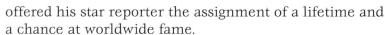

Among his African assistants, Henry Morton Stanley was known as Bula Matari, which means Rock Breaker. He is pictured here with his assistant, Kalulu.

caravan large group of people traveling together, often with pack animals, across a desert or other dangerous region

offered his star reporter the assignment of a lifetime and a chance at worldwide fame.

Bennett wanted Stanley to track down the Scottish missionary and explorer David Livingstone, who had vanished into the African interior two years before. Stanley, however, did not share his publisher's excitement about the project. Stanley thought that the task was impossible, and he worried that failure would ruin his reputation as a journalist. His trip was not scheduled to start for about a year, and in the meantime, he privately hoped that Livingstone would reappear. When a year passed with no sign of the Scotsman, Stanley reluctantly began his journey.

Finding the Missing Livingstone

The Stanley expedition employed nearly 200 people. Splitting into five groups, they left the island of Zanzibar, off the east coast of Africa, in March 1871. Stanley headed to Bagamoyo, on the mainland, and then west to Tabora (both in present-day Tanzania). His destination was Ujiji, a **caravan** station that Livingstone had reportedly planned to visit.

The expedition moved slowly. Stanley was unfamiliar with the difficult terrain of mountains, swamps, and rain forest. He also faced hostility from African tribes and disobedience from his own men. Stanley had yet another worry: he had been warned in Zanzibar that Livingstone might not want to be found.

When the journalist heard from eastbound travelers that Livingstone had recently arrived at Ujiji, he forced his men to march faster. Stanley did not want to give the famous explorer a chance to avoid the search party. On November 10, the expedition took Livingstone by surprise. A jubilant Stanley wrote this account of their meeting:

> *I would have run to him, only I was a coward in the presence of such a job,—would have embraced him, only, he being an Englishman, I did not know how he would receive me; so I did what cowardice and false pride suggested was the best thing—walked deliberately to him, took off my hat, and said:*
>
> *"Dr. Livingstone, I presume?"*
>
> *"Yes," said he, with a kind smile. . . .*

Stanley spent four months with Livingstone, and the two men became friends. The doctor was very sick, but Stanley could not persuade him to leave Africa. Livingstone insisted that he must stay until he learned whether the Lualaba River joined the Nile or the Congo. Unfortunately, he never found out, for he died a year later.

Crossing a Continent

After leaving Livingstone in March 1872, Stanley made a triumphant trip to England. He was on a new assignment in West Africa when he heard of Livingstone's death, and he resolved to complete the work

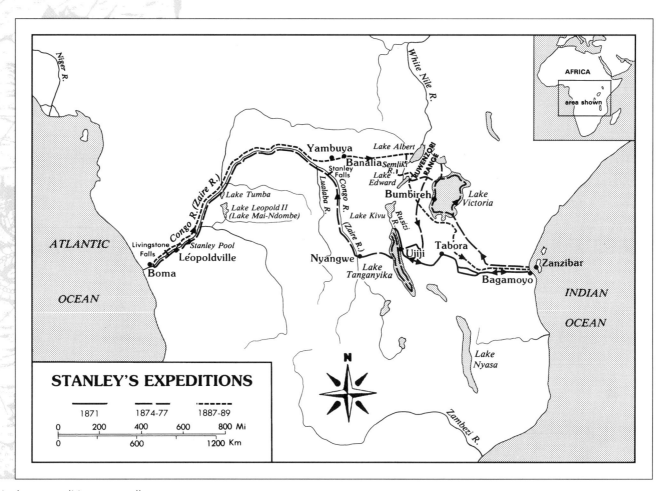

STANLEY'S EXPEDITIONS

| 1871 | 1874-77 | 1887-89 |

| 0 | 200 | 400 | 600 | 800 Mi |
| 0 | | 600 | | 1200 Km |

Stanley's three expeditions were all intended to search for or compete with other explorers: Livingstone, Cameron, and Schnitzer.

mission settlement founded by priests in a land where they hoped to convert people to Christianity

of the man who had made him famous. In 1874 Stanley launched an expedition to the interior from Bagamoyo. The trip was sponsored by the *New York Herald* and the London *Daily Telegraph.* Stanley had mapped out a series of explorations, and he wanted to complete them quickly because he was eager to return to his new fiancée in England. He also wanted to finish his work ahead of the English explorer Verney Lovett CAMERON, who had similar objectives.

Along the caravan route to Tabora, Stanley turned north, taking a shortcut to Lake Victoria, which he reached in January 1875. While circumnavigating the lake, he met with King Mtesa of Buganda and made plans for a Christian **mission** there. Stanley's explorations of Lake Victoria added evidence to John Hanning SPEKE's belief that the White Nile River began there. Stanley hoped to reach Lake Albert, to the northwest, but Mtesa's warriors blocked his path, and he narrowly escaped being killed.

Stanley proceeded south to Lake Tanganyika. He arrived in May and circled the entire lake by boat. He confirmed that the lake is not linked to the Nile River system. He then turned west toward the Lualaba River. He reached it in October 1876 and set off downriver in January 1877. The Lualaba led him to the Congo River, which he followed to the Atlantic Ocean, braving tribal attacks and dangerous rapids. Stanley arrived on Africa's west coast in August, the third European explorer to cross the continent. Livingstone had done so in 1856, and Cameron, Stanley's rival, had completed the journey in late 1875.

Stanley (left) found a weary and sick Livingstone (right) among a group of Arabs in the African town of Ujiji.

A Question of Loyalty

After sailing south to Cape Town, South Africa, Stanley sent the story of his trip to the newspapers that had sponsored him. One of his avid readers was King Leopold II of Belgium. In late 1877, agents of the king met Stanley in Marseilles, France. They asked him to help Belgium set up a colony in the Congo River region. However, Stanley was loyal to his homeland, and he refused to accept the assignment until he had offered to colonize the Congo for Britain. Stanley was famous in Britain as an adventurer and a writer, but British officials did not consider him a serious explorer. They rejected his offer, so he agreed to work for Belgium.

Stanley returned to the Congo in 1879 and spent five years creating the Belgian Congo Free State (now the Democratic Republic of Congo). He negotiated treaties with the region's tribal chiefs and also found time for exploration. In 1883 he discovered Lake Tumba and Lake Leopold II, which he named after the king of Belgium (it was later renamed Mai-Ndombe). On the north bank of the Congo River, a town was named Stanleyville in his honor (it is now the city of Kisangani). Stanley's relentless drive to settle the area earned him the nickname "Bula Matari," meaning Rock Breaker, among his overworked assistants. To the rest of the world, he became known as the "Congo King."

Chosen for Another Rescue

After his work in the Congo, Stanley returned to Europe to rest. But in 1886 word reached Britain of a crisis in Africa involving Eduard SCHNITZER (also known as Emin Pasha). Schnitzer, the governor of the Egyptian province of Equatoria (in modern Sudan) was under attack by rebels. The British public demanded that their country come to Schnitzer's rescue, and they clamored for Stanley—who had succeeding in finding Livingstone—to lead the expedition.

Stanley arrived in Africa in 1887 and managed to locate Schnitzer at Lake Albert the following year. As in his attempt to rescue Livingstone, Stanley found himself trying to convince a reluctant and stubborn man to leave Africa. Schnitzer only wanted help fighting the rebellion and had no intention of returning to Europe. The two men grew angry with each other, but Schnitzer eventually agreed to go with Stanley. During this expedition, Stanley found time to explore Mount Ruwenzori and the Semliki River. He was also able to clarify how Lake Albert and Lake Edward were linked to the White Nile River. He negotiated treaties for England with African peoples in the region, leading to the establishment of English settlements there.

Shortly after he returned from this mission, Stanley settled in England. Although his earlier absence had cost him his first fiancée, he was married at last to a daughter of a member of Parliament. He reclaimed his British citizenship in 1892 and later served in Parliament himself. Stanley was knighted in 1899, five years before he died of a stroke at the age of 63.

SUGGESTED READING Ian Anstruther, *I Presume: Stanley's Triumph and Disaster* (Bles, 1973); John Bierman, *Dark Safari: The Life Behind the Legend of Henry Morton Stanley* (Knopf, 1990); Byron Farwell, *The Man Who Presumed: A Biography of Henry M. Stanley* (Greenwood Press, 1974); Richard S. Hall, *Stanley: An Adventurer Explored* (Houghton, 1975); Steven Sherman, *Henry Stanley and the European Explorers of Africa* (Chelsea House, 1993).

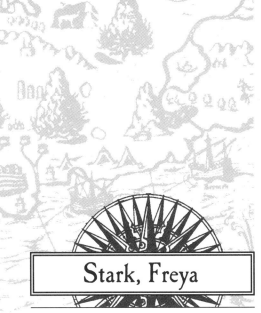

Stark, Freya

English
b January 31, 1893; Paris, France
d May 9, 1993; Asolo, Italy
Explored and wrote about Middle East

Freya Stark traveled tirelessly all her life. At age 70, she crossed the Himalaya mountain range, which she called "the last terrestrial footsteps to infinity."

Freya Stark was a lifelong traveler who often wrote about her journeys. Her published works include 14 travel books, 8 volumes of letters, and a 3-volume autobiography. All of these reveal her passion for travel and her captivating writing style.

A Woman of Many Talents
Stark's parents were painters, and her family was constantly moving from place to place, visiting relatives in England and Italy. They finally settled in Italy, where Freya and her sister were raised by nannies. Freya learned to be self-reliant, teaching herself Latin and reading classic books. At age 15, she moved to London to study, and by 21 she had earned a degree in history. Stark also spoke Italian, French, and German. When World War I began, she went back to Italy to train as a nurse but caught a serious fever and almost died. When she was well enough to travel, she returned to London.

Dreams Come True
For her ninth birthday, Stark had received a copy of *The Arabian Nights,* and ever since she had dreamed of exploring distant Arabia. Since she was now old enough to "travel single-mindedly for fun," as she put it, she learned Arabic and then set out for the Middle East, in November 1927. Although her health was poor, she was willing to take risks to reach her goal. Unlike many other explorers, who wanted to conquer the lands they visited, she only desired to observe the beauty around her and to share those wonders with others through her unique writings.

Stark made her way across Lebanon to Damascus, Syria. She then wandered south into the land of the Bedouin nomads, who rode camels as they traveled across the Arabian desert. Stark wrote enthusiastically about her first experience in this barren land:

Camels appeared on our left hand: first a few here and there, then more and more, till the whole herd came browsing along, five hundred or more. . . . The great gentle creatures came browsing and moving and pausing, rolling gently over the landscape like a brown wave just a little browner than the desert that carried it. . . . I never imagined that my first sight of the desert would come with such a shock of beauty and enslave me right away.

Tracing the Steps of the Assassins
Stark traveled on to Egypt and then to Baghdad, Iraq. She decided to write an article combining her observations with an account of

Stark (center) overcame injury and poor health to cross Middle Eastern deserts with simple means and few companions.

malaria disease that is spread by mosquitoes in tropical areas

dysentery disease that causes severe diarrhea

the history of the fortresses of the Assassins. In the 1200s, this violent band of outlaws had built a series of castles from Aleppo (in present-day Syria) to the border of Persia (present-day Iran).

Stark spent part of the winter of 1927 learning Persian; she then trekked alone to the castle at Alamut. The fortress had been the Assassins' headquarters until their defeat by the Mongols in 1256. Stark was the first European woman to travel in this area, and her presence aroused great curiosity among the local people. Although she battled both **malaria** and **dysentery,** the trip was a great success. After she returned to Britain, the Royal Geographical Society encouraged her to go back and map the area. In 1931 Stark returned to the region and discovered a previously unknown Assassin castle. The article she had planned to write eventually became a book, *The Valley of the Assassins,* which was published in 1934.

Further Travels and Writing

Stark spent the 1930s continuing her exploration of the Middle East. When World War II began in 1939, she offered her knowledge and expertise to the British government of Aden (now southern Yemen). Two years later, she went to Baghdad again and became involved in the politics of the region. She traveled to the United States to speak about British policy in Palestine (the area that is now Israel and Jordan) and later visited India. By the late 1940s, she had also written 10 travel books. Stark then turned her attention to the classical world, studying ancient Greece and Rome. These interests led to more travels and more books, including her last major work, *Rome on the Euphrates.*

SUGGESTED READING Freya Stark, *The Valley of the Assassins and Other Persian Travels* (Jeremy P. Tarcher, 1983).

Stefansson, Vilhjalmur

Canadian-American
b November 3, 1879; Arnes, Canada
d August 26, 1962; Hanover, New Hampshire
Explored Arctic Ocean

Vilhjalmur Stefansson traveled widely in the Arctic Ocean and discovered the last unknown major landmasses in the Canadian Arctic. Best known for his unusual methods of survival in the polar region, Stefansson insisted that explorers of the Arctic should adapt to the environment and learn to live off the land instead of bringing their own supplies. Stefansson's prediction that the northern regions of North America would become economically valuable was eventually proven true.

Unexpected Changes

Stefansson was the son of Icelanders who moved to Canada and then settled in the United States. He showed his independent nature at a young age, stirring up trouble while studying at the University of North Dakota, so that he was expelled from the school. He eventually graduated from the University of Iowa. Stefansson

During World War II, Vilhjalmur Stefansson used his expertise on the Arctic Ocean to advise the U.S. Navy.

anthropology the scientific study of human societies

Inuit people of the Canadian Arctic, sometimes known as the Eskimo

zoologist scientist who studies animals

anthropologist scientist who studies human societies

sledge heavy sled, often mounted on runners, that is pulled over snow or ice

then earned a scholarship to Harvard Divinity School, where he studied religion and **anthropology.**

Stefansson next made preparations to go to Africa. Before he departed, he received an unexpected invitation to join the Anglo-American Polar Expedition to Victoria Island in the Canadian Arctic. Stefansson accepted the offer and began his career as an Arctic explorer.

In 1906 he traveled overland to the Canadian cities of Toronto, Winnipeg, and Edmonton. In Edmonton he boarded a boat heading down the Mackenzie River to Herschel Island, where he planned to meet the other members of the expedition. While journeying downriver, he studied the Indians who lived in the region. When he reached his destination, Stefansson learned that the expedition's ship could not sail to Victoria Island because it was trapped in ice. Unfortunately, when the ice melted, the ship sank.

Since his first mission had been canceled, Stefansson decided to spend six months living with an **Inuit** family on the Arctic coast of Canada's Yukon Territory. During this time, he learned the family's language and culture, and he formed the belief that it was possible for white explorers to live off the land as the Inuit did. His experience in the Yukon inspired his lifelong devotion to the polar region.

Living off the Land

Stefansson returned to the United States in the fall of 1907. With the sponsorship of the American Museum of Natural History and the Geological Survey of Canada, he began to plan another trip to Victoria Island. He wanted to prove his theory that explorers could find plenty of food in the Arctic, so he did not make arrangements for supplies. Accompanied by the **zoologist** Rudolph Anderson, Stefansson disappeared into the western Canadian Arctic from 1908 to 1912.

While traveling along Coronation Gulf, Stefansson and Anderson studied the local people. The explorers called them Copper Eskimos because of the copper tools they used. Also known as Blond Eskimos, they bore a slight resemblance to Europeans. Some **anthropologists** had suggested that these Inuit were descendants of the Norse, a European people from Scandinavia. The Norse had established a thriving colony in Greenland during the Middle Ages but had mysteriously disappeared from that area.

Arctic Discoveries

From 1913 to 1918, Stefansson joined Anderson on another expedition, sponsored by the Canadian government, to explore Canada's Northwest Territories. Anderson led a group over the continental mainland from Alaska to Coronation Gulf. Meanwhile, Stefansson's group had become stuck in the ice off the coast of Alaska. He left most of his crew on board their ship, the *Karluk,* and headed north. Traveling with two companions, six dogs, and one **sledge,** Stefansson journeyed some 500 miles over the Arctic ice. Along the way, his small team mapped large areas of formerly unexplored territory, including the previously unknown Borden, Meighen, and Lougheed Islands. In 1918 Stefansson set up a floating research station on drifting ice in the Beaufort Sea. This method became an accepted way of making long-term observations of the region.

During this time, the *Karluk* drifted westward with the ice pack and eventually sank. The ship's captain, R. A. Bartlett, led the crew over the sea ice to Wrangel Island. He then proceeded to Siberia, and from there to Alaska, to seek assistance.

Lifelong Devotion

Stefansson maintained a strong interest in the Arctic although his activities in the region were not always successful. In the early 1920s, without first obtaining permission from the Canadian government, he tried to set up a Canadian colony on Wrangel Island, north of Siberia. The would-be settlers died tragically, and the **Soviet Union** took possession of the island.

Stefansson later served as a consultant to a commercial airline that wanted to offer flights in the polar region. He finished his career at Dartmouth College, in the Department of Northern Studies. He wrote many books throughout his life, including an autobiography, and died in New Hampshire at the age of 82.

SUGGESTED READING Richard J. Diubaldo, *Stefansson and the Canadian Arctic* (McGill-Queens University Press, 1978); Alexander Gregor, *Vilhjalmur Stefansson and the Arctic* (Book Society of Canada, 1978); Vilhjalmur Stefansson, *Discovery: The Autobiography of Vilhjalmur Stefansson* (McGraw-Hill, 1964) and *The Friendly Arctic* (Macmillan, 1943).

Soviet Union nation that existed from 1922 to 1991, made up of Russia and 14 other republics in eastern Europe and northern Asia

Stein, Mark Aurel

Hungarian
b November 26, 1862; Budapest, Hungary
d October 26, 1943; Kabul, Afghanistan
Explored central Asia

plateau high, flat area of land

caravan large group of people traveling together, often with pack animals, across a desert or other dangerous region

surveyor one who makes precise measurements of a location's geography

Mark Aurel Stein was one of the leading modern explorers of central Asia, a region of deserts, windswept plains, high **plateaus,** and rugged mountain ranges. Following in the footsteps of Nikolai PRZHEVALSKI and Sven HEDIN, Stein was an archaeologist who shed new light on the civilizations that had once flourished along the Silk Road, the ancient **caravan** route across Asia. One of his discoveries was among the most important archaeological finds ever made in central Asia.

The Scholarly Explorer

From childhood Stein had been interested in the routes by which ALEXANDER the Great and other ancient Greeks had taken their armies and their culture into Asia. Thanks to his parents' wealth, he received an excellent education in Hungary, Germany, and Britain. His studies centered on Asian languages, history, and civilizations, and he obtained a degree in archaeology. Stein also served for a year in the Hungarian army, where he learned the skills of a **surveyor.**

After his parents died, Stein went to India, then a British colony, as a school official in 1888. In Lahore and Calcutta, Stein spent many years as an enthusiastic and well-liked educator. But his attention was often drawn to central Asia, north of India, and he won government support for the long, adventurous expeditions that became his greatest work.

For a dozen years, Stein's travels were limited to the mountains and valleys on the borders of India. In 1900, however, he made a longer journey. Sven Hedin had found traces of a lost city in the

Takla Makan, a harsh desert in western China, north of Tibet. Stein uncovered the few visible ruins and found the entire lost city as well as traces of other settlements near the town of Hotan. His work resulted in historians' vivid new awareness of the Silk Road as it had existed hundreds of years earlier—before drifting sand had covered the abandoned towns.

The Caves of the Thousand Buddhas

In 1906 Stein made a second expedition to the Takla Makan. He visited the city of Dunhuang in western China, the site of an ancient religious shrine called the Caves of the Thousand Buddhas. He was accompanied by a trusted assistant named Chiang. A remarkably hard worker, Stein liked to keep his expeditions small and limited himself to one or two assistants. Often these men collapsed from exhaustion, but some, like Chiang, became loyal, long-term companions.

The caves had long ago been turned into temples by monks, who had filled them with images of the Buddha—Siddhartha Gautama, the founder of Buddhism. Stein did not discover these caves; religious pilgrims had known of them for centuries, and a few Europeans had visited them as well. But Stein and Chiang found something that no earlier visitors had seen.

One of the monks who remained at the nearly deserted shrine had found a room full of old manuscripts hidden behind a wall. Although the monk, named Wang, quickly hid the manuscripts again, rumors about them leaked out and caught Stein's attention. Hoping to persuade Wang to share his find, Stein told him of his great admiration for XUAN Zang, a famous Buddhist monk of the 600s. Wang reluctantly agreed to let Stein see a few manuscripts. By Stein's great good fortune, the very first ones that Wang pulled from the hiding place had been written by Xuan Zang himself. Chiang convinced Wang that this coincidence was a sign that Stein was meant to have at least some of the manuscripts.

The materials that Wang eventually turned over to Stein—for a price—had been sealed up and forgotten for about 900 years. The carefully prepared rock chamber had served its purpose, and as Stein later wrote, "these masses of manuscripts had lain undisturbed for centuries." Stein's treasures were sent to India and Britain. Among them, scholars later discovered, is a scroll thought to be the world's oldest printed book—a Buddhist text called the *Diamond Sutra* that was printed in China in 868. Although the Chinese and others have accused Stein of stealing a national treasure, many of the manuscripts he left behind were later stolen or destroyed.

The Restless Traveler

Stein's discovery earned him honors and praise from around the world. He continued with his work, which he described in two books. In 1907 Stein journeyed again to the Takla Makan, losing the toes of his right foot to frostbite after exploring the mountains of China's Kunlun Shan. In 1920 the British government of India named Stein head of the Archaeological Survey of India, but Stein

Mark Aurel Stein's discovery of ancient Buddhist manuscripts in a desert cave was a remarkable episode in the history of scientific exploration.

did not settle down at a desk. He began his longest journey three years later, traveling into northwestern China, where he discovered more ancient documents in Tibetan and other languages. He took a long route back to India through Persia (now Iran), Afghanistan, and Pakistan.

Revolutions in China and Russia soon closed much of central Asia to exploration. Stein then turned his attention to Alexander's routes through Persia and the Middle East. Stein looked forward to traveling again in Afghanistan, but he died a few days after he arrived there.

SUGGESTED READING Wilfrid Blunt, *The Golden Road to Samarkand* (Viking Press, 1973); Peter Hopkirk, *Foreign Devils on the Silk Road* (University of Massachusetts Press, 1980); Jeanette Mirsky, *Sir Aurel Stein: Archaeological Explorer* (University of Chicago Press, 1977); Rebecca Stefoff, *The Accidental Explorers: Surprises and Side Trips in the History of Discovery* (Oxford University Press, 1992).

Stuart, John McDouall

Scottish
b September 7, 1815; Dysart, Scotland
d June 5, 1866; London, England
Explored southern Australia; crossed Australia

John McDouall Stuart was the first European to reach the center of the continent of Australia. He was also one of the first to cross it from south to north. The trail he blazed for a telegraph line from Adelaide to what is now Darwin unified Australia through communications and eventually linked it with the rest of the world.

Trek to the Center

Stuart was born in Scotland in 1815 and moved to South Australia in 1838. He worked as a surveyor for the British colonial government, and in 1844 he joined the English explorer Charles STURT in an unsuccessful attempt to reach the center of the continent. In 1858 Stuart headed out on his own, journeying through South Australia between Lake Torrens and Streaky Bay. The next year, he made two surveys of land west of Lake Eyre. On the second trip, he experienced periods of near blindness, a problem that would trouble him on later expeditions as well.

In 1860 the South Australian Parliament offered a reward to the first person who could establish an overland route for a telegraph line across the continent. Stuart and two companions accepted the challenge. On March 2, they left Chambers Creek and headed north. By April 22, the party had reached the geographical center of the continent, approximately 125 miles north of Alice Springs. Stuart named a nearby hill Central Mount Sturt in honor of Charles Sturt the man who was nicknamed the "father of Australian exploration." The peak was later renamed Central Mount Stuart after its discoverer.

Stuart and the other men continued north for another 175 miles, until they reached Tennant Creek. Weakened by **scurvy** and hunger—and under attack by Aborigines—the men turned back. Once again Stuart was nearly blind for most of the journey. The team arrived at Chambers Creek, below Lake Eyre, on September 1.

scurvy disease caused by a lack of vitamin C and once a major cause of death among sailors; symptoms include internal bleeding, loosened teeth, and extreme fatigue

Crossing the Continent

The parliament soon gave Stuart money for another attempt at crossing Australia. He left from a farm near Lake Eyre on January 11, 1861, traveling with 13 men and 49 horses. By April 25, he had reached Tennant Creek, only 300 miles south of the Gulf of Carpentaria. However, a wall of thick shrubs prevented him from entering the gulf or the Victoria River to the west. Stuart called it "as great a barrier as an inland sea." He had traveled 100 miles farther than on his last expedition. But on July 12, short of food and water, he was again forced to end his mission.

Stuart reached the southern coast of Australia in September, three months after the death of the Irish explorer Robert O'Hara BURKE, who had been the first person to make the south-to-north crossing of the continent. In October, with fresh supplies, Stuart made a third attempt at the journey, and this time he was successful. In July 1862, he reached the mouth of the Adelaide River on Van Diemen Gulf. There he stripped the branches from a small tree and on it raised the British flag with his name sewn across the center.

Stuart started back almost immediately after his triumph on the northwest coast. His health had failed. He wrote: "I completely lost the use of my limbs and had to be carried about like an infant" on a stretcher hung between two horses. He suffered from night blindness and scurvy, and he could eat only boiled flour. When Stuart returned home in December, he was rewarded with cash and land as well as the gold medal of Britain's Royal Geographical Society. However, he never fully recovered from his illnesses. He lost his memory and the ability to speak, and he died, near poverty, in England in 1866.

Less than a decade after Stuart's trek, the overland telegraph line was erected along his route. From Darwin, on the northwest coast of Australia, a line was run across the sea, linking the continent with Java (now in Indonesia), Asia, and—finally—Europe.

SUGGESTED READING Ian Mayleston Mudie, *The Heroic Journey of John McDouall Stuart* (Angus and Robertson, 1968).

John McDouall Stuart struggled through Australia's harsh interior in order to find a route for a telegraph line.

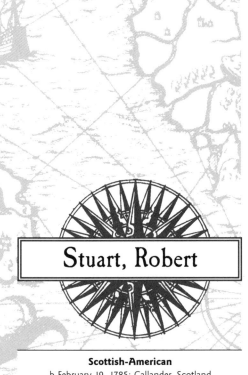

Stuart, Robert

Scottish-American
b February 19, 1785; Callander, Scotland
d October 29, 1848; Chicago, Illinois
***Explored American West;
discovered South Pass***

From 1812 to 1813, Robert Stuart journeyed east to St. Louis from Astoria (in what is now Oregon). During his travels, he discovered South Pass, a 20-mile-wide opening in the Rocky Mountains. Twelve years later, the Mountain Man Jedediah SMITH rediscovered the pass and put it on the map of the United States. South Pass eventually became the main gateway for settlers headed for the west coast.

A Guide Points the Way

Stuart left his homeland of Scotland and settled in Montréal, Canada, in 1807. Three years later, he became a partner in the Pacific Fur Company, a new fur-trading venture. John Jacob Astor, the company's founder, wanted to establish a series of trading posts along the route taken by Meriwether LEWIS and William CLARK from 1804 to 1806. Astor also planned to construct the company's headquarters at the mouth of the Columbia River. In 1810 Wilson Price HUNT, also a partner in the company, led an overland expedition to

the Columbia while Stuart and several others sailed around South America's Cape Horn and landed on the coast of what is now Oregon. Stuart's group arrived before Hunt's. After helping to build a trading post, which he named Astoria, Stuart led a band of trappers into the valley of the Willamette River.

Near the end of June 1812, Stuart was given the important task of carrying messages back to Astor in New York. Setting out with a small group, Stuart followed the route that Hunt had taken to the coast. In what is now southwestern Idaho, Stuart and his companions met a lone Indian, who told them of a path across the Rocky Mountains that was shorter than the one Hunt had followed. The party rode east, through dry land covered with what Stuart called "sage brush and its detested relations." They were following the route that would later become the Oregon Trail.

Caution and Conflict

On the Bear River, a group of Crow Indians began to menace Stuart and his men. Although the Indians did not attack, they did take the group's horses. In an effort to avoid a hostile encounter with the Crow, Stuart turned east from the river and wandered into the mountains. Eventually, the explorers came upon the Greys River, which they correctly assumed would bring them to the Snake River. When they reached the Snake, they built rafts and headed downstream, hoping to find Snake Indians who would be willing to sell them horses. However, they did not meet any Indians along the way, so they abandoned the rafts and proceeded farther east on foot.

Traveling toward Teton Pass, in what is now western Wyoming, Stuart found signs that Blackfoot Indians were nearby. By that time, the explorers were hungry and eager to hunt the plentiful game in the area. But they could not risk firing their rifles, because the noise would attract the attention of the Blackfoot, who had a reputation for violence. Unfortunately, by the time the expedition had left Blackfoot territory, there were no animals to be found. After three days without food, one member of the group suggested that they draw straws to choose one person to kill and eat. Upon hearing this notion, Stuart aimed his rifle at the man, who then fell to his knees, begging for forgiveness and promising not to mention cannibalism again. Luckily, the next day, a buffalo appeared, and the men slaughtered it for a feast.

Gateway to the West

From the Teton Pass, the party headed southeast, moving parallel to the Wind River Range. At that point, the group was only about 100 miles from where they had left the Bear River a month earlier. Stuart and his men had traveled over 400 miles in a useless U-shaped path. However, they were approaching the pass about which they had been told. On October 22, 1812, they made the first known crossing of South Pass by non-Indians.

After leaving the Rockies, the party came upon the Sweetwater River. They built a cabin near what is now Casper, Wyoming, where they planned to spend the winter. On December 12, a group of

Arapaho Indians discovered the site. Although the Indians appeared to be friendly, Stuart acted cautiously and moved his men from the cabin to a location closer to the Nebraska border. In the spring of 1813, the party reached St. Louis, where they received a lively reception that rivaled the one given to Lewis and Clark at the end of their historic journey seven years earlier.

On May 16, Stuart left St. Louis on horseback; he arrived in New York City about one month later. He met Astor and gave him a report of the journey. Stuart understood the significance of finding South Pass, and he correctly predicted that wagons would be able to travel to the Pacific Ocean on the path he had followed east.

His insights, however, remained hidden from the public for many years. Astor regarded Stuart's information as a trade secret, and he kept Stuart's journal to himself. News of a pass through the Rockies did reach a few newspapers, but Americans' westward migration began many years later than it might have if more people had known about Stuart's trail.

SUGGESTED READING LeRoy Hafen, editor, *Mountain Men and Fur Traders* (University of Nebraska Press, 1982); Theodore J. Karamanski, *Fur Trade and Exploration: Opening the Far Northwest, 1821–1852* (University of Oklahoma Press, 1983); John Upton Terrell, *Furs by Astor* (William Morrow, 1963).

Sturt, Charles

English
b April 28, 1795; Bengal, India
d June 16, 1869; Cheltenham, England
Explored rivers of southeastern Australia

tributary stream or river that flows into a larger stream or river

Charles Sturt has been praised as the father of Australian exploration. He was one of the first Europeans to explore Australia's interior, and he solved some of the mysteries surrounding the continent's largest river system. His efforts on the Darling, Murrumbidgee, and Murray Rivers opened up vast new regions of Australia to British settlers.

Questions in a New Homeland

Sturt was born in 1795 in Bengal, India, which was then ruled by Britain. After studying in England, he joined the army and earned the rank of captain. He served in Spain, Canada, and Ireland before arriving in New South Wales, Australia, in 1826 to help guard convicts. Sturt liked the rugged country immediately and developed an interest in its geography. He also became friendly with several explorers.

Sturt was appointed to work for the colony's governor, Sir Ralph Darling, who sent him on several journeys into unknown country. Sturt took careful notes, and his accurate charts and descriptions added much to what was known of the continent. In 1828 Sturt took part in his first major expedition, joining Hamilton HUME to explore the lands beyond the Macquarie River. The party left Sydney in November and crossed the Blue Mountains to the Macquarie Marshes. Proceeding northwest, Sturt discovered and named the wide Darling River. The water was salty, leading Sturt to believe mistakenly that there was a great inland sea nearby. Nevertheless, he correctly determined that the Castlereagh, Macquarie, and Bogan Rivers are all **tributaries** of the Darling.

Hazards and Heroes

In November 1829, Sturt left on another expedition. He and his companions planned to follow the Murrumbidgee River to see

In 1833 Sturt publicized his journey on Australia's Murray River. Three years later, settlers followed his route and founded the city of Adelaide.

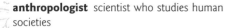

anthropologist scientist who studies human societies

whether it emptied into a sea or joined the Darling River. Describing the landscape he found west of Sydney, Sturt wrote: "Neither bird nor beast inhabited these lonely and inhospitable regions, over which the silence of the grave seemed to reign. We had not, for days past, seen a blade of grass." He reached the Murrumbidgee in the last days of December, and within a week, he assembled a 27-foot vessel and started downriver.

Sturt's ride down the Murrumbidgee was made dangerous by rapids and floating trees. On the second day, the explorers lost a small boat that carried many of their supplies. After a week, Sturt noted that the river took a sudden and twisting turn to the south. The party soon came to a point where the Murrumbidgee met a "broad and noble river." Not realizing that Hume had found this river in 1824, Sturt named it the Murray River in honor of Sir George Murray, Britain's secretary of state for colonies.

A week later, on January 21, 1830, about 600 armed Australian Aborigines appeared along the river, chanting war songs. The current kept the boat out of their reach, but the warriors followed behind. As the uneasy explorers began to wonder what to do, a second tribe appeared and drove off the first. **Anthropologists** later explained that Sturt's rescuers believed him to be a legendary hero of their tribe.

In early February, the explorers found that the Murray River empties into a small coastal lake, which Sturt named Lake Alexandrina. The river's water passes through the lake into the Gulf of St. Vincent and the Indian Ocean. The exhausted men returned upstream to the Murrumbidgee River. With the river flooded, they had to pull their boat against the current for three weeks. The strain of that effort temporarily blinded Sturt. On May 25, 1830, the explorers returned to Sydney as heroes, having opened 2,000 miles of waterway to navigation.

The Desert Interior

During a brief trip to Britain, Sturt married and then resigned from the army. He returned to Australia in 1834, and after failing at farming and ranching, he took a job with the government office in charge of surveying the province of South Australia. In 1844 he set out on his last major expedition—an attempt to reach the center of the continent.

On August 10, his team of 16 men, including John McDouall STU-ART, headed north from the mouth of the Murray River. As they proceeded into the interior, temperatures reached 119° Fahrenheit in the shade. They dug an underground room and were forced to spend six months there, trying to stay cool. In July they moved on to the Simpson Desert and became the first people of European descent to set foot in that vast wasteland. But they failed to reach the continent's midpoint, and they returned to Adelaide in January 1846. Two men had died of **scurvy,** and the ordeal had ruined Sturt's own health. He retired from government service in 1851 and spent his last years in England.

SUGGESTED READING Charles Sturt, *Journals of the Central Australian Expedition, 1844-5* (Caliban Books, 1984).

scurvy disease caused by a lack of vitamin C and once a major cause of death among sailors; symptoms include internal bleeding, loosened teeth, and extreme fatigue

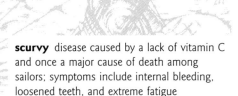

Sverdrup, Otto Neumann

Norwegian
b October 31, 1854; Bindal, Norway
d November 26, 1930; Oslo, Norway
Explored Greenland and northern Canadian Arctic

fjord narrow inlet where the sea meets the shore between steep cliffs

Inuit people of the Canadian Artic, sometimes known as the Eskimo

sledge heavy sled, often mounted on runners, that is pulled over snow or ice

Otto Neumann Sverdrup served as chief assistant to fellow Norwegian explorer Fridtjof NANSEN on two famous Arctic expeditions. Sverdrup also led his own mission to the Canadian Arctic from 1898 to 1902. On that journey, he displayed calmness, confidence, and expertise as he charted enormous expanses of territory in Canada's northernmost island chains.

Calm Under Pressure

Sverdrup was born on a farm in northern Norway. Nansen later wrote of Sverdrup's upbringing: "Accustomed from childhood to wandering in the forest and on the mountains . . . Otto learned early to look after himself and to stand on his own legs." Growing up on a **fjord,** Sverdrup was fascinated with the sea, and at 17 he became a sailor. During the next 15 years, he perfected his navigational skills and rose to the rank of captain.

Sverdrup's background made him an excellent candidate for Arctic exploration, and in 1888 he was given the opportunity to join an expedition. He was living at the time with Nansen's brother, Alexander, who informed him that Nansen was looking for skiers to accompany him across Greenland's ice cap. Sverdrup's talent as a strong and agile skier had impressed Alexander, who recommended Sverdrup for the trek.

Nansen's crossing of Greenland marked the first time that Europeans had actually discovered territory in the Arctic, instead of mapping land frequently traveled by the **Inuit.** The journey began with a difficult landing on pack ice, 12 miles from the east coast of Greenland. Sverdrup impressed Nansen with his strength, endurance, and calmness under pressure. He demonstrated his resourcefulness by constructing a sort of iceboat from **sledges.** With tent canvas for sails, the craft raced across the ice, reducing the expedition's planned traveling time by six days.

In 1890 Nansen recruited Sverdrup to captain his new ship, the *Fram.* Nansen's plan was to allow a vessel to be frozen in the ice pack north of Siberia and drift with the ice over the North Pole to Greenland. This unique voyage required a vessel with a shallow, rounded hull that would allow the expanding ice to slip directly under it rather than crush it. Sverdrup supervised the construction of this revolutionary craft, which looked more like a bathtub than a normal ship.

Master of the **Fram**

The *Fram* sailed from Vadsø, Norway, on June 26, 1893. Although the expedition was Nansen's idea, and he continued to direct it, Sverdrup guided the ship on its remarkable three-year voyage. While Nansen left the *Fram* to make his famous sledge trip toward the pole, Sverdrup stayed with the vessel. His most difficult task was to remove the ship from the ice so that the party could return to Norway before they ran out of supplies. The crew members spent 28 days blasting and cutting ice to open a 180-mile stretch of water. According to an editor of Sverdrup's account of the trip, this feat "at once made him a living legend among mariners."

Nansen easily obtained funds for a second voyage and gave his assistant complete command. Sverdrup planned to sail up the west coast of Greenland and through Robeson Channel to the frozen Arctic Ocean in order to explore the north coast of Greenland.

Peary and the Pole

While Sverdrup was heading for the Arctic, the American explorer Robert PEARY was striving to become the first person to reach the North Pole. Peary felt threatened by Sverdrup's presence in the area. Although the Norwegian's stated goal was to scout for islands north of Greenland, it was likely that he would try to reach the pole himself if he had the opportunity. As a member of Nansen's expedition across Greenland's ice cap, Sverdrup had already denied Peary the glory of making the first crossing of that island.

During the winter of 1898 to 1899, Peary and Sverdrup met at Cape Sabine on the east coast of Canada's Ellesmere Island. The American was not happy to see his rival, and he did not discuss his plans for exploration. Nevertheless, Sverdrup acted like a gentleman, offering Peary a cup of coffee, which he refused. Sverdrup later wrote that he "rejoiced at having shaken hands with the bold explorer, even though his visit had been so short that we hardly had time to pull off our mittens."

Fortunately for Peary, Sverdrup was unable to cut through the ice and head northward. Since Sverdrup could not carry out his original plan, he decided to travel west. For the next three years, he used the *Fram* as a base for exploring Jones Sound and Ellesmere Island. He also discovered what are now called the Sverdrup Islands, which he claimed for his home country, though Norway later gave them to Canada. In 1903 Sverdrup received a medal from England's Royal Geographical Society for his efforts on this trip.

The following year, he published an account of his travels in the Canadian Arctic. He later worked for the Russian government, commanding ships and leading rescue missions in northern waters. Sverdrup was not the last explorer to use the *Fram*. His countryman Roald AMUNDSEN took the ship on a historic journey to Antarctica in 1910. Later, however, the ship sat in port and started to rot, so Sverdrup began a campaign to save it. He died in 1930, five years before the preserved ship was put on display near Oslo.

SUGGESTED READING T. C. Fairley, editor, *Sverdrup's Arctic Adventures* (Longmans, 1959).

Tasman, Abel Janszoon

Dutch
b 1603; Lutjegast, the Netherlands
d 1659; Batavia (present-day Jakarta, Indonesia)
*Discovered Tasmania,
New Zealand, and Fiji Islands*

archipelago large group of islands or a body of water with many islands

On two great voyages of discovery in the 1600s, Abel Janszoon Tasman proved that Australia was not part of an enormous landmass that was believed to exist in the Southern Hemisphere. He also discovered the islands of Tasmania and New Zealand as well as several **archipelagos** in the southern Pacific Ocean. However, Tasman's sponsors considered his missions to have failed, because he had not found any treasure or new opportunities for trade.

The Ambitions of a Trading Company

Tasman was born and raised in the Netherlands. He arrived in the Dutch colony of Batavia (present-day Jakarta, Indonesia) around 1632 and took a job as a ship's captain for the powerful Dutch East India Company. At the time, the company was the dominant European force in Southeast Asia. For most of the next seven years, Tasman sailed throughout the region, visiting places such as Japan, Cambodia, and Formosa (modern-day Taiwan).

In 1642 the governor of Batavia chose Tasman to lead a major expedition into the southern Pacific Ocean. Earlier in the century, Dutch explorers such as Dirck HARTOG and Willem JANSZ had discovered separate stretches of coastal land south of Indonesia. These coasts were believed to belong to a large landmass known as the Great South Land (later called Australia). Tasman's orders were to explore the known parts of this territory to see whether it was part of a mythical southern continent called *Terra Australis Incognita.* The East India Company encouraged Tasman to trade with any people he met in order to learn about new sources of spices and other goods. The Dutch also hoped that he would find a southern ocean route that would give them easy access to the riches of Chile in South America.

With these ambitious instructions in hand, Tasman left Batavia on August 14, 1642. His expedition included two ships named the *Heemskerk* and the *Zeehaan,* a crew of about 110 men, supplies to last 18 months, and cargo to trade along the way. He sailed first for Île de France (present-day Mauritius) in the Indian Ocean. Tasman believed that traveling east from that island would be an easier way to find a route to Chile than sailing from Batavia.

Tasman still had to decide just what course to take from Île de France. He could have sailed almost directly eastward to reach Eendrachtsland, the part of the Great South Land's western coast discovered by Hartog in 1616. Another option was to take a much more southerly route in hopes of finding *Terra Australis Incognita.* Tasman preferred to attempt the latter, but severe weather to the south led him to choose a course roughly halfway between the two options he had considered.

Smoke in the Distance

Tasman wrote in his log that about three months after leaving Batavia, the explorers found "the first land we had met with in the South Sea." For a week, the two ships circled a large island, which Tasman named Van Diemen's Land after the Dutch governor of Batavia.

Tasman anchored the ships on December 1, 1642, and sent a landing party ashore. The crewmen found abundant fruit trees and other plant life growing wild. The sailors heard sounds and saw smoke in

The accomplishments of Abel Tasman (shown here with his wife and daughter) were long kept secret by the Dutch East India Company.

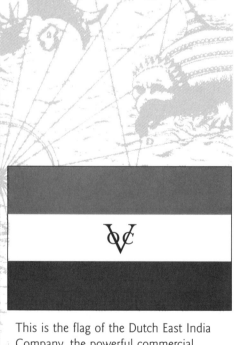

This is the flag of the Dutch East India Company, the powerful commercial enterprise that sponsored the explorations of Tasman and many other Dutch navigators.

the distance. Tasman reported that they saw no other human beings, "although we surmise some were not far away and were with watching eyes observing our goings-on."

Tasman decided to claim the island for the Dutch East India Company and tried to send out another landing party. However, rough waters kept the small boat from reaching the shore, so the expedition's carpenter swam ashore, holding a pole with which to mark the Dutch claim. Since the island seemed to have no spices or other riches, the explorers set sail again on December 4, continuing their eastward course. The island was not visited again until a French ship anchored there, 130 years later.

After nine days spent crossing what is now called the Tasman Sea, the Dutch sighted more land. Tasman named it Staaten Land and believed—incorrectly—that it was connected to the Great South Land. In fact, it is an island, known today as South Island, New Zealand. Tasman then mistook the strait that separates New Zealand's two main islands for a bay. When a landing party went ashore there, Maori tribesmen killed four of the Dutch sailors, so Tasman named the place Murderers Bay and departed.

A Circle of Islands

Tasman sailed north and then northeast from Staaten Land. His course took him to the islands of Tongatapu and Nomuka in the group now called the Tonga Islands (also known as the Friendly Islands). There Tasman obtained fresh food and water and traded with the islanders, exchanging nails for coconuts. Sailing northwest from the Tongas, Tasman was the first European to see what are now called the Fiji Islands. After passing the Ontong Java island group (north of the Solomon Islands) and the north coast of New Guinea, he returned to Batavia on June 15, 1643.

Although Tasman had not seen the Australian landmass at all, he had taken a nearly circular route around it. Geographers therefore believed that it was too small to be *Terra Australis Incognita,* which was expected to be as large as Europe and Asia put together. Tasman's voyage was therefore quite valuable as geographic exploration, but his employers considered it a commercial failure.

Mistaken Map

The Dutch East India Company soon decided to send Tasman on another voyage. This time his mission was to see whether New Guinea was attached to the north coast of the Great South Land. The Dutch had not yet discovered the Torres Strait, which separates New Guinea from Australia.

On February 29, 1644, Tasman set sail with three ships. When he reached New Guinea, he missed the Torres Strait and sailed down the western side of the Australian peninsula that is now called Cape

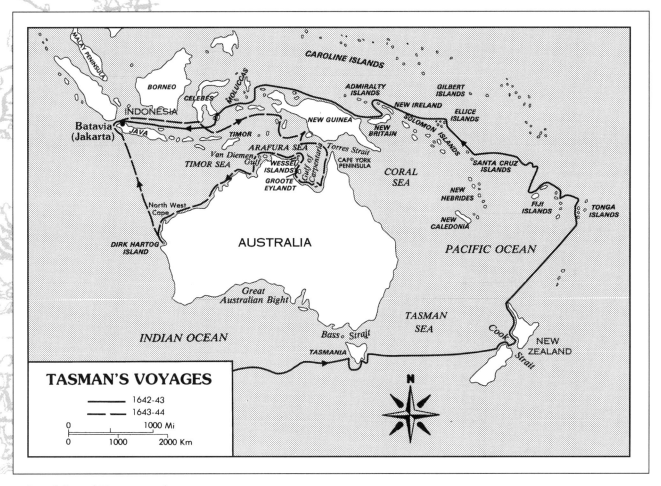

TASMAN'S VOYAGES

——— 1642-43
— — — 1643-44

0   1000 Mi
0   1000   2000 Km

No other explorer followed Tasman south of Australia for 100 years. The dangerous waters and poor trade possibilities made it seem too risky.

York. He followed the coastline of what is now the Gulf of Carpentaria, but the gulf's reefs and sandbars kept him far from shore. He traveled as far west as the island now known as Dirk Hartog Island, but he made many mistakes along the way as he tried to identify the coastal geography.

Although no journal of that voyage survived, Tasman's mistakes were reflected in a map made after his return to Batavia. Even so, he had navigated an estimated 8,000 miles of dangerous and uncharted coastline that the Dutch had never before seen. Tasman's money-minded employers were once again displeased. A company report took a pessimistic view of trade with the inhabitants of the Great South Land. According to the report, the only people Tasman had seen were "naked, beach-roving wretches, destitute even of rice . . . miserably poor, and in many places of very bad disposition."

Return to a Merchant's Life

Apparently, the Dutch East India Company believed that Tasman's accomplishments outweighed his failures. Although he never again sailed as an explorer, he continued to work for the company. In 1647 he commanded a trading fleet to Siam (now Thailand), and upon his return, he led an attack on the Spanish in the Philippines. Tasman also served on a government council in Batavia. He retired in 1653 and lived in Batavia until his death, six years later.

The company remained silent about Tasman's voyages and never published an account of them. The Dutch preferred to let the rest of the world believe that there was nothing of value in the southwestern Pacific Ocean. They still hoped that they would find riches in the Great South Land, and they did not want to compete with other nations. However, much of the area later came under British control. The island of Van Diemen's Land was renamed Tasmania in 1856.

SUGGESTED READING Andrew Sharp, *The Discovery of Australia* (Clarendon Press, 1963) and *The Voyages of Abel Janszoon Tasman* (Cambridge University Press, 1968).

Tavares, Antonio Rapôso de. *See Rapôso de Tabares, Antonio.*

Teixeira, Pedro de

Portuguese
b between 1570 and 1593; Castanheira, Portugal
d June 4, 1640; São Luis do Maranhão, Brazil
Explored Amazon River

bandeira Portuguese raid into the South American interior to capture Indians as slaves during the 1600s

tributary stream or river that flows into a larger stream or river

In the early 1600s, Captain Pedro de Teixeira went to Brazil on a military mission to remove English, Dutch, and French forces from Spanish and Portuguese territories in the region. By the 1630s, the Portuguese had defeated all of their foreign rivals in Brazil and had begun to concentrate on strengthening their influence in the rest of South America. In 1637 Teixeira led an expedition across the continent by way of the Amazon River. He went from Pará (present-day Belém, Brazil) to Quito (in present-day Ecuador) and back. As a result of Teixeira's journey, Portugal gained control over the entire Amazon River region.

Fighting for Control

Pedro de Teixeira was born into a noble family in the town of Castanheira, Portugal. His exact date of birth is unknown, and there are no records of his early life. He came to Brazil sometime in the early 1600s in military service. From 1615 to 1616, Teixeira assisted in the forced removal of the French from the coastal town of São Luis do Maranhão. Between 1618 and 1622, Teixeira served as governor of the territory of Pará.

During the following five years, Teixeira led several military raids against the English and the Dutch, destroying their settlements along the Xingu River. He then went on a **bandeira** up the Amazon to the Tapajós River, and he later mapped the lower Amazon River. In 1629 Teixeira commanded a major campaign against Portuguese competitors who had settled in the territory around Manacapuru. Sailing up the Amazon with a crew of 120 Portuguese and 1,600 Indians in 98 canoes, Teixeira captured English, Dutch, and Irish settlements. As a result of these journeys, he learned a great deal about the lower Amazon and many of its **tributaries.** He also became familiar with the Indian tribes of the region.

By that time, the Portuguese in Brazil had conquered all of their foreign competitors. However, since South America was still dominated by Spain, the Portuguese had to find a way to extend their influence beyond Brazil. Although both Spain and Portugal were then under the rule of a Spanish king, the Portuguese in Brazil were still very loyal to their homeland. When two Spanish friars from Peru arrived unexpectedly in Pará, the Portuguese recognized an opportunity to pursue their goals.

Teixeira was chosen to lead an expedition up the Amazon River to escort these priests back to Quito. But his orders from the governor of Maranhão revealed a broader plan to explore the river. The captain was instructed to establish friendly relations with the Indians and to look for good places to build forts. He was also sent to found a Portuguese settlement and to mark the boundaries between Spanish and Portuguese territories, which had been set by the **Treaty of Tordesillas** in 1494.

A Slow Journey

Teixeira set out from Pará on October 28, 1637, with 47 canoes carrying 70 soldiers and almost 2,000 slaves—the largest party ever sent to navigate the length of the Amazon. The men encountered few problems as they made their way upstream. However, their progress was slow because they were paddling against a very strong current. Teixeira also had to send scouting parties ahead to determine which of the river's many forks to take. Moreover, the Indians who lived along the Amazon could not feed such a large group, so the party often had to stop to hunt, fish, and gather fruits. As a result of these delays, it took Teixeira's expedition eight months to reach the first Spanish settlement along the Amazon.

Teixeira's greatest problem on the journey was to keep the slaves rowing. They became frustrated and exhausted by the amount of effort they had to exert against the current. In order to persuade the men to continue, he assured them that they were close to their destination. Teixeira made his claims seem true by sending small parties ahead of the canoes as if to announce the expedition's arrival. Actually, these parties were going ahead only to observe the river's course.

When the canoes reached the upper Amazon and the territory of the Omagua Indians, Teixeira left some of his men there to build a camp and wait for his return. With the rest of the group, he pushed ahead to the Napo River and entered the land of the Quijos Indians. At that point, Teixeira sent an advance party of eight canoes to find the best river route to Quito. They first chose the Quijos River, believing it to be the shortest route. However, the river's current was too fast and strong, so they were forced to complete the journey on foot. They climbed through the Andes mountain range and arrived in Quito in 1638.

The people of Quito welcomed Teixeira and his men by holding parties and bullfights in their honor. The Spanish authorities, however, realized the significance of Teixeira's journey, and they encouraged him to return to Pará as soon as possible. The officials also decided to send a Spaniard on the trip back to Brazil in order to determine how much power Portugal had seized in the Amazon region. Father Cristóbal de ACUÑA, the brother of the governor of Quito, was appointed to observe, record, and map the Amazon for future Spanish expeditions. He kept a very detailed account of the trip from Quito to Pará, and his journal is the main source of historical information about Teixeira's return voyage. The Portuguese captain also agreed to

Treaty of Tordesillas agreement between Spain and Portugal dividing the rights to discovered lands along a north-south line

take along a group of Spanish soldiers, who had been ordered to build a fort to protect Peru from possible English or Dutch invasions.

A Bold Declaration

The group left Peru on February 16, 1639, following the Napo River until it reached the Amazon. When Teixeira arrived at the site where he had left some of his men behind, he discovered that they had fought many battles with an unfriendly tribe of Omagua Indians. He quickly attacked and slaughtered the Indians and then founded a town, which he named Franciscana. During the dedication ceremony, Teixeira claimed the surrounding lands for Portugal, and none of the Spaniards objected. Somewhere near the settlement, he dug a hole in which he placed a carved log to show the border between Spanish and Portuguese territory. Historians are unsure of the site, since this town no longer exists.

The expedition continued downriver. When the party stopped to rest at the mouth of the Río Negro, many of the men—including Teixeira—wanted to capture slaves in the area. Father Acuña objected, stating that this activity was morally wrong and that he wanted to reach Pará as soon as possible. Teixeira chose to support Acuña, and the canoes continued down the Amazon without further delay. When the expedition finally reached Pará on December 12, 1639, Teixeira was honored for his accomplishments. The following year, he was named governor of the province of Pará, but he died a few months later.

As a result of Teixeira's transcontinental journey, the Portuguese established control over the entire Amazon River region—a large part of South America. By the time King John IV regained the Portuguese throne from Spain in 1641, his country possessed most of the river valley, in territory that had been granted to Spain by the Treaty of Tordesillas.

SUGGESTED READING John Hemming, *Red Gold: The Conquest of the Brazilian Indians* (Harvard University Press, 1978); Clements R. Markham, editor and translator, *Expeditions into the Valley of the Amazons* (Hakluyt Society, 1859); Anthony Smith, *Explorers of the Amazon* (Viking, 1990).

Tereshkova, Valentina Vladimirovna

Russian
b March 6, 1937; Maslennikovo, Russia
living
First woman in space

orbit stable, circular route; one trip around; to revolve around

Soviet Union nation that existed from 1922 to 1991, made up of Russia and 14 other republics in eastern Europe and northern Asia

cosmonaut Russian term for a person who travels into space; literally, "traveler to the universe"

Valentina Tereshkova was the first woman—and the tenth person—to **orbit** the earth. Her flight in 1963 was a triumph for the space agency of the **Soviet Union.** It also opened the way for women to take part in space exploration.

A Volunteer for Space

Tereshkova was born on a farm near the city of Yaroslavl in Russia. After her father was killed in battle in World War II, she and her mother moved to Yaroslavl. At 16 Tereshkova went to work in a tire factory while attending classes at a night school. Within a few years, she had discovered an exciting hobby—parachute jumping. She joined a local club, began making jumps, and eventually became a certified instructor.

The idea of space travel fascinated Tereshkova. In 1961, after the Soviet **cosmonaut** Yuri GAGARIN became the first person to fly in

Cosmonaut Valentina Tereshkova was neither a pilot nor a scientist. Her government wanted to show that it could send a woman factory worker into space.

capsule small early spacecraft designed to carry a person around the earth

rocket vehicle propelled by exploding fuel

space, Tereshkova wrote to the Soviet space agency, volunteering to be trained. By most standards, she had no chance of being chosen. She lacked scientific training and did not even know how to fly an airplane. But Soviet leaders saw a chance to score a victory over their American rivals by being the first to send a woman into space. The Soviets also wanted to publicize the heroism of ordinary citizens, so they decided to turn a working woman into a cosmonaut. In 1962 the agency told Tereshkova and four other women to report to a training center called Star City.

Sea Gull in Orbit

The strong and energetic Tereshkova did well at her physical training, but she had more trouble mastering the science of space flight. However, she studied hard, and her efforts were rewarded. On June 16, 1963, she climbed into the Vostok 6 **capsule** *Sea Gull* and rode a **rocket** into space. Another cosmonaut, Valeri Bykovsky, was already orbiting the earth in the Vostok 5 capsule *Hawk*.

Using her code name, Sea Gull, Tereshkova radioed back to earth: "I see the horizon. A light blue, a blue band. This is the earth. How beautiful it is! Everything goes fine." When Bykovsky flew nearby in his own capsule, the two cosmonauts spoke and even sang together by radio. Tereshkova also carried out experiments to find out how weightlessness would affect her. The only trouble she reported was a bout of motion sickness. After almost three days, Tereshkova had circled the earth 48 times, covering 1.2 million miles. The capsule began its return to earth, and at a height of about 4 miles, she exited the spacecraft and parachuted safely into a field in the Soviet Union.

Tereshkova's flight won her the title of Hero of the Soviet Union, her country's highest honor. A few months later, she married another cosmonaut. Their daughter was the first child whose parents had both traveled in space. For many years after her historic mission, Tereshkova toured the world, making speeches to promote space flight and women's rights.

SUGGESTED READING Carole S. Briggs, *Women in Space: Reaching the Last Frontier* (Lerner Publications, 1988); Tony Lothian, *Valentina: First Woman in Space* (Pentland Press, 1993); Mitchell Sharpe, *"It Is I, Sea Gull": Valentina Tereshkova, First Woman in Space* (Crowell, 1975).

Thesiger, Wilfred Patrick

English
b June 1910; Addis Ababa, Abyssinia (now Ethiopia)
living
Lived among tribes in Arabia, Africa, and Asia

For almost 50 years, Wilfred Thesiger lived among tribal peoples in distant and often dangerous parts of the world— in the deserts of Africa and Arabia, in the swamps of the Upper Nile River, in the marshes of Iraq, and in the high mountain ranges of India and Pakistan. His motives and methods were different from those of most explorers, as he explained:

While I was with the Arabs I wished only to live as they lived, and now that I have left them I would gladly think that nothing in their lives was altered by my coming. Regretfully, however, I realize that the maps I made helped others with more material aims to visit and corrupt a people whose spirit once lit the desert like a flame.

Wanderings and Warfare

The oldest son of a British missionary in Addis Ababa, Abyssinia (now Ethiopia), Thesiger traveled with his family in the deserts and highlands of Africa and India. He was educated at the best schools in England and then returned to Abyssinia to explore the Awash River and the Aussa region to the north. From 1935 to 1939, he served the British government of the Sudan region and explored parts of what later became Sudan and Chad. During World War II, he assisted Britain and its allies in the defense of Ethiopia, Syria, and North Africa.

The Empty Quarter

After the war, Thesiger began a series of treks across the Rub' al-Khali, also known as the Empty Quarter, a desert in the Arabian Peninsula. It had first been crossed a few years earlier by Bertram Thomas and Harry St. John Philby. But Thesiger's goal was less the crossing of the desert than the experience of being there. Along the way, he befriended the bedouin, the camel-herding nomads who made the desert their home, and gained a great respect for their way of life.

In the 1950s, Thesiger spent seven years living in and exploring the Iraqi marshes near the mouths of the Tigris and Euphrates Rivers. From 1968 to 1994, he spent most of his time in Kenya. He then moved to London, where he was knighted in 1995.

SUGGESTED READING Michael Asher, *Thesiger* (Penguin, 1995); Wilfred Thesiger, *Arabian Sands* (Collins, 1983), *The Last Nomad* (E. P. Dutton, 1980), and *The Marsh Arabs* (Allen Lane, 1964).

Thompson, David

English
b April 30, 1770; London, England
d February 10, 1857; Longueil, Canada
Explored Canadian West and Columbia River

surveyor one who makes precise measurements of a location's geography

A tireless traveler, David Thompson covered more than 50,000 miles in his career as a fur trader, **surveyor,** geographer, and explorer. Wherever he went, he made detailed maps of his routes and the surrounding regions. Thompson surveyed over 9,000 square miles east of the Rocky Mountains in Canada. In 1807 he crossed the Rockies through Saskatchewan Pass and followed the Columbia River to its source. Over the next four years, Thompson traveled every inch of the Columbia, mapping it to its mouth on the Pacific Ocean.

The Impossible Border

Thompson was only 2 years old when his father died, leaving the family in poverty. Educated at a school for the needy, Thompson showed a special talent in mathematics. When he was 14 years old, he became an apprentice to fur traders with the Hudson's Bay Company. During the 13 years he worked for the company, he navigated and surveyed many of the rivers that empty into Hudson Bay. However, his superiors did not recognize the value of his explorations, and they encouraged him to devote more time to the fur trade.

In 1797 Thompson left the Hudson's Bay Company to join its rival, the North West Company. On one of his first assignments, he journeyed from the Assiniboine River (in present-day Manitoba) to the Mandan villages on the Missouri River in what is now North Dakota. Thompson then explored the source of the Mississippi River in what is now northern Minnesota. At that time, the boundary

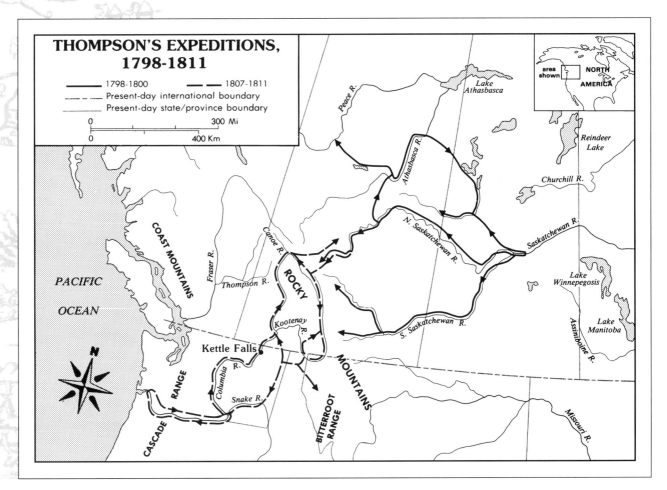

THOMPSON'S EXPEDITIONS,
1798-1811

—— 1798-1800   — · — 1807-1811
— · · — Present-day international boundary
———— Present-day state/province boundary

0   300 Mi
0   400 Km

area shown — NORTH AMERICA

One authority in the field of surveying has called David Thompson "the greatest practical land geographer that the world has produced."

between the United States and Canada was supposed to run west from the Lake of the Woods to the Mississippi. Thompson's survey showed that the source of the Mississippi was probably south of the Lake of the Woods. Therefore, a line running due west from this lake would never intersect the river.

The Piegan and the Kootenay

In the early 1800s, Thompson explored the upper waters of the Saskatchewan and Athabasca Rivers of western Canada. The officials of the North West Company then wanted him to find a safe route across the Rocky Mountains to the Pacific Ocean. They hoped to transport goods overland from the coast to trading posts in the mountains.

Thompson had done some trading with a tribe of Blackfoot Indians called the Piegan, who lived in the eastern foothills of the Rockies. In the winter of 1800, they told him that a group of Kootenay Indians was camped in Piegan territory. The Piegan did not want Thompson to trade goods—especially guns—with their longtime enemies, who lived west of the mountains. The Piegan tried to keep him from making contact with the Kootenay, but Thompson was eager to learn about the territory on the other side of the Rockies. After he held a secret meeting with the Kootenay, two of his trappers returned with these Indians to their homes to investigate the area.

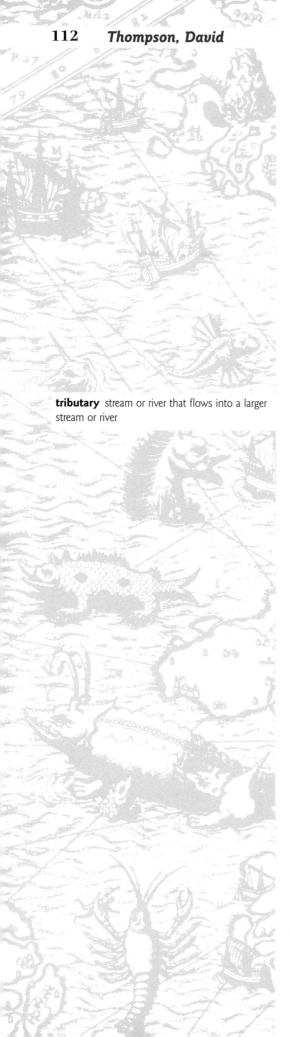

tributary stream or river that flows into a larger stream or river

Over the Mountains

The scouts brought back valuable information, but Thompson was not able to use it for several years. Engaged in competition with other traders, Thompson had to concentrate on his fur venture. However, in 1807 the North West Company ordered him to seek business with the Indians on the western slopes of the Rockies. Thompson assembled a large party, including his wife (who was half Indian) and their three children. When Thompson arrived at Saskatchewan Pass, he met a group of Piegan, who had been stationed there to prevent him from crossing. Thompson and his party waited until the Indians left to fight in a battle. The explorers then crossed the mountains and soon reached a river flowing north, which Thompson named the Kootenay. This river was actually the Columbia, which had been discovered and named by Captain Robert GRAY in 1792. Thompson did not recognize it as the Columbia because he expected that river to flow south. He was not aware that it flows north before making a horseshoe turn and continuing south. Thompson later realized that he had actually found the upper Columbia. The name Kootenay was then given to the main **tributary** of the Columbia.

Thompson and his companions built canoes and paddled upstream to what is now Lake Windermere. Near the lake, Thompson built a fort, which he and his party later used in fighting off an attack by the Piegan. In the spring of 1808, Thompson continued south on the river, traveling upstream. He found the source of the Columbia River in what is now Columbia Lake. From there he followed the Kootenay River into what is now Idaho. He eventually established trading posts in Idaho and western Montana.

For three years, Thompson explored various rivers west of the Rockies and built several trading posts to gain the business and loyalty of the region's Indians. In 1809 he met a rival from the Hudson's Bay Company, who had been exploring the upper Columbia. Facing this evidence of serious competition, Thompson decided to focus on his fur business rather than make a planned journey along the Columbia.

Race to the Pacific

In the spring of 1810, Thompson received a message that John Jacob Astor's Pacific Fur Company had sent Robert STUART and Wilson Price HUNT to build a trading post at the mouth of the Columbia River. The North West Company ordered Thompson to travel down the Columbia to the Pacific coast, perhaps in order to get there before Astor's men. However, Thompson seems to have been more interested in his fur trade than in exploration—he did not begin his expedition down the river until more than a year later.

Thompson spent the winter of 1810 to the spring of 1811 at the juncture of the Columbia and Canoe Rivers (in present-day British Columbia). In the spring, he canoed down the Kootenay, then traveled over land to the Columbia at Kettle Falls, in what is now northeastern Washington. Thompson left Kettle Falls on July 3 and headed west. Twelve days later, he arrived at the Pacific Ocean and discovered that the Pacific Fur Company had already established a trading post there. Welcomed by his rivals, Thompson remained at the post for a week and then returned to the Columbia River. From there he traveled north and explored the parts of the Columbia that he had never seen, finally completing the survey that he had begun in 1807. He was the first European to follow the Columbia all the way from its source in the Rockies to its junction with the Snake River. Meriwether LEWIS and William CLARK had already explored the Columbia west of the Snake on their journey in 1804 to 1806.

Thompson retired from the fur trade in the spring of 1812. But his exploration of North America was not finished. In 1817 he accepted a position as surveyor and astronomer for a joint project of the U.S. and Canadian governments. He was given the duty of surveying the boundary between the two countries—a difficult task at which he worked for 10 years.

SUGGESTED READING Victor G. Hopwood, editor, *David Thompson: Travels in Western North America* (Macmillan of Canada, 1971); Jack Nisbet, *Sources of the River: Tracking David Thompson Across Western North America* (Sasquatch Books, 1994); David Thompson, *David Thompson's Narrative 1784–1812* (Champlain Society, 1962).

Thomson, Joseph

Scottish
b February 14, 1858; Penpont, Scotland
d August 2, 1895; London, England
Explored central Africa

geologist scientist who studies the earth's natural history

species type of plant or animal

geology the scientific study of the earth's natural history

sultan ruler of a Muslim nation

The scientist Joseph Thomson was the first European to enter some parts of eastern central Africa. On his most notable journey, he traveled through the homeland of the Masai tribe, whose violent defense of their territory had turned back all previous European visitors. Thomson was a **geologist** and naturalist by training, and his name was given to Kenya's Thomson Falls as well as to a **species** of antelope, Thomson's gazelle. Late in his brief career, he gained recognition as a diplomat and trade negotiator in Africa.

A Growing Reputation

Thomson had long been fascinated with the natural sciences when he went to study with the noted scientist Archibald Geikie, who recommended him for an expedition in 1879. The 21-year-old Thomson served as geologist on a journey to central Africa sponsored by Britain's Royal Geographical Society. Six months into the mission, the party's leader died, and Thomson took command. The group traveled through what is now southern Tanzania, reached the north shore of Lake Nyasa, and headed north to Lake Tanganyika. Thomson then tried to travel into the Congo region to the west, but a hostile tribe forced him to turn around. He discovered Lake Rukwa before returning to the east coast in 1880.

In the same year, Thomson published a two-volume book describing his detailed scientific observations. This work was highly valued for its explanations of central Africa's geography and **geology.** Thomson's new expertise led the **sultan** Barghash of Tanzania to hire him in 1881 to search for coal around the Ruvuma River. However, that expedition was unsuccessful.

Unarmed Among the Masai

Thomson returned to England, and he received a second commission from the Royal Geographical Society in 1882. His assignment, which was to find the shortest route between Tanzania and Uganda, required him to cross the land of the feared Masai tribe. He started at the coastal city of Mombasa and then traveled—unarmed—through Masai territory to the northeast. Passing Mount Kilimanjaro, he discovered Lake Baringo and arrived safely in December 1882 at Lake Victoria. The society honored him with its Founder's Medal when he returned to England in 1883.

A Career Cut Short

Thomson found himself much in demand for his knowledge of Africa's geography and his ability to establish good relations with African peoples. He earned a reputation as an excellent diplomat when he negotiated a trade treaty for a British company in Nigeria. In the late 1880s, he visited Morocco and the Atlas Mountains of western North Africa, and he published a book about the region in 1889.

The following year, Thomson was again asked to negotiate a treaty, this time for mining and trade in southern Africa. His career in Africa seemed to hold much promise for the future. However, he could not withstand the physical strain of exploration. He returned to England in failing health and died there at the age of 37.

SUGGESTED READING Robert J. Rotberg, *Joseph Thomson and the Exploration of Africa* (Oxford University Press, 1971).

Joseph Thomson was the first European to travel unharmed through Masai territory in what is now western Kenya.

Tinné, Alexine

Dutch
b October 17, 1835; The Hague, The Netherlands
d August 1, 1869; near Ghat, Libya
Explored Nile River, central Africa, and Sahara

tributary stream or river that flows into a larger stream or river

Alexine Tinné was a wealthy Dutch heiress with a passion for exploration. She led several expeditions along the Nile River and its **tributaries** and visited previously uncharted territory in central Africa. Tinné was also the first European woman to attempt a crossing of the Sahara.

Desire for Adventure

Tinné was born the richest heiress in the Netherlands. Raised by nannies and taught by tutors, she loved to read and was particularly talented in science. Her interest in geography was strengthened further by the long vacations she took with her family every summer.

Tinné visited Africa for the first time at the age of 19. In 1855 she and her mother took a tour of Europe and then traveled to Egypt. Although Tinné led an active social life in Cairo and Alexandria, she had more ambitious goals for this trip. After learning some Arabic, she hired a crew of 14 and rented a 90-foot-long Egyptian boat for a voyage up the Nile River to Aswan. Upon arriving there, she and her mother left the boat to travel east by camel to Al-Quseir, on the Red Sea. After this 10-week journey, the pair returned to Cairo, and Tinné began preparations for a second voyage the following winter. She wanted to go upriver to Khartoum (in present-day Sudan), but she was warned that this trip was impossible without a steam-powered riverboat. Since there were no such vessels available, Tinné had her furniture, food, and livestock loaded onto an even bigger boat than the one she had taken on her first voyage, hired a larger crew, and headed up the Nile.

One writer described Dutch heiress Alexine Tinné as an explorer "without any other motive than her passion for unknown things."

caravan large group of people traveling together, often with pack animals, across a desert or other dangerous region

botanist scientist who studies plants

specimen sample of a plant, animal, or mineral, usually collected for scientific study or display

The boat stopped at Asyut and then at Luxor, where Tinné tried to arrange a tour of the surrounding desert by camel **caravan.** But the area's bedouin nomads refused her request. When Tinné and her party reached Aswan, waterfalls forced them to transfer to a smaller boat. After another week, they came to Abu Simbel, an enormous temple that had been built in honor of the Egyptian king Ramses II. Tinné then made a second request for a caravan tour, but again it was denied. Disappointed, she and her companions decided to turn back rather than proceed to Khartoum. They arrived in Cairo in March 1857.

Traveling in Style

During the next several years, Tinné continued to travel, visiting Lebanon, Turkey, Italy, and Austria. In 1860 she returned to Cairo with the goal of sailing farther up the Nile River. By January 1862, she had assembled her largest expedition yet: three boats, with supplies for a year. Her mother's sister also joined the group. When the party stopped at Korosko to begin the long-awaited tour of the desert, 102 camels were needed just to carry the luggage. After 12 weeks on the Nile, they arrived at Khartoum.

They set out again on May 11, and within a week, they came to the trading station at Jebel Dinka. Tinné hired a new steamboat and took it upriver to Lake No. From there she and her party proceeded along the Bahr al-Jebel, a tributary of the White Nile River. The expedition made its way slowly up the narrow waterway for 150 miles. When the steamboat reached Rejaf (now in southern Sudan), the river became too rough to navigate safely, and one of the crew members drowned. Tinné had to decide whether to continue the journey. Since her aunt was begging to return home, and she herself had fallen ill, the expedition went back to Khartoum.

A Tragic Journey

After recovering from her illness, Tinné began to prepare for an even more daring adventure. She hoped to sail up another tributary of the White Nile, the Bahr al-Ghazal, and then trek to the central highlands of Africa—possibly as far south as the equator. In February 1863, she set out with her mother, her aunt, 6 servants, a **botanist,** and 71 soldiers. The party traveled in one steamboat and seven smaller boats. They brought along enough ammunition and supplies for 6 months. But the crew had to battle against storms and floods, extending the difficult trip to 11 months. Tinné's mother and aunt, the botanist, and two of the family's longtime maids died of fever and exhaustion. Overcoming her grief, Tinné explored uncharted territory and brought back a collection of plants. She later described these **specimens** and her travels in a book titled *Plantae Tinneanae*.

Tinné lived in Cairo and Algiers for several years. In 1869 she began a trip across the Sahara desert region, but along the way, she was murdered by a group of Tuareg bandits. Impressed by her bravery, the famous Scottish explorer David LIVINGSTONE commented: "The work of SPEKE and Grant is deserving of the highest commendation. . . . But none rises higher in my estimation than the Dutch lady, Miss Tinné, who, after the severest domestic afflictions, nobly persevered in the teeth of every difficulty."

SUGGESTED READING Penelope Gladstone, *Travels of Alexine: Alexine Tinné, 1835–1869* (John Murray, 1970).

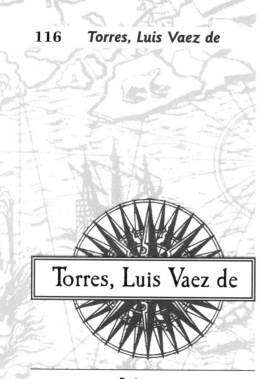

Torres, Luis Vaez de

Portuguese
b ?; Portugal
d 1613; ?
Discovered strait between New Guinea and Australia

Luis Vaez de Torres solved one of the major geographical puzzles of his time. In 1605 he sailed through the strait between the lands that are now New Guinea and Australia. This voyage proved that New Guinea is an island, not a part of the continental landmass then known as the Great South Land. However, Torres did not seem to realize the importance of his discovery.

Solving the Mystery

Little is known about Torres's life before or after his famous voyage. Sailing in the service of Spain, he was appointed second-in-command under his countryman Pedro Fernandez de QUIRÓS. The purpose of the expedition was to establish a Spanish colony in the southern Pacific Ocean and to discover *Terra Australis Incognita,* the legendary southern continent. Torres was given command of the *San Pedrico,* which left Callao, Peru with two other ships in December 1605.

The explorers remained at sea for months, stopping at various islands and eventually reaching an island that became known as Espíritu Santo (in the present-day New Hebrides). Three weeks after their arrival, Quirós sailed away suddenly and without any explanation. After an extensive but unsuccessful search for his commander, Torres decided to proceed to Manila in the Philippines. On the way, he came across what is now called the Louisiade Archipelago, east of New Guinea. It took him 34 days to navigate the maze of reefs and sandbars in the waters of the island chain.

When he reached the eastern tip of New Guinea, he tried to sail north of it, as other explorers had done. But strong winds forced him to travel southwest, along the island's south side. He then passed through the strait that now bears his name. Torres landed in Manila in the summer of 1607, and on July 12, he wrote a letter to the king of Spain, describing his journey. Six years later, the king received another account of the voyage from an officer named Diego de Prado y Tovar, who today is usually credited as the other discoverer of what is now called Torres Strait.

Recognition at Last

Notes on a Dutch map made in 1622 mention Torres's route. However, the Dutch did not rediscover the strait for about 50 years. Torres was not given credit for the discovery until 1762, when Manila was captured by the British, who found records of his voyage.

SUGGESTED READING Sir Clements Markham, *The Voyages of Pedro Fernandez de Quirós* (Hakluyt Society, 1904).

Tristão, Nuño

Portuguese
b ?; Portugal
d 1447; Gambia River (now in Gambia)
Explored West Africa;
discovered Arguin Island and Cape Blanc

During the 1440s, Nuño Tristão explored a large portion of Africa's west coast in a series of expeditions commissioned by Portugal's Prince Henry the Navigator. Credited with the discoveries of the island of Arguin and nearby Cape Blanc, Tristão was also one of the first Europeans to engage in African slave trading. He never returned from the last and longest of his voyages to the Gambia River.

Taking Prisoners

In 1441 Prince Henry outfitted two ships for separate journeys down the west coast of Africa. Tristão, a young knight, was given command of one ship, and the other was captained by Antâo Gonçalves. Sailing south, Tristão encountered Gonçalves at Río de Oro in Western Sahara, and the two commanders decided to capture some of the local people and take them back to Portugal.

After they raided a site that they named Porto de Cavaleiro, the Portuguese killed 3 members of a local tribe and captured 10 more. Gonçalves sailed back to Portugal with the captives, who included a high-ranking leader and 2 wealthy youths. Tristão continued south and reached a cape at the northern border of what is now Mauritania. He named it Cape Blanc for its white sands. Since his supplies were running low, he then decided to head home.

Revenge Against the Raiders

Pleased with Tristão's discoveries and his capture of the Africans, Prince Henry sent him on another expedition in 1442. On this voyage, Tristão journeyed past Cape Blanc and discovered the island of Arguin. However, high waves prevented him from making any other landings, and his supplies were again low, so he returned to Portugal.

Tristão reported his latest findings to the Prince. The news of Arguin excited Portugal's merchants, adventurers, and slave traders. The island soon became a busy slave trading station, the first European venture of that kind in Africa. During the next few years, Tristão made a series of slave raids on the coast of West Africa.

Meanwhile, the African leader and the wealthy young men who had been captured in the first raid begged for their freedom. They promised that in exchange for each of them, they would send back five other villagers. Prince Henry agreed to the deal and allowed the captives to return home. But the freed tribesmen disappeared and did not send others in their place. The Portuguese used this incident as an excuse to raid other West African villages and capture slaves. As the slave trade became a significant economic force in the region, the tribes grew resentful that their people were being stolen—rather than bought. By the time Tristão set out on his third voyage of exploration, the Africans were ready to take revenge.

Tristão sailed beyond what is now the Senegal River and passed Cape Verde, the westernmost point of Africa. His ship reached the mouth of the Gambia River in 1446. Rowing upstream, Tristão and his men were suddenly surrounded by canoes filled with tribesmen, who shot poison-tipped arrows at them. Some crew members died before they could retreat to the mouth of the river. Tristão reportedly died aboard his vessel within the first day of the return voyage.

SUGGESTED READING C. Howard and J. H. Plumb, editors, *West African Explorers* (Oxford University Press, 1952).

Tudela, Benjamin of.   See *Benjamin of Tudela.*

Urdaneta, Andrés de

Spanish
b 1498; Villafranca de Oria, Spain
d June 3, 1568; Mexico City (now in Mexico)
Charted eastward route across Pacific Ocean

New Spain region of Spanish colonial empire that included the areas now occupied by Mexico, Florida, Texas, New Mexico, Arizona, California, and various Caribbean islands

galleon large sailing ship used for war and trade

circumnavigation journey around the world

latitude distance north or south of the equator

The Spanish navigator and priest Andrés de Urdaneta was the first person to sail and chart the sea route from the islands of Southeast Asia (known as the East Indies) to **New Spain.** Known as Urdaneta's Passage, the route suddenly enabled navigators to cross the Pacific Ocean from west to east. It therefore had a great effect on the destiny of Spain's colonial empire—for the next 300 years, Spanish **galleons** regularly carried treasure and goods between the Philippine Islands and what is now Mexico.

Conflict and Christianity

One of the Basque people of northeastern Spain, Urdaneta sailed for Asia with a fellow Basque seaman, Juan Sebastián de ELCANO, at the age of 27. The two men joined a Spanish expedition to claim and conquer the Spice Islands, also known as the Moluccas (an island group that is now part of Indonesia). By the time the Spaniards reached the islands, they had lost five of their seven ships and two-thirds of the crew. They had also lost both of the commanders. Elcano, who four years earlier had completed Ferdinand MAGELLAN's **circumnavigation,** was among the dead. Urdaneta and the other survivors took up a position on the island of Tidore, where they fought off the Portuguese for several years. They eventually surrendered and were sent to Portugal before being returned to Spain.

In 1538 Urdaneta sailed to Mexico, intending to join an expedition led by Pedro de ALVARADO. In 1541 both men fought rebellious Indians in the Mixtón War. Alvarado died, and when the fighting ended, Urdaneta decided to remain in Mexico as a government official. He also earned a reputation as a geographer and strengthened his Christian faith. He joined the religious Order of Saint Augustine in 1552 and became a priest five years later.

Urdaneta's Passage

In 1559, Spain's King Phillip II asked the 61-year-old Urdaneta to pilot a fleet of five ships to the East Indies under the command of Miguel López de LEGAZPI. The expedition left Mexico on November 21, 1564, and the smallest ship, the *San Lucas,* was soon separated from the others at sea. Captained by Alonso de Arellano, the *San Lucas* visited several island groups before sailing north. At a **latitude** of about 40° north, Arellano found a current (now called the Japan Current) that carried his ship eastward, across the Pacific Ocean to North America. However, Arellano failed to chart his route, and his success provided no guidance for other navigators.

Meanwhile, Urdaneta led the other four ships to the island of Cebu and helped Legazpi win over the inhabitants to Spanish rule and to Christianity. Expanding his control over most of the other islands in the group, Legazpi named them the Philippines in honor of the Spanish king. Urdaneta left the islands on June 1, 1565, aboard the *San Pedro.* Without knowing of Arellano's success, he sailed as far north as 42°, using both the Japan Current and the **westerlies** to cross the ocean along a wide, curving route. Urdaneta reached what is now California on September 18, 1565, and then sailed south to Acapulco.

The six-month, 11,000-mile eastward voyage took twice as long as the trip westward, but after Urdaneta made it known to other navigators, it opened tremendous new trade possibilities. Until then, sailors had had to travel west from the East Indies, returning to Europe or the Americas by way of Africa. Arellano and Urdaneta were the first to succeed in crossing the Pacific from west to east. The trading galleons that used this route became a principal lifeline of the Spanish empire. They were also a primary target for English **buccaneers,** such as Francis DRAKE, who sought to disrupt Spain's dominion over Pacific waters.

SUGGESTED READING Mairin Mitchell, *Friar Andrés de Urdaneta* (Macdonald and Evans, 1964).

westerlies winds that blow from west to east midway between the equator and each of the poles

buccaneer pirate, especially one who attacked Spanish colonies and ships in the 1600s

Vaca, Álvar Núñez Cabeza de. See *Cabeza de Vaca, Álvar Núñez.*

Vaez de Torres, Luis. See *Torres, Luis Vaez de.*

Vancouver, George

English
b June 22, 1757; King's Lynn, England
d May 10, 1798; Petersham, England
Surveyed Pacific coast of North America

Northwest Passage water route connecting the Atlantic Ocean and Pacific Ocean through the Arctic islands of northern Canada

Between 1792 and 1794, George Vancouver completed an extensive scientific survey of the Pacific coast of North America. He charted every bay, cape, and channel from San Francisco to Cook Inlet, Alaska. Vancouver also proved that there was no **Northwest Passage** south of the Arctic Ocean.

Learning from the Captain
Vancouver entered Britain's Royal Navy at the age of 13. He was then chosen by Captain James COOK to join an expedition to search for the legendary southern continent, *Terra Australis Incognita.* During that three-year voyage, Vancouver studied with the noted astronomer William Wales, who was also on board. In 1776 Cook selected Vancouver to accompany him on a search for the outlet of the Northwest Passage on the Pacific Ocean.

In March 1778, Vancouver and some of his shipmates became the first Europeans to land on the coast of what is now British Columbia. Later in the voyage, Vancouver was almost killed in a battle against the people of the Sandwich Islands (now Hawaii). Unfortunately, Captain Cook did not escape death. The expedition returned to England in October 1780. Over the next nine years, Vancouver served primarily in the Caribbean Sea and was promoted to first lieutenant.

In the late 1700s, the British began to recognize the commercial potential of the northwest coast of North America. However, they had to contend with Spain's claim to control of the entire coastline

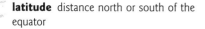

Vancouver's ship, the *Discovery*, was too large for safe navigation of the small inlets of Puget Sound.

latitude distance north or south of the equator

as far north as Prince William Sound (in present-day Alaska). In an effort to strengthen their presence in the region, the British decided to send an expedition to survey the Pacific coast of North America, with Vancouver as second-in-command. Britain also wanted the expedition to resolve the lingering question of the existence of a Northwest Passage. Although Cook had not found such a route above the **latitude** of 55° north, the possibility of a passage south of that line had not yet been fully investigated.

Troubles with Spain

Before Vancouver and his crew departed from England, important news reached London. Several British trading ships had been seized by the Spanish in Nootka Sound. The British strongly protested this aggressive act. Since the Spanish did not want a war over the incident, they signed the Nootka Sound Convention on October 28, 1790. This treaty required Spain to give the stolen property back to its British owners. More important, Spain surrendered its claim to complete control of the Pacific coast.

After this crisis had been resolved, the British resumed their plans for a survey of the northwest coast of North America. This time Vancouver was given command of the expedition. He was also instructed to ensure that the stolen British property was returned at Nootka and to complete Cook's unfinished survey of the Sandwich Islands.

Two ships, the *Discovery* and the smaller *Chatham,* set out from Falmouth, England, on April 1, 1791. The ships sailed south, rounded Africa's Cape of Good Hope, and proceeded to New Holland (now known as Australia), New Zealand, Tahiti, and the Sandwich Islands. On April 17, 1792, they reached the Pacific coast of North America, at a point about 110 miles north of San Francisco.

Vancouver sailed north and began his survey. He quickly and easily mapped the coasts of what became present-day Oregon and

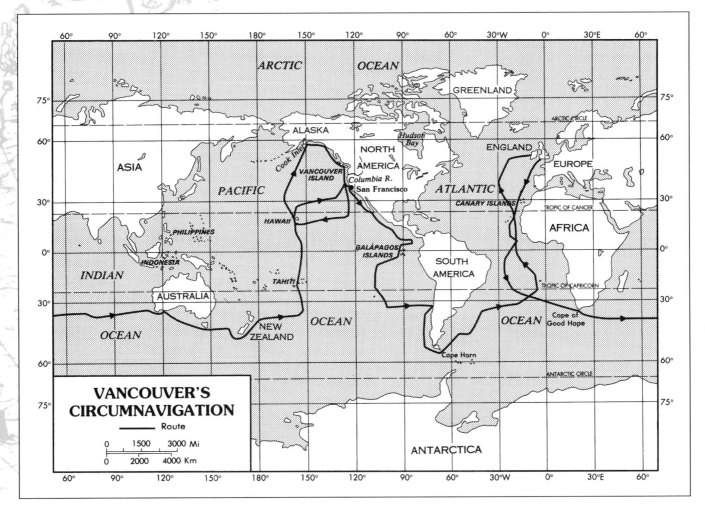

VANCOUVER'S CIRCUMNAVIGATION
— Route
0   1500   3000 Mi
0   2000   4000 Km

In under five years, George Vancouver's survey expeditions traveled about 75,000 miles.

Washington. By April 29, he had arrived at the Strait of Juan de Fuca (between present-day Washington State and Vancouver Island). At this point, the survey became more difficult. Vancouver had been ordered to make a detailed examination of the strait. He was determined to trace every inlet completely to verify whether it was the opening of a Northwest Passage. Although the *Chatham* had been sent on this voyage to navigate waters that were too narrow for the *Discovery,* Vancouver soon learned that even the *Chatham* was not safe in many small inlets of what is now Puget Sound. To continue north, he had to use the small boats from the two ships, making the survey more dangerous than he had expected.

Friendly Enemies

Near the end of June, Vancouver encountered two Spanish vessels. He was disappointed to discover that they had already explored the Strait of Juan de Fuca and the Strait of Georgia (between present-day Vancouver Island and the Canadian mainland). However, since the Spanish had not yet mapped Puget Sound, the British commander continued up the east coast of what is now Vancouver Island. Sailing between the island and the mainland, he arrived in Queen Charlotte Strait. In this way, he proved that the large landmass was indeed an island. After rounding its northern coast, Vancouver headed down the west coast until he reached Nootka Sound. There he met the Spanish commander Juan Francisco de la BODEGA Y QUADRA, who had also been appointed to carry out the terms of the Nootka Sound Convention.

Although Vancouver and Bodega y Quadra became close friends, they could not agree on the requirements of the treaty. They decided to wait for more detailed instructions from their governments. Meanwhile, Bodega y Quadra entertained his British guests in grand style. Vancouver then sailed south to San Francisco and Monterey, where he met the Spanish governor of California, also a generous host. Since winter was approaching, Vancouver and his men sailed west to map the Sandwich Islands.

By May 1793, Vancouver had returned to the northwest coast of North America, and in June he explored Dean Channel. By September he had reached the latitude of 56° north. He then sailed south again to California, hoping that his friend Bodega y Quadra had received word about how to settle the Nootka Sound Convention. But Bodega y Quadra was not there, and the new Spanish governor did not receive the British warmly. Vancouver soon departed and traveled south to 30° north—the southernmost limit of his survey. That winter he completed his exploration of the Sandwich Islands.

Port Conclusion

In the spring of 1794, Vancouver decided to head north to Cook Inlet—the northernmost point of his survey. From there he turned south, and on August 19, he completed his expedition in a bay off Baranof Island. He named this body of water Port Conclusion and threw a party for his crew to celebrate the end of the mission. The ships sailed around South America's Cape Horn and arrived in England on October 20, 1795. Less than three years later, Vancouver died at the age of 40 as he was preparing his journals for publication.

Vancouver left his mark on the Pacific Northwest with the place names he gave to several hundred physical features in the region. For example, he named Puget Sound after the lieutenant of the *Discovery,* and he named Mount Rainier after an officer he had known in the Caribbean. Vancouver Island was originally called Quadra and Vancouver's Island, in honor of the explorer's Spanish friend.

SUGGESTED READING Bern Anderson, *Surveyor of the Sea* (University of Toronto Press, 1960); James Stirrat Marshall and Carrie Marshall, *Vancouver's Voyage* (Mitchell, 1967); John M. Naish, *The Interwoven Lives of George Vancouver, Archibald Menzies, Joseph Whidbey, and Peter Puget: Exploring the Northwest Coast* (Edwin Mellen Press, 1996); Ronald Syme, *Vancouver: Explorer of the Pacific Coast* (William Morrow, 1970).

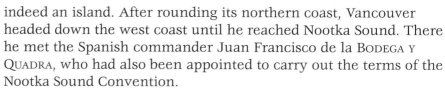

Van Linschoten, Jan Huyghen. See *Linschoten, Jan Huyghen van.*

Varennes, Pierre Gaultier de. See *La Vérendrye, Pierre Gaultier de Varennes de.*

Varthema, Ludovico di

Italian
b 1465?; Bologna, Italy
d 1517; Rome, Italy
Explored Middle East, India, and Southeast Asia

pilgrimage journey to a sacred place
sultan ruler of a Muslim nation

In 1502 Ludovico di Varthema left behind his home, his wife, and his child in the Italian city of Bologna. Driven by a desire for adventure—rather than fame or fortune—he traveled to Cairo, Egypt, and to Damascus, Syria. Along the way, he studied Arabic in order to pose as a Muslim. In this disguise, he joined a military force in Damascus, and as a soldier, he took part in a **pilgrimage** to Mecca and Medina, the holy cities of Islam that were barred to Christians. Varthema was the first European in centuries to publish a description of these cities.

Varthema then set out to reach India by way of the Red Sea. He was arrested on the coast of Yemen and charged with being a Christian spy. The **sultan** of San'a held him prisoner, but one of the sultan's wives helped him to escape. Varthema then explored southwestern Arabia before heading for Persia (present-day Iran); there he befriended a merchant, who agreed to travel with him to India by ship. They visited the city of Calicut and the island of Ceylon (now Sri Lanka) before going on to Burma (now Myanmar), Sumatra, and Java.

Varthema returned to India and parted from his Persian friend. He joined a Portuguese force in a battle against the inhabitants, and he was knighted for his military service. Varthema left India in late 1507 and traveled home by way of the east coast of Africa and around the Cape of Good Hope, reaching Italy in late 1508. Within two years, he published a highly popular account of his travels.

SUGGESTED READING Ludovico de Varthema, *The Itinerary of Ludovico di Varthema of Bologna* (reprint, Da Capo Press, 1971).

Vásquez de Coronado, Francisco. See *Coronado, Francisco Vásquez de.*

Vélez de Escalante, Silvestre. See *Escalante, Silvestre Vélez de.*

Verrazano, Giovanni da

Italian
b 1485?; near Florence (now in Italy)
d 1528?; Guadeloupe?
Explored Atlantic coast of North America

Giovanni da Verrazano was an Italian navigator who sailed in the service of France. He explored the Atlantic coast of North America from the area that is now North Carolina to what is now Maine; he may even have sailed as far north as Newfoundland. Among his discoveries were Narragansett Bay, Block Island, New York Bay, and the mouth of the Hudson River. Verrazano's expedition also established France's claim to territory in North America.

A Future in France

Most historians believe that Verrazano was born on the estate of the wealthy, noble Verrazano family, about 30 miles from Florence (then an independent city-state and now part of Italy). He was well educated and showed particular talent in mathematics. Around the year 1506, Verrazano moved to France.

At that time, the French were interested in Italian culture, and King Francis I had surrounded himself with Italian thinkers and artists. Seeing the opportunity to make a name for himself,

Verrazano greatly advanced the mapping of North America's east coast, but he made a geographical error that was copied on maps for over 100 years.

Verrazano entered the service of France and made several voyages to the eastern Mediterranean region. He also became a successful pirate, capturing Spanish treasure ships for France.

In 1524, King Francis chose Verrazano to lead a small fleet across the Atlantic Ocean. Francis hoped to find both a northern sea passage to China and land for the French to colonize. Verrazano was instructed to explore the vast unknown area between Florida, which had been claimed by Spain, and Newfoundland, which had been claimed by England. His four ships left in late 1524 or early 1525 with the financial support of French and Italian bankers and merchants. Verrazano's brother, Girolomo, sailed with him aboard his flagship, *La Dauphine.* No record exists of the other men who sailed with the Verrazanos. In an official letter to the king, written after the voyage, Giovanni simply referred to his crew as "the maritime mob."

American Shores

Two of Verrazano's ships were wrecked shortly after leaving Europe; and a third sailed back to France with treasure captured from foreign vessels. Only *La Dauphine* reached North America, arriving near what is now Cape Fear, North Carolina, around March 1, 1525. From there Verrazano sailed south for another 50 miles, looking for a harbor. However, he soon turned back in order to avoid any Spanish vessels that might be found in waters to the south.

Heading north along the coast, the explorers sighted a harbor, probably what is now called Chesapeake Bay. The Verrazano brothers mistook the bay to be a strait leading to the Pacific Ocean and named it the Verrazano Sea. This geographical error appeared for over 100 years on maps that showed North America in the shape of an hourglass, with the Verrazano Sea at the narrowest part. Verrazano did not attempt to penetrate the bay, choosing instead to continue his exploration of the coast.

Verrazano then sailed along the shores of what are now Delaware and New Jersey. These waters are often rough and dangerous, but he enjoyed calm sailing in mild spring weather. He discovered what is now New York Bay on April 17, 1525, and anchored in a narrow channel leading to the upper section of the bay. This waterway is now called the Verrazano Narrows. The Italian navigator described the upper bay as a "pleasant lake" and named it Santa Margarita in honor of the king's sister. In honor of King Francis, he gave the name Francesca to all the land that he explored on his voyage.

Continuing north, Verrazano then discovered what is now called Block Island (off the coast of the present-day state of Rhode Island) and sailed into Narragansett Bay to avoid bad weather. He permitted a local Indian to guide him to a sheltered area (now Newport Harbor) where the ship could anchor safely. Verrazano stayed in the harbor for about two weeks and sent search parties up to 30 miles inland. They noted the fertile soil and the forests of oak and walnut trees. Verrazano also traded with the Wampanoug Indians. He considered them "goodliest people, and of the fairest conditions that we have found in this our voyage." He wrote that the Wampanoug women were "very handsome" and "as well mannered . . . as any woman of good education."

Modern Times

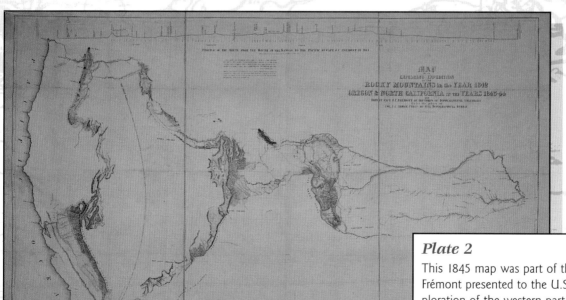

Plate 3

In the 1800s, polar exploration commanded considerable resources and attention. But progress was often slow as men hauled sledges across the ice. This painting by A. H. Markham shows the team he led in George Nares's expedition to Greenland and Ellesmere Island in 1875 to 1876.

Plate 4

European explorers learned to adopt the techniques of the people native to the Arctic. Here, an Aleut travels and hunts by kayak in the Bering Sea.

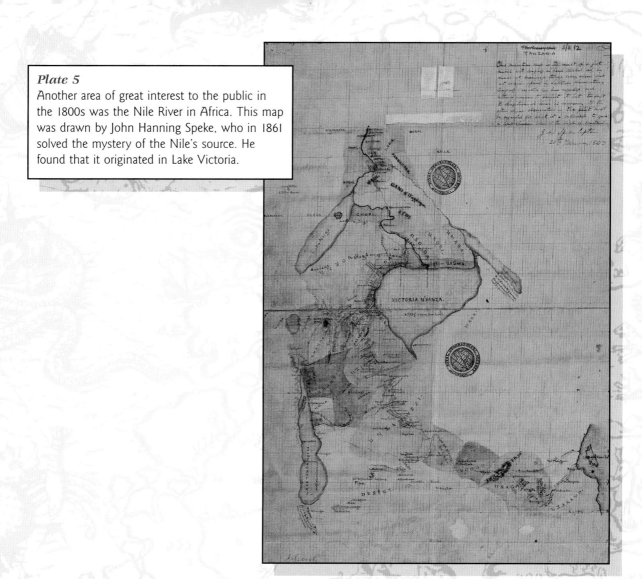

Plate 5
Another area of great interest to the public in the 1800s was the Nile River in Africa. This map was drawn by John Hanning Speke, who in 1861 solved the mystery of the Nile's source. He found that it originated in Lake Victoria.

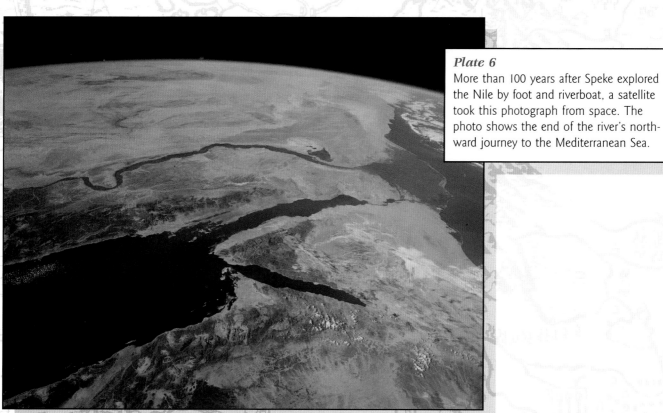

Plate 6
More than 100 years after Speke explored the Nile by foot and riverboat, a satellite took this photograph from space. The photo shows the end of the river's northward journey to the Mediterranean Sea.

Plate 7
The steamboat gave river explorers greater speed and range than sailboats and canoes. *Walk-in-the-Water,* the first steamboat on the Great Lakes, was in service from 1818 to 1821.

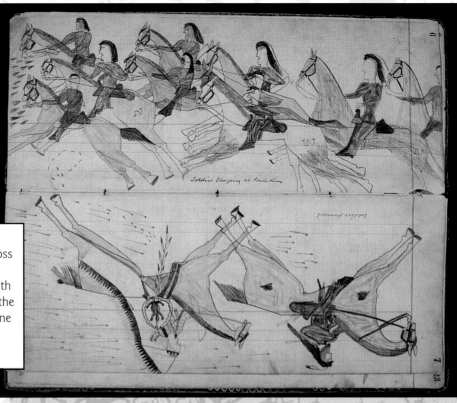

Plate 8
As explorers pushed west across North America, they were involved in numerous battles with Indian tribes. This page from the "ledger books" of the Cheyenne is called "Soldiers Charging at Powder River."

Plate 9
Despite technological advances, explorers continued to struggle with nature for their survival. In this illustration from the 1820s, a European in Libya rides a camel into a violent sandstorm.

Plate 10
The British explorer Samuel White Baker captured the fury of an African elephant in this picture, titled "The Last Charge."

Plate 11
By the mid-1900s, explorers were using highly specialized vehicles to travel in the harshest environments. Vivian Fuchs rode snow tractors across Antarctica.

Plate 12
Small metal capsules carried early astronauts and cosmonauts through space. On the Gemini 8 mission, Neil Armstrong (right) and David Scott splashed down in the ocean and were picked up by the U.S. Navy.

Plate 13
Space missions require vast support networks of people and equipment on the ground, including today's Mission Control Center in Houston, Texas.

Plate 14
On the moon's surface in 1969, Neil Armstrong took this photograph of his fellow astronaut Edwin Aldrin, Jr.

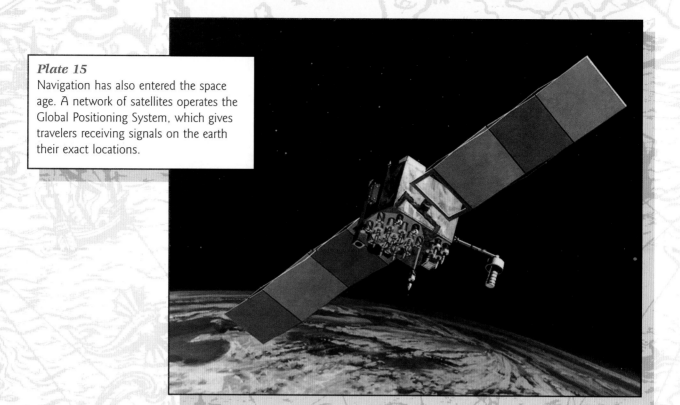

Plate 15
Navigation has also entered the space age. A network of satellites operates the Global Positioning System, which gives travelers receiving signals on the earth their exact locations.

Plate 16
The space shuttle continues to link the earth and space. Its missions include the construction of a space station that could serve as a base for future exploration of the planets.

Verrazano headed north again on May 5 or 6, navigated through waters that are now called Vineyard Sound and Nantucket Sound, rounded Cape Cod, and eventually landed at Casco Bay (in present-day Maine). There he encountered the Abnaki Indians, whom he described as "crude" and as having "evil manners." He named the area the Land of Bad People, but he was deeply impressed with its natural beauty. He may have gone as far north as Newfoundland before returning to France on July 8, 1525.

Plans Unfulfilled

Verrazano tried to organize a second expedition to the Americas, but France was at war, and his backers were pessimistic about the new land's potential for profit. He did sail to the coast of Brazil in 1527 to obtain brazilwood, but he did not undertake another voyage of exploration until the following year.

The Verrazano brothers then returned to North America to continue the search for a water route to Asia, this time south of the regions they had explored in 1525. However, Girolomo returned to France without Giovanni, bearing the only information now available about this voyage. According to Girolomo, the expedition reached the coast of Florida and then headed southeast along the Caribbean **archipelago** called the Lesser Antilles. The ships anchored off one of the islands (probably Guadeloupe), and Giovanni went ashore in a small boat, not realizing that the inhabitants were cannibals. Girolomo watched in horror as his brother was killed and eaten by the islanders.

Giovanni da Verrazano failed to find a passage to Asia, but his explorations of the North American coastline were invaluable for the future settlement of the continent by Europeans. In 1529 Girolomo drew a world map showing Verrazano's routes and discoveries, and later visitors to those lands were as much impressed as the brothers had been. In his letter to the king, Giovanni summed up his feelings about the North American seaboard, saying: "We greatly regretted having to leave this region, which seemed so delightful and which we supposed must also contain great riches."

SUGGESTED READING Henry Cruse Murphy, *The Voyage of Verrazano: A Chapter in the Early History of Maritime Discovery of America* (reprint, Books for Libraries, 1970); Lawrence Counselman Wroth, *The Voyages of Giovanni da Verrazano, 1524-1528* (Yale University Press, 1970).

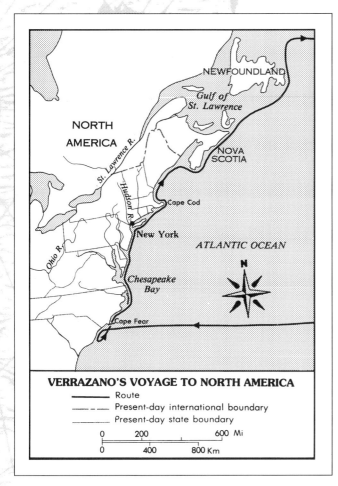

VERRAZANO'S VOYAGE TO NORTH AMERICA

After exploring North America's Atlantic coast in 1525, Giovanni da Verrazano wrote that he regretted leaving the "delightful" land and "turquoise sea."

archipelago large group of islands or a body of water with many islands

Vespucci, Amerigo

Italian
b March 9, 1451?; Florence (now in Italy)
d February 22, 1512; Seville, Spain
Explored coast of South America

In 1502, after making two voyages to what is now called South America, the Italian explorer Amerigo Vespucci came to a startling conclusion—that the lands discovered by Christopher COLUMBUS were not part of Asia but a separate landmass. Vespucci called this continent *Mundus Novus*, which in Latin means New World, and argued for his theory in a published account of his explorations. His idea was so well received by Europeans of his day that the German

cartographer mapmaker

cosmography the scientific study of the structure of the universe

Italian explorer Amerigo Vespucci's name was given to both North America and South America.

cartographer Martin Waldseemüller named the new continent America in his honor.

Controversy has long surrounded Waldseemüller's decision. Vespucci's reputation suffered centuries of attack from people who believed that the newfound land should have been named after Columbus. In the late 1800s and the 1900s, however, scholars have presented a more balanced—positive—view of Vespucci. According to them, he was a man of ideas whose interests lay in art and science; he did not seek conquest, fame, or fortune. They also point out that Vespucci was a friend of Columbus and a trusted adviser to the powerful Medici family of Florence, the monarchs of Spain and Portugal, and the other great navigators of his day.

Friends in High Places

Vespucci was born in Florence on March 9, 1451, into a family of wealthy bankers and merchants. As a youth, he developed an intellectual curiosity that directed the course of his life. He collected maps and books and became especially interested in **cosmography** and astronomy. Vespucci's own business career began in 1479, when he became one of the Medici family's representatives to the king of France. He returned to Florence in 1480 and continued to serve the family as a banker. In about 1492, they sent him to Seville, Spain, to help direct a shipping company that provided supplies for Spanish voyages of exploration. There is evidence that Vespucci met Columbus in Seville in 1496, after Columbus's second voyage.

Vespucci soon became an explorer himself, but historians are not certain when he sailed on his first voyage or how many voyages he actually made. Very little firsthand evidence exists. A letter dated 1504, from Vespucci to a Florentine official, states that Vespucci made a total of four voyages and that on his first voyage, in 1497, he reached land in what is now Central America. If Vespucci did indeed make that journey, it occurred one year before Columbus discovered Venezuela and would make Vespucci the first European to have reached the American mainland. However, many scholars now believe this letter to have been faked by supporters of Vespucci. The only other evidence is three letters written by Vespucci to the Medici family. These documents, which are regarded as authentic, describe only two voyages—Vespucci's journey with Alonso de OJEDA, from 1499 to 1500, and his own expedition from 1501 to 1502.

Crossing the Equator

Vespucci joined Ojeda as a financial representative, but Ojeda also made him pilot of one of the ships. They departed from Spain on May 16, 1499, and separated sometime after the fleet passed the Cape Verde Islands. Ojeda headed up the northwest coast of what is now South America. Meanwhile, Vespucci sailed southwest as far as Cape Santo Agostinho on the eastern coast of what is now Brazil before turning back to the northwest. During the journey, Vespucci sighted the mouths of several rivers, probably including the Amazon, the Pará, and the Orinoco. Vespucci and his crew may have been the first Europeans to reach Brazil and also to cross the equator in American waters.

Eventually, however, supplies ran low, the ships' hulls began to rot, and the winds turned unfavorable. Vespucci was forced to sail to Hispaniola (the island now occupied by Haiti and the Dominican Republic) to rejoin Ojeda before returning to Spain.

Disproving Columbus's Claim

At the end of 1500, Vespucci entered the service of King Manuel I of Portugal. On May 13, 1501, Vespucci left Lisbon and traveled to the Cape Verde Islands, where he met fellow explorer Pedro Álvares CABRAL. When Cabral described his recent discovery of Brazil, Vespucci realized that it was the same land that he himself had explored during Ojeda's expedition. Columbus too had visited that area, but he had claimed that it was part of Asia. Though he had at first accepted Columbus's theory, Vespucci was now uncertain, and he decided to return to those shores.

Vespucci reached Brazil at the **latitude** of 5° south, naming the site Cape São Roque. He then followed the coast of South America for about 2,400 miles in a southwesterly direction. Passing Cape Frio, he discovered Guanabara Bay (the site of present-day Rio de Janeiro) and the Río de la Plata (located between present-day Uruguay and Argentina). Some historians think that Vespucci went no farther than Cape Frio, but others accept his account that he reached the latitude of 49° south in Patagonia.

The Name Game

Vespucci returned to Lisbon on July 22, 1502, convinced that the lands that he and Columbus had explored were not part of Asia. Instead, Vespucci insisted, they were part of a separate and previously unknown landmass, which he called *Mundus Novus.* Vespucci also identified stars that were visible only in the Southern Hemisphere and showed that the accepted cosmography of PTOLEMY was at least partially wrong or else incomplete. The written account of Vespucci's findings was so popular that it went through more than 20 editions in several languages before 1508. The German mapmaker Martin Waldseemüller called the newfound continent "the land of Amerigo, or America, after Amerigo, its discoverer, a man of great ability." Waldseemüller included the name in his geography book and map of 1507. Despite much disagreement, the designation *America* prevailed. In 1538 Gerhardus Mercator became the first geographer to name both North America and South America on a world map.

Vespucci did not play a role in this naming, and in any case, Columbus himself never felt that Vespucci had stolen any of his fame. In a letter to his son Diego, Columbus said of Vespucci: "It has always been his wish to please me; he is a man of good will; . . . his labors have not brought him the rewards he in justice should have."

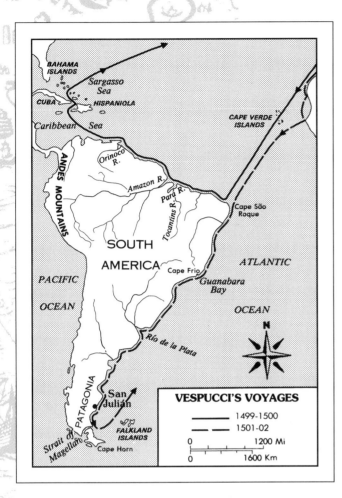

Vespucci realized that the lands that Christopher Columbus had discovered were not part of Asia.

latitude distance north or south of the equator

In 1505 Vespucci married and settled permanently in Seville. King Ferdinand II appointed him Spain's first pilot major. In this post, Vespucci trained and tested other navigators and prepared and updated the official map of the newly discovered lands. Vespucci died in Seville in his early 60s.

SUGGESTED READING Germán Arciniegas, *Amerigo and the New World: The Life and Times of Amerigo Vespucci*, translated by Harriet de Oris (reprint, Octagon Books, 1978); Frances Salter Nilsen, *Amerigo!: The Amerigo Vespucci Story* (Shamrock Press Publishing Company, 1992); Amerigo Vespucci, *Letters From a New World: Amerigo Vespucci's Discovery of America*, translated by David Jacobson (Marsilio Publications, 1992).

Vial, Pedro

French
b between 1746 and 1755; Lyons, France
d 1814; Santa Fe, New Mexico
Established Santa Fe Trail

For 200 years, the only way to reach Santa Fe (in modern-day New Mexico), was through Chihuahua (in northern Mexico). In 1786 Pedro Vial blazed new routes that linked Santa Fe with the cities of San Antonio, New Orleans, and St. Louis. These paths through the wilderness made possible a great increase in travel and settlement in what was to be the southwestern United States. The route between Santa Fe and St. Louis became famous as the Santa Fe Trail.

Nomad of the Wilderness

Born in France, Pedro Vial (also known as Pierre Vial) made his way to North America and lived among the Indians of Natchitoches (in what is now Louisiana) for several years. Little else is known about his early life. By 1786 he had entered the service of Spain.

Spanish officials hired him to open an overland trail from San Antonio (in present-day Texas) to Santa Fe. He left on October 26, 1786, with one companion. They headed in a straight line for Santa Fe, crossed nearly 1,200 miles of uncharted wilderness, encountered at least five tribes of Indians, and reached Santa Fe on May 26, 1787. About a year later, Vial blazed trails eastward from Santa Fe to New Orleans (in present-day Louisiana) and westward from New Orleans to San Antonio.

Captives on the Santa Fe Trail

Pedro Vial set out on his most famous journey—from Santa Fe to St. Louis—on May 21, 1792. He survived a month of difficult travel through lands that are now Oklahoma and Kansas before he and his two companions were captured by Kansas Indians. The pioneers were beaten and threatened for six weeks, until an Indian who spoke French recognized Vial and arranged for the prisoners' release. They started their journey again on September 11, traveling with a French trader along the Kansas and Missouri Rivers in a **pirogue.** In October 1792, they arrived at St. Louis, having established the Santa Fe Trail.

Five years later, Vial left the service of Spain and went to live with Comanche Indians near St. Louis. By 1805, however, he was working for Spain again. He died nine years later in Santa Fe.

SUGGESTED READING Noel M. Loomis and Abraham P. Nasatir, *Pedro Vial and the Roads to Santa Fe* (University of Oklahoma Press, 1967).

pirogue canoe usually made from a hollow tree trunk

Vizcaíno, Sebastián

Spanish
b 1550?; Corcho, Spain
d 1628?; ?
Explored coast of California

New Spain region of Spanish colonial empire that included the areas now occupied by Mexico, Florida, Texas, New Mexico, Arizona, California, and various Caribbean islands

militia armed force made up of citizens who are not professional soldiers but who may be called upon to serve the military

galleon large sailing ship used for war and trade

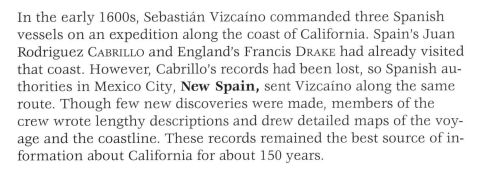

In the early 1600s, Sebastián Vizcaíno commanded three Spanish vessels on an expedition along the coast of California. Spain's Juan Rodriguez CABRILLO and England's Francis DRAKE had already visited that coast. However, Cabrillo's records had been lost, so Spanish authorities in Mexico City, **New Spain,** sent Vizcaíno along the same route. Though few new discoveries were made, members of the crew wrote lengthy descriptions and drew detailed maps of the voyage and the coastline. These records remained the best source of information about California for about 150 years.

A Failed Fortune in Pearls

Scholars think that Vizcaíno was born in Corcho, Spain, into a family of commoners. He claimed to have served with the royal army in Portugal in 1567, but he may only have belonged to a **militia.** Like many other Spanish men of his time, Vizcaíno hoped to make his fortune in the Americas. He arrived in what is now Mexico around 1585 and became a merchant.

Spain had been developing profitable trade across the Pacific Ocean, with **galleons** carrying cargo between Manila (in the Philippine Islands) and Acapulco (on the west coast of Mexico). Vizcaíno may have made at least one voyage to Manila and back. He then turned to pearl fishing in the Gulf of California, the long bay that separates Baja California from the mainland of Mexico. He joined a company that received official permission to look for pearls in return for a promise to give one-fifth of them to the Spanish king. In the 1590s, Vizcaíno made two unsuccessful attempts to find pearls in the gulf. The authorities denied his request for a third chance and sent him instead on a mission of exploration.

The California Expedition

The Spanish authorities gave Vizcaíno clear instructions. The expedition's purpose was to study the California coast in detail. Special attention would be paid to making accurate maps and locating ports that the galleons could use as shelters from pirates and storms. Although Vizcaíno was in charge, two councils made up of navigators and military officers sailed with him, and he was obliged to consult with them and to follow their rulings.

On May 5, 1602, the expedition sailed from Acapulco with three ships. From the start, the ships encountered poor sailing conditions. Antonio de la Ascension, a missionary on board who wrote an account of the voyage, described constant winds that made sailing "an insufferable labor." From the sea, the coast of California presents a stern and unwelcoming face. Its rocky, wave-pounded shores and its miles of dry mountains and cliffs are broken by very few suitable places to land. Pushing northward along the coast, the Spanish investigated these few harbors, many of which had been seen and named by earlier explorers. Contrary to his instructions, Vizcaíno gave some of the sites new names. He may have hoped that he would be credited with discovering new places, or he may not have been aware of the earlier discoveries.

Ascension's record of each landing is filled with details about the availability of food, water, and firewood, and also about whether the

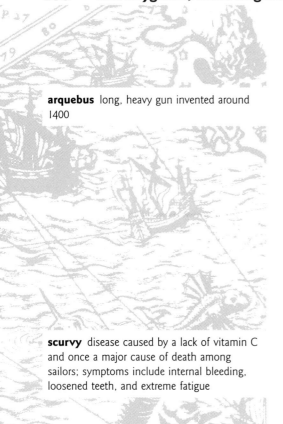

arquebus long, heavy gun invented around 1400

scurvy disease caused by a lack of vitamin C and once a major cause of death among sailors; symptoms include internal bleeding, loosened teeth, and extreme fatigue

local Indians were "ferocious and savage" or "of good disposition, meek and grateful." In one passage, he described a fight that broke out after some Indians tried to steal a small boat and other items. When the Indians put arrows to their bows, the Spanish began firing their **arquebuses,** "as it was not fitting to allow the Indians to shoot them." They killed several tribesmen. The remaining Indians became friendly—although, as Ascension wrote, "they never took their eyes off the arquebuses."

In November, the expedition stopped in San Diego Bay, an excellent port that was already known to the Spanish. There the men gathered wood and water, repaired their vessels, and rested. When the ships left the bay, winds continued to hinder their progress, but soon the explorers discovered the island of Santa Catalina to the northwest. The inhabitants of the island were skilled fishers and sailors, and Ascension wrote optimistically of the chances of converting them to Christianity. Farther up the coast, the expedition made its most important discovery, Monterey Bay, on December 15. Ascension called it "a very good port and well protected from all winds."

By then many crewmen were suffering from **scurvy.** Vizcaíno sent one of his ships, carrying the sick men and a request for more men and supplies, back to Mexico. Continuing northward, the remaining two ships became separated. Despite storms at sea and disease among the crew members, each vessel reached Cape Mendocino and then turned back toward Mexico. Vizcaíno arrived at the port of Mazatlán on February 18, 1603.

Maps and Legends

According to some historians, one other goal of Vizcaíno's expedition had been to find the western end of the Strait of Anian. This waterway was thought to flow through North America, connecting the Atlantic Ocean with the Pacific Ocean. The reports of Vizcaíno's voyage suggested that the Strait of Anian did not exist, but it remained on many maps, and explorers continued to search for it for nearly 200 years. Adding to this confusion, Ascension created a new geographic myth by proposing that California was a very long island rather than the coast of a continent. This mistake also appeared on maps for many years.

Vizcaíno recommended that Spain build a settlement at Monterey Bay, but the Spanish authorities chose San Diego Bay instead and turned down his request to be put in charge. Vizcaíno made one more long voyage, across the Pacific Ocean to Japan and back. He probably ended his days as a landowner in New Spain.

SUGGESTED READING W. Michael Mathes, *Vizcaíno and Spanish Expansion in the Pacific Ocean, 1580–1630* (California Historical Society, 1968); Henry R. Wagner, *Spanish Voyages to the Northwest Coast of America in the Sixteenth Century* (California Historical Society, 1929).

von Drygalski, Erich Dagobert. See *Drygalski, Erich Dagobert von.*

von Kotzebue, Otto. See *Kotzebue, Otto von.*

von Krusenstern, Adam Ivan. See *Krusenstern, Adam Ivan von.*

von Payer, Julius. See *Payer, Julius von.*

von Richthofen, Ferdinand Paul Wilhelm. See *Richthofen, Ferdinand Paul Wilhelm von.*

Walker, Joseph Reddeford

American
b December 13, 1798; Virginia?
d October 27, 1876; Contra Costa County, California
Blazed overland route to California

Joseph Reddeford Walker was once described in his own time as a man whose "chief delight" was to explore "unknown regions." He made a yearlong trek from the Green River (in what is now western Wyoming) across the rugged mountains of the Sierra Nevada to the Pacific Ocean. On the return trip, Walker discovered a pass through the Sierra Nevada. This mountain pass, which now bears his name, became the main route by which settlers reached California.

Trappers, Explorers, or Spies?
Raised in Tennessee, Walker moved to Independence, Missouri, when he was 21 years old. He later joined the expedition that surveyed and mapped what was to become the Santa Fe Trail, which connected Missouri to what is now New Mexico. In 1831 Walker met Captain Benjamin BONNEVILLE, who was leading a group of men on a westward journey to trap furs. Walker signed on with Bonneville as field commander of a party of 110 men. They traveled to the Snake and Salmon Rivers in search of beaver, but their efforts were largely unsuccessful.

The party then headed to the Green River in 1833 for the rendezvous, an annual meeting of mountain men and their suppliers. While there, Bonneville instructed Walker to recruit men for an expedition to the West. The true purpose of that journey has never become clear. Bonneville may have wanted the men to search for new beaver hunting grounds, or he may have been seeking a route to the Pacific Ocean. However, some historians believe that he was spying on Mexican territory for the United States government.

In August 1833, Walker set out from the Green River with about 50 men and a large number of horses. The party traveled across barren plains for a month before reaching what is now called the Humboldt River (in present-day Nevada). The men followed the river to a series of marshy lakes called the Humboldt Sinks and then proceeded southwest to the Sierra Nevada. Walker and his men trudged across the mountains for three tiring weeks, suffering from severe cold and hunger. After they reached the top ridge of the mountains, they were rewarded with a breathtaking sight—what is now called Yosemite Valley.

Meteors and Earthquakes
The explorers descended the Sierra Nevada and soon found themselves in California. New sights and experiences dazzled them.

Joseph Walker was amazed by California's meteor showers, earthquakes, and enormous redwood trees.

They saw giant redwoods and a meteor shower, and they heard the rumbling of what was probably an earthquake. Walker mistook the noise of the earthquake for the roar of the ocean, which was still 70 miles away. When the men finally reached the Pacific, they found whales stranded on the shore. From there the party traveled south to Monterey, the capital of Mexico's California territory. The Americans were well received by Mexican officials, who fed and entertained them for a month. When the explorers returned to Wyoming in January 1834, they were full of praise for California.

Walker was determined to find an easier route through the Sierra Nevada. He led his men back to the mountain range and followed it south until they came to a pass. At that point, they crossed at a height of 5,200 feet, which was relatively low in a range whose mountains often topped 10,000 feet. But difficult times still lay ahead. Out of water in the dry, elevated lands of Nevada, the men became so thirsty that they drank the blood of horses that died on the trail. Despite such hardship, Walker attended the 1834 rendezvous with all the members of his original party, proving his skill as a leader and organizer.

The Walker Pass

Soon after Walker blazed the trail between the Rocky Mountains and California, it became the most important route to the west coast. Other explorers had failed to find a practical way to reach the Pacific Ocean. Jedediah SMITH had twice followed a route that proved to be of little use to others, and 26 men had died on his two expeditions. But Walker did not lose a single man, and his trail became the main route for settlers heading west. He personally led some of these settlers into the land he regarded as a kind of paradise, and he himself finally moved to California at the age of 69.

SUGGESTED READING Bil Gilbert, *Westering Man: The Life of Joseph Walker, Master of the Frontier* (Atheneum, 1983).

Wallace, Alfred Russel

English
b January 8, 1823; Usk, Wales
d November 7, 1913; Broadstone, England
*Explored Amazon River basin
and Malay Archipelago*

botany the scientific study of plants

zoology the scientific study of animals

specimen sample of a plant, animal, or mineral, usually collected for scientific study or display

species type of plant or animal

surveyor one who makes precise measurements of a location's geography

Alfred Russel Wallace's scientific work ranks him with Charles DARWIN as one of the outstanding naturalists of the 1800s. He made important contributions to the fields of scientific exploration, natural history, **botany,** and **zoology.** Wallace was a self-educated man who pursued his interest in natural history through explorations of the Amazon River system in Brazil and the Malay Archipelago in Southeast Asia. He collected **specimens** of insects, butterflies, and birds. He also began to work on a theory of evolution, the idea that animal and plant **species** change over time to fit their environment.

An Education Without a School

Alfred Russel Wallace was one of nine children in a poor family. He was forced to drop out of school at the age of 14 and to earn money by working for his brother William, a **surveyor,** for six years. It was during that time that he became interested in the natural world.

In the rain forests of Brazil and Southeast Asia, the naturalist Alfred Russel Wallace gathered evidence for his theory of evolution.

socialism system of government in which the state owns or controls the manufacture and distribution of goods and services

malaria disease that is spread by mosquitoes in tropical areas

While visiting London, Wallace spent time at the Hall of Science, a club where teachers met and exchanged ideas. There he learned about **socialism,** which became one of his many lifelong interests. He read eagerly and widely, especially travel books, biographies, and works by writers of ancient Greece and Rome. Wallace was influenced by Darwin's and Alexander von HUMBOLDT's accounts of their scientific explorations.

When the demand for surveyors lessened in 1844, Wallace turned to teaching to make a living, and he qualified to serve as a schoolmaster in Leicester, England. There he met and befriended Henry Walter BATES. The two men went on beetle-collecting expeditions together in a nearby forest and frequently discussed all aspects of natural science. Wallace's brother died in 1845, and Wallace returned to surveying, but he stayed in touch with Bates. In 1847 Wallace was greatly intrigued by a book, written by W. H. Edwards, about a voyage on the Amazon River. Edwards's account inspired Wallace to ask Bates to join him on an expedition to the Amazon River basin. They planned to support themselves by collecting specimens to sell to museums.

The Amazon Rain Forest

On May 28, 1848, Wallace and Bates arrived at Pará (present-day Belém), Brazil, near the mouth of the Amazon River. Together they explored the region around Pará and journeyed along the Tocantins River and the Río Negro. While exploring the Tocantins, Wallace lost part of his hand near the wrist because of an accidental gunshot. Despite the injury, Wallace was able to explore Mexiana Island (near Marajó on the equator), where he found many exotic birds, such as toucans and herons.

In late 1848, the two friends decided to separate for a while in order to explore different areas. Wallace journeyed up the narrow channels that connect the Pará River with the Amazon. He then continued up the Amazon, stopping at Santarém and Óbidos along the way. He and Bates reunited on January 22, 1850, at Barra do Rio Negro (present-day Manaus). They explored the area together and then separated again; it was the last time they would see each other on this expedition.

Wallace continued north along the Río Negro, passed the mouth of the Casiquiare River, and then hiked to the town of Yavita, Venezuela. There he discovered 40 species of butterflies previously unknown to European scientists. He also traveled as far west as Micúru on the Uaupés River. During his explorations, Wallace carefully observed and noted the areas where different plants and animals flourished. He was the first scientist to identify such regions in South America.

Overcoming Disaster

Wallace became ill and decided to return to Britain in 1852, but the journey home was a disaster. First he suffered an attack of **malaria.** Then, in the Caribbean Sea, fire engulfed the ship he had boarded, and he was forced to drift for 10 days in a small boat before being rescued. He eventually made it back to Britain, but he had lost all of his specimens and notes from his four years in South America. Though unable to publish his detailed scientific findings, he did manage to write and publish two books about the expedition.

Wallace refused to be discouraged by his bad luck and left for the Malay **Archipelago** of Southeast Asia in 1854. For the next eight years, he explored the islands that now make up Indonesia and Malaysia. He traveled more than 14,000 miles altogether and collected about 127,000 specimens. Wallace returned to England in 1862 and published a book, *The Malay Archipelago,* in 1869, winning international fame.

Sharing the Spotlight

During his Malay expedition, Wallace developed a theory of evolution that described the way in which species change over time. Through a process called natural selection, he argued, the members of a species that are better suited to their environment are the ones that survive. He sent his essay on the subject to Darwin, who realized that Wallace's ideas were almost exactly the same as his own. About 15 years earlier, Darwin had written an essay about evolution, but he had never published it. Darwin and Wallace decided to publish their articles at the same time in 1858, and both men were recognized for their work.

In his later years, Wallace became actively involved in political causes such as socialism and women's rights. He stayed in public view—even, at the age of 84, coming forward to challenge an astronomer's theory that intelligent life existed on Mars. He also experienced a renewal of faith in God. Wallace died in 1913, widely praised as one of the greatest scientists of his time.

SUGGESTED READING Penny Van Oosterzee, *Where Worlds Collide: The Wallace Line* (Reed, 1997); Alfred Russel Wallace, *The Malay Archipelago: The Land of the Orang-utan and the Bird of Paradise* (reprint, Oxford University Press, 1989) and *A Narrative of Travels on the Amazon and Río Negro,* revised edition (Ward and Locke, 1911).

---

archipelago large group of islands or a body of water with many islands

Wallis, Samuel

English
b 1728; Fentonwood, England
d January 21, 1795; London, England
Sailed around the world; explored Tahiti

frigate small, agile warship with three masts and square sails

scurvy disease caused by a lack of vitamin C and once a major cause of death among sailors; symptoms include internal bleeding, loosened teeth, and extreme fatigue

---

Samuel Wallis was a British naval commander who led the *Dolphin* on its second voyage to the southern Pacific Ocean, from 1766 to 1768. He made many discoveries but is perhaps best known for his monthlong exploration of Otaheite. Now known as Tahiti, it is the largest of the Society Islands.

Chaos in the Strait

Born in southwestern England in 1728, Wallis joined Britain's Royal Navy at the age of 20. In 1766 Wallis, who was by then a captain, was given command of the *Dolphin,* a fast **frigate** with a copper hull. With orders to search for the undiscovered southern continent known as *Terra Australis Incognita,* the *Dolphin* left Plymouth, England, in August. It was accompanied by a second ship, the *Swallow,* commanded by Philip CARTERET. By December they had reached the Strait of Magellan at the southern tip of South America. The expedition spent four months navigating the dangerous waterway in very bad weather. When they finally reached the Pacific Ocean, a

Samuel Wallis and his crew enjoyed their visit to the tropical island of Tahiti, but it was only one stop on their two-year voyage around the world.

mate assistant to the commander of a ship

For a map of Wallis's route, see the profile of Louis-Antoine de BOUGAINVILLE in Volume 1.

archipelago large group of islands or a body of water with many islands

gust of wind carried the *Dolphin* far ahead of the *Swallow,* and the two ships were never reunited.

By that time, many of the sailors had **scurvy,** so Wallis was anxious to find land. In early June 1767, he reached two islands in the southern Pacific Ocean and claimed them for Britain. But neither island offered a safe harbor, so Wallis sailed on. One foggy evening a few weeks later, he arrived at another island and entered a bay where he was able to anchor his ships. In the morning, the mist lifted, and Wallis and his crew saw the inhabitants of the island surrounding the *Dolphin* in hundreds of wooden canoes.

At first the islanders were friendly and curious, and many of them boarded the *Dolphin.* However, when a goat that was on deck butted one of them, they all jumped overboard. When some started to throw stones at the *Dolphin,* the British opened fire with guns. Eventually, though, the two groups made peace. Since Wallis was ill at the time, he sent his second lieutenant, Tobias Furneaux, ashore. The lieutenant claimed the island for Britain and named it King George the Third's Island. The local people called it Otaheite, and it is now known as Tahiti.

Trading Nails

The British and the islanders traded with each other—iron cooking pots for pigs, fruit, and vegetables. When the islanders requested nails, the sailors pried some from the wood on the ship. To keep his crewmen from taking the *Dolphin* apart, Wallis finally had to forbid them to leave the ship. Furneaux and the first **mate** explored the island, which they reported to be "pleasant." About a month after their arrival, Wallis and his men departed, leaving many of the Tahitian women crying on the shore. Unfortunately, the close relations between the women and the sailors may have spread disease among the islanders.

Wallis then sailed west, discovered several other islands, and proceeded to Batavia (present-day Jakarta, Indonesia), where he planned to have his ship repaired. Along the way, the *Dolphin* passed through a small **archipelago,** which the crew named the Wallis Islands. The expedition finally reached England in May 1768. Wallis was later appointed commissioner of the navy and served in that post from 1782 until his death in London, 13 years later.

SUGGESTED READING Hugh Carrington, editor, *The Discovery of Tahiti: A Journal of the Second Voyage of H.M.S. "Dolphin" Round the World by George Robertson, 1766–1768* (Hakluyt Society, 1948).

Wegener, Alfred Lothar

German
b November 1, 1880; Berlin, Germany
d November 1930; Greenland
Explored Greenland;
proposed theory of continental drift

Alfred Lothar Wegener was a German scientist who entered the field of exploration through his work in **meteorology.** His studies of the effects of heat and other forms of energy on the atmosphere of the earth took him to Greenland on four separate expeditions between 1906 and 1930. Despite the strain and danger that Wegener endured in the polar region, his research resulted in his theory of continental drift, which was a breakthrough in the science of **geology.**

Alfred Wegener's expeditions in Greenland led to his theory that the continents had once been a single landmass.

---

meteorology the scientific study of weather and weather forecasting

geology the scientific study of the earth's natural history

latitude distance north or south of the equator

sledge heavy sled, often mounted on runners, that is pulled over snow or ice

Treks in the Polar Region

In 1906 Wegener joined a Danish expedition to study the northeast coast of Greenland. On March 13, 1908, the party discovered an ice-free area about 24 miles from the coast. Wegener named it Dronning Louise Land. During the two winters the men spent in the Arctic region, they made several more geographical discoveries as well as many corrections to the charts made earlier by the American explorer Robert PEARY.

In 1912 Wegener again traveled to Greenland on a Danish expedition that crossed the island at its widest point. After wintering near Dronning Louise Land, the party made a 700-mile trip to the west coast at a **latitude** of about 77° north. They used ponies rather than dogs to pull the **sledges** and reached an altitude of 9,800 feet on their journey.

The Original Landmass

After Wegener returned to Germany, he published *The Origin of Continents and Oceans* in 1915. In this work, he described his theory of continental drift, which argued that the seven continents were originally one large landmass. He claimed that magnetic and tidal forces had caused the continents to separate gradually and drift apart. Although Wegener's ideas at first were criticized, they had a major impact on the field of geology after his death.

On his final expedition in 1930, he departed from the west coast of Greenland near Disko Bay. As he journeyed inland, he measured the depth of the ice with echo-sounding equipment and traveled using sledges that were powered by airplane engines and propellers. Later that year, he established a research station on the ice cap of central Greenland. In November 1930, the 50-year-old Wegener died of exhaustion on his way from the station to the west coast.

SUGGESTED READING American Association of Petroleum Geologists, *Theory of Continental Drift: A Symposium on the Origin and Movement of Land Masses, Both Inter-Continental and Intra-Continental, As Proposed By Alfred Wegener* (University Microfilms, 1979).

Wentworth, William Charles

Australian
b October 26, 1790?; Norfolk Island?, Australia
d March 20, 1872; Winborne, England
Explored Australia's Blue Mountains

William Charles Wentworth is remembered primarily as a writer, publisher, and Australian patriot. In 1813 he set out on a journey to find fertile grazing lands and made the first crossing of Australia's Blue Mountains. Wentworth published two books describing his experiences, which persuaded the growing British colony that the lands west of the mountains were worthy of exploration.

Searching for Greener Pastures

The exact date and place of Wentworth's birth are unknown. He was probably born on Norfolk Island, a prison colony off the coast of New South Wales, where his father worked as a surgeon and his

William Charles Wentworth was able to cross the previously impassable Blue Mountains by traveling along the ridges rather than through the valleys.

mother was a prisoner. His father sent him to Greenwich, England, to be educated. William returned to Australia in 1810 and became a landowner.

By the time he was 23 years old, Wentworth already owned one of Australia's largest estates. Facing financial ruin as the result of a drought, he joined his countryman Gregory BLAXLAND on an expedition to search for new grazing lands in 1813. The men became the first settlers to cross the Blue Mountains, part of the Great Dividing Range that separates Australia's east coast from the rest of the continent. They were able to accomplish this feat because they hiked along the ridges instead of in the valleys, where others had traveled in the past.

Influence and Activism

In 1816 Wentworth returned to England to study British law. Three years later, he published two volumes about his homeland, describing a green valley that he and Blaxland had sighted beyond the Blue Mountains. He stated that this land would be a good place to raise sheep for Australia's thriving wool industry. What Wentworth did not realize was that he and Blaxland had not crossed the main range of the Blue Mountains; they had only seen a wide valley in the mountains. They were also unaware that fertile plains are not common in the continent, which is dominated by barren desert.

Wentworth returned to Sydney, Australia, in 1824. He became active in the country's movement for self-government and was one of the authors of Australia's constitution. For many years, Wentworth traveled between England and Australia. He finally settled in England in 1862 and died there 10 years later. Despite the inaccuracy of Wentworth's description of Australia's geography, his account encouraged settlers to move beyond the east coast of the continent. He and Blaxland also demonstrated a useful technique for crossing the area's mountains.

SUGGESTED READING Jo Jensen, *Blaxland, Lawson and Wentworth* (Future Horizon Publishing, 1997); Arthur W. Jose, *Builders and Pioneers of Australia* (J. M. Dent and Sons, 1928).

Wheeler, George Montague

American
b October 9, 1842; Hopkinton, Massachusetts
d May 3, 1905; New York, New York
Surveyed American West

surveyor one who makes precise measurements of a location's geography

As a **surveyor** with the United States Army Corps of Engineers, George Montague Wheeler conducted geographical surveys of the American West between 1871 and 1879. He and his teams crossed 175,000 square miles of territory. They worked from the northern border of Mexico to Oregon and from the mountain range known as the Sierra Nevada to eastern Colorado.

Flexing Military Muscle

Wheeler graduated from the U.S. military academy at West Point, New York, in 1866. Several years later, when the army was trying to find a more direct route for moving troops south to Arizona, Wheeler proposed a general survey of the West. At that time, three western survey expeditions were already being led by civilians—

George Wheeler (center) posed for this photograph with the crew of one of the boats he used to explore the American West on behalf of the U.S. Army.

geology the scientific study of the earth's natural history

Whymper, Edward

English
b April 27, 1840; London, England
d September 16, 1911; Chamonix, France
Explored Andes, Alps, and Rocky Mountains

glacier large, slowly moving mass of ice
fossil trace left in rocks by a plant or animal that lived long ago

Ferdinand Hayden, Clarence KING, and John Wesley POWELL. Yet Wheeler argued persuasively that because these men were most interested in **geology,** their work would not be useful to the army. He believed that the army needed maps that focused on man-made features such as mines, farms, villages, roads, railroads, and dams.

Wheeler won the army's support, and he was sent into the field in 1871 to survey territory that included parts of eastern Nevada and Arizona. Wheeler and his party made a difficult survey of Death Valley, where they labored in overwhelming heat. Soon afterward, they set out on an exploration of the Colorado River. The men traveled upstream on flat-bottomed boats, which they often had to tow. Powell had already made a journey downriver, but Wheeler declared that Powell's work was not useful for the army's purposes. Unfortunately, Wheeler's journey up the Colorado did not produce much new information, and his men spent most of their time on the river struggling to stay alive.

Wheeler soon recommended a broader survey of the West, which he began in 1873. By this time, his efforts were overlapping those of the civilian surveyors. Their dislike of Wheeler and their desire to damage his reputation led in 1874 to a congressional hearing on his activities. Although Wheeler was allowed to continue his survey, Congress later agreed that he was duplicating the efforts of others and that his project should no longer be funded. Instead the United States Geographical Survey was created in 1879 to centralize all survey work under one agency.

Those who disliked George Wheeler described him as an unskilled surveyor who was only seeking power for the army in its rivalry with civilians. On the other hand, Wheeler's supporters argue that if he had been allowed to complete his work, the country would have had a useful map of the West much earlier.

SUGGESTED READING Doris Ostrander Dawdy, *George Montague Wheeler: The Man and the Myth* (Swallow Press, Ohio University Press, 1993).

Edward Whymper was a famous mountain climber and explorer who studied the effects of altitude on plant and animal life. He scaled daunting mountain ranges in South America, Europe, and Greenland. In his 60s, he explored the Great Divide of the Rocky Mountains.

An Unhappy Beginning

Whymper showed an early talent for art as well as a love of nature. In 1860 he was working for a London publisher, making sketches of mountain peaks in the Alps. He developed a fascination with the mountains, and from 1861 to 1865, he made several ascents in the Alps. He was the first person to reach the summit of the famous Matterhorn in Switzerland—on his seventh attempt. But his success ended in tragedy when four members of his party died on the way down the mountain.

In this illustration, Edward Whymper dodges falling rocks on the Matterhorn, a towering peak in the Swiss Alps.

Mountain Sickness

Whymper also made two expeditions to the **glaciers** on the mountains of Greenland, in 1867 and 1872, and collected rare plants and **fossils.** In 1879 he traveled to the Andes of Peru, hoping to learn why climbers in South America seemed to experience mountain sickness at lower altitudes than did climbers in Europe. Ascending the mountain Chimborazo, he found that it had not only glaciers but also two peaks rather than one. By the time they had set up their second camp, everyone in Whymper's party was suffering from the fever and headaches of mountain sickness. Slowly, however, they adjusted to the altitude and moved on, sometimes crawling on their hands and knees to keep from sinking too deeply into the snow. In January 1880, they became the first people to have reached both summits, the higher of which is 20,561 feet above sea level.

After climbing other peaks in Ecuador and collecting more data on mountain sickness, Whymper returned to England in late 1880. He concluded that mountain sickness is caused mainly by low air pressure, not simply by high altitude. Whymper found that people could become accustomed to these conditions by climbing in gradual stages. Twenty years later, while he was in his 60s, he explored the Great Divide of the Rocky Mountains—the boundary between rivers that flow eastward and those that flow westward. He died in France a few years later.

SUGGESTED READING Edward Whymper, *Scrambles Amongst the Alps*, second edition (John Murray, 1892) and *Travels Amongst the Great Andes of the Equator* (John Murray, 1892).

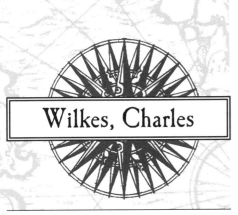

Wilkes, Charles

American
b April 3, 1798; New York, New York
d February 7, 1877; Washington, D.C.
Commanded first American voyage around the world

circumnavigation journey around the world

Naval officer Charles Wilkes commanded the U.S. South Seas Exploring Expedition from 1838 to 1842, completing the first American **circumnavigation.** The expedition was one of the first to reach Antarctica, and it produced a vast amount of geographical and scientific data. Moreover, it proved that the young American republic had the ability to launch a successful scientific voyage similar to those of the British and the French.

The Dreams of a Young Nation

Wilkes was born into a prominent New York family. As a young man, he often spent time at his father's place of business, watching the merchant ships in New York Harbor. After he expressed an interest in going to sea himself, his father arranged for him to join the merchant marine in 1815. Even though he was treated harshly in the service, Wilkes joined the navy three years later as a midshipman. He was stationed in Boston, the Baltic Sea, the Mediterranean Sea, and South America. On April 26, 1828, he married Jane Jeffrey Renwick, and two days later, he was promoted to lieutenant commander.

Charles Wilkes of the U.S. Navy won a reputation for toughness and courage, but his quick temper often got him into trouble.

hydrography the scientific study of bodies of water to make navigation easier

species type of plant or animal

longitude distance east or west of an imaginary line on the earth's surface; in 1884 most nations agreed to draw the line through Greenwich, England

specimen sample of a plant, animal, or mineral, usually collected for scientific study or display

Wilkes developed a strong interest in astronomy and surveying, and he became an expert in **hydrography.** By 1828 the United States was eager to undertake a seagoing expedition to make a name for itself in scientific exploration. The French had recently sent Jules-Sébastien-César DUMONT D'URVILLE on a voyage to the southern Pacific Ocean, and Britain's James COOK had already made significant discoveries in that region as well. Wilkes volunteered for the government-sponsored voyage. Meanwhile, he was placed in charge of the navy's Department of Instruments and Charts. In 1837 the U.S. government was ready to begin the proposed expedition, and Wilkes was appointed to a post in its astronomical department. After several officers had been named commander and had then resigned, Wilkes was asked to lead the mission himself. On April 20, 1838, President Martin Van Buren approved the appointment.

Scientific Studies in South America

The government provided Wilkes with six ships, 12 civilian naturalists, and a large group of naval officers. The vessels, however, were old and not prepared for a voyage through dangerous, icy waters. Only three of the ships would return from the journey.

The fleet left Norfolk, Virginia, on August 18, 1838. After stops at Madeira and the Cape Verde Islands, the ships arrived at Rio de Janeiro, Brazil, on November 24. Six weeks later, they sailed south to Tierra del Fuego. Wilkes established a base camp at Orange Harbor, near Cape Horn at the southern tip of South America. By mid-February—the nesting season in that part of the world—the naturalists found many **species** to observe, including penguins, geese, seals, and wolves. From this camp, Wilkes took two ships to explore the waters between the South Orkney Islands and the Antarctic peninsula. However, like others before him, he was unable to navigate through the wall of ice at the **longitude** of 100° west, and he had to return to South America.

Islands and Ice

The fleet next headed north to Valparaiso, Chile, a place Wilkes had visited 18 years earlier. The small village had since become a busy town frequented by tourists from many nations. The naturalists gathered **specimens** in the Andes mountain range, and then the ships sailed west. By that time, one of the original ships had been lost, and another had had to be sent back to the United States. The remaining vessels sailed through the Tuamotus, Tahiti, Samoa, and other Pacific islands on their way to Australia. In all of these places, they saw evidence of the impact of European visitors, especially Christian missionaries. For instance, in response to missionary influence, the Tahitians whom Wilkes met were fully clothed.

Wilkes arrived in Sydney, Australia, in November 1839 and sent his naturalists ashore to investigate Australia and later New Zealand. The following month, he sailed south on the *Vincennes* and encountered icebergs on January 10, 1840. Nine days later, he

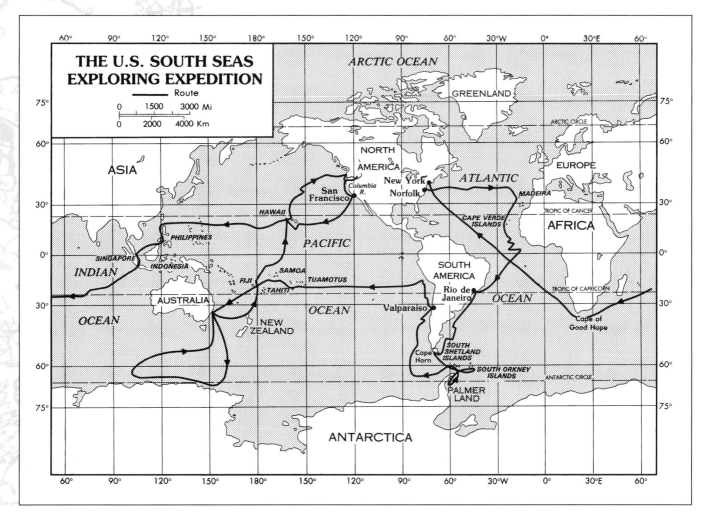

THE U.S. SOUTH SEAS EXPLORING EXPEDITION

Route

0   1500   3000 Mi
0   2000   4000 Km

The U.S. South Seas Exploring Expedition was the first American voyage around the world.

archipelago large group of islands or a body of water with many islands

saw what he believed to be land, and he therefore claimed to have been the first to sight the Antarctic continent. Other explorers and scholars later contested his claim, but a large portion of Antarctica is now named Wilkes Land in his honor. After navigating around icebergs and through severe storms for 10 days, he was able to land and collect mineral samples. The *Vincennes* then returned to New Zealand to reunite with the other ships in the expedition.

The Pacific Northwest

From New Zealand, Wilkes and his men traveled north to Fiji. While they were surveying the island, two of the men were attacked and killed by the local people. This mishap caused the expedition to leave in early August. Wilkes then proceeded to Oahu, in the Sandwich Islands (present-day Hawaii). He stayed aboard the *Vincennes* to explore that **archipelago** while the remaining ships continued to map and chart other islands in the southern Pacific Ocean. After returning to Oahu in April 1841, the entire fleet set out for the northwest coast of North America. For most of the summer, the explorers surveyed Puget Sound (in the present-day state of Washington) and more than 100 miles of the Columbia River. A small party remained in the region to explore the coast of Oregon on foot, and the rest of the crew sailed south to San Francisco,

California. In November the entire expedition headed home, arriving in New York City on August 9, 1842.

In 3 years and 10 months, Wilkes and his men had covered over 80,000 miles and charted more than 300 Pacific islands, 800 miles of rivers and coastline in Oregon, and 1,600 miles of Antarctica's coastline. The mission helped the young United States to claim its place in exploration alongside European powers such as Britain and France. Much of the credit for this accomplishment goes to Wilkes's navigational and scientific skills, as well as to his willpower and leadership.

From 1845 to 1861, Wilkes was placed in charge of the expedition's collections and reports, and he personally prepared the five-volume account of the journey. He also contributed to books about hydrography and **meteorology.** In 1844 he achieved the rank of commander, and in 1848 he received the Founder's Medal of Britain's Royal Geographical Society.

meteorology the scientific study of weather and weather forecasting

"The Stormy Petrel"

Despite his strengths as a leader, Wilkes had weaknesses as well. At times he was impulsive, arrogant, and even cruel to his men. When he returned from the U.S. South Seas Exploring Expedition, he faced a trial for illegally punishing his crew, although he was eventually found innocent. Wilkes was nicknamed "The Stormy Petrel"—a species of seabird that flies far from land—as much for his character as for his willingness to sail in rough seas. He may have been the inspiration for Captain Ahab in the American author Herman Melville's novel, *Moby-Dick.*

During the Civil War, Wilkes's temper again created problems. As commander of the Union navy's *San Jacinto,* he sparked an international incident by seizing two Confederate officials from the British steamboat *Trent* in 1861. His act violated Britain's status as a neutral observer of the war. The following year, he broke neutrality agreements again while commanding a fleet in the Caribbean Sea. Once more he was brought to trial, but this time, he was found guilty and was removed from active duty. Wilkes died on February 7, 1877, and is buried in Arlington National Cemetery in Washington, D.C.

SUGGESTED READING Daniel C. Hashell, *The United States Exploring Expedition, 1838-1842, and its Publications, 1844-1874* (reprint, Greenwood, 1968); William J. Morgan and others, editors, *Autobiography of Rear Admiral Charles Wilkes, U.S. Navy, 1798-1877* (Naval History Division, Department of the Navy, 1978); William Stanton, *The Great United States Exploring Expedition of 1838-1842* (University of California Press, 1975); Herman J. Viola and Carolyn Margolis, editors, *Magnificent Voyagers: The U.S. Exploring Expedition, 1838-1842* (Smithsonian Institution Press, 1985).

Wilkins, George Hubert

Australian
b October 31, 1888; Mount Bryan East, Australia
d November 30, 1958; Framingham, Massachusetts
*Explored Arctic and Antarctica
by plane and submarine*

George Hubert Wilkins's fame rests not only on his career as a polar explorer but also on his widely respected work as a photographer, filmmaker, author, and scientist. He was the first to fly airplanes over both the Arctic Ocean and Antarctica—and also the first to dive under the Arctic ice cap in a submarine. With both still and motion picture cameras, he photographed expeditions in the Arctic as well as battles in the Balkans and France. A self-taught scientist, Wilkins also pioneered the idea that weather could be accurately predicted by setting up a worldwide network of weather stations. Despite his many skills, he was a modest man who rarely sought publicity, and he was often overshadowed by the reputations of explorers such as Richard BYRD and Lincoln ELLSWORTH.

Learning from Nature and Experience

Wilkins grew up on a sheep and cattle ranch in the remote interior of South Australia. Early in his life, he showed the restless energy and resourcefulness of a pioneer. He learned the basics of natural science from the Australian Aborigines who lived off the land outside white settlements in Australia. After receiving a general education in Adelaide, he took up the exciting new art of filmmaking.

Wilkins left Australia for England at the age of 20, planning to work as a filmmaker. After stowing away on a ship to Algiers (in present-day Algeria), he was kidnapped by Arab gun smugglers. He escaped and made his way to London, where he worked as a journalist and cameraman. He covered events all over Europe, and he barely escaped death many times while covering the Balkan Wars of 1912 and 1913; he also found time to learn how to fly an airplane. He then joined Vilhjalmur STEFANSSON as a reporter and photographer on the Canadian Arctic Expedition. On this trip, he learned Arctic survival skills that he would put to good use in his later explorations.

War Takes Priority

In 1916 Wilkins was still in the Arctic with Stefansson when they learned that World War I had broken out two years earlier. Wilkins left the expedition and joined the Royal Australian Flying Corps as an aerial photographer. His work earned him much praise and a promotion to the rank of captain. After the war, he made preparations to participate in a major aerial expedition to the Arctic, but the plans collapsed when the organizer of the trip was unable to raise enough money.

In 1920 Wilkins served as second-in-command of the British Imperial Antarctic Expedition. That adventure was soon followed by a job as naturalist for Ernest SHACKLETON in Antarctica. When he returned, the British Museum chose him—despite his lack of advanced formal education—to lead a survey of plant and animal life in northern Australia. He completed that mission in 1923 and published an illustrated book titled *Undiscovered Australia*.

From the Air Above

Wilkins flew an airplane over the Beaufort Sea (north of Canada's Yukon Territory) in both 1926 and 1927 to prepare for a flight across the Arctic Ocean. The experience he gained was not limited to flying, since he also had to make three emergency landings on the frozen sea. On April 15, 1928, he and his pilot, Carl Ben Eielson, made the first flight across the Arctic Ocean. Flying from Point Barrow, Alaska, to Spitsbergen, Norway, in 20 hours, they covered 2,500 miles—1,000 of which had never before been seen by humans. Wilkins reported that no undiscovered islands existed in that stretch of the ocean. Britain honored his achievement by making him a knight.

In his busy life, George Hubert Wilkins won acclaim as an explorer, photographer, filmmaker, author, and scientist.

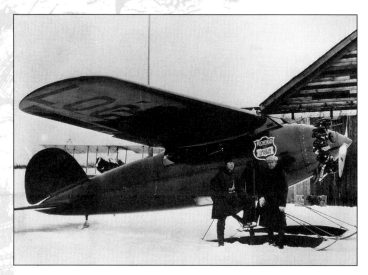

Sponsored by the *Detroit News*, George Wilkins (left) and his pilot Carl B. Eielson (right) flew a Lockheed Vega airplane over the Arctic Ocean.

dirigible large aircraft filled with a lighter-than-air gas that keeps it aloft; similar to a blimp but with a rigid frame

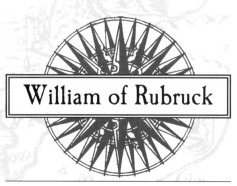

William of Rubruck

French
b 1215?; Rubrouck, near St.-Omer, France?
d 1295?; ?
Wrote detailed account of trip across Asia to Mongol Empire

Not content to rest, Wilkins and Eielson also made the first flight over Antarctica on November 16, 1928, a round trip of 1,200 miles along the coast of the Antarctic Peninsula. Richard Byrd was also on the southern continent at the time, preparing for his own aerial explorations. Although Wilkins and Eielson lacked Byrd's extensive resources, their flight preceded his by two months.

Shortly afterward, Wilkins participated in the round-the-world flight of the **dirigible** *Graf Zeppelin*. On a return visit to Antarctica in 1929, Wilkins proposed that Graham Land was an island and not part of the Antarctic Peninsula. This theory was later proven incorrect; the ice he had seen lies over land, not water.

Deep Beneath the Ice

Wilkins continued to amaze the public. In 1931 he purchased a submarine from the U.S. Navy and named it *Nautilus* after the submarine in Jules Verne's novel *20,000 Leagues Under the Sea.* The navy had planned to scrap the vessel, so Wilkins was able to buy it for only one dollar. He hoped to explore the polar ocean floor, surfacing from time to time to broadcast radio messages and make weather observations. However, the submarine suffered from many mechanical problems, and Wilkins could only make a few short dives under the ice. Yet he had proved the possibility of polar exploration by submarine. He lived to see his plan successfully carried out when a U.S. Navy nuclear-powered submarine—also named *Nautilus*—reached the North Pole by traveling under the ice cap in 1958.

Wilkins remained active in polar exploration throughout the 1930s. He took part in Lincoln Ellsworth's four expeditions to the Antarctic and also served the U.S. government in many roles. In all, he spent 26 winters and 5 summers in the Arctic and 8 summers in the Antarctic. After his death in 1958, the nuclear-powered submarine *Skate* took his cremated remains to the Arctic, surfacing through the ice at the North Pole. After an official naval funeral, Wilkins's ashes were scattered to the winds.

SUGGESTED READING John Grierson, *Sir Hubert Wilkins* (Robert Hale, 1960); Lowell Thomas, *Sir Hubert Wilkins* (McGraw-Hill, 1961); Sir Hubert Wilkins, *Flying the Arctic* (G. P. Putnam, 1928).

William of Rubruck was a Franciscan friar who undertook a two-year diplomatic mission to the Mongol Empire from 1253 to 1255. His descriptions of the Mongols and their customs are regarded by many historians as the finest written by any Christian traveler of the Middle Ages. Although he was not the first to visit the land of the Mongols—another Franciscan, Giovanni de Plano CARPINI, had returned from there just six years earlier—William made several geographical and historical discoveries on his journey. He became the first European to offer convincing proof that the Caspian Sea was not a part of an ocean. He was also the first to learn the truth behind the legend of Prester John and the lost Asian Christians.

The top of this medieval illustration shows William of Rubruck and another monk with King Louis IX. Below, the two monks begin their journey to Mongolia.

alliance formal agreement of friendship or common defense

crusade Christian holy war

khan title of an Asian ruler

Seeking the Aid of the Mongols

In the mid-1200s, Palestine (now Israel and Jordan) was controlled by the Saracens, a nomadic people from the Arabian deserts. King Louis IX of France was looking for a way to drive the Saracens out of Palestine, which he considered to be sacred Christian territory. The king hoped to form an **alliance** with the Mongols, an Asian people who had invaded eastern Europe in 1241. He thought that the Mongols could attack the Saracens from lands north and east of Palestine while Christians launched a **crusade** from the island of Cyprus.

Louis had already sent one representative to the Mongols, a man named Andrew of Longjumeau. While the king was in the Palestinian port of Acre, waiting for reinforcements for his campaign against the Saracens, Andrew returned and reported that his mission had failed. William of Rubruck immediately volunteered to attempt another trip. Like many friars of his time, William was well educated, and he also had a gift for learning foreign languages. He felt that he would have a better chance of gaining the favor of the Mongols if he approached them as a private citizen and missionary rather than as an official ambassador. The king agreed, and William and a few companions left from Constantinople (now Istanbul, Turkey) on May 7, 1253.

Taking the Long Way

The group sailed across the Black Sea to the port of Sudak. There they met Mongols who gave them carts and oxen for their long journey to the camp of Batu, the Mongol conqueror of eastern Europe. Batu's son, Sartach, was said to be sympathetic to the Christian cause. But when the party arrived at the camp, Batu ordered William and another friar in the group to travel to the court of the Great Khan at Karakorum in central Mongolia. It took the pair 3½ months to make the difficult 5,000-mile journey to the east. William later wrote of the trip: "There was no end to hunger and thirst, cold and exhaustion."

The **khan** met William on January 3, 1254, and treated him with respect. He gave William a letter, which recommended that King Louis send official ambassadors to the Mongol court so that the khan would know whether the French wanted peace or war with the Mongol Empire. William remained with the khan until July, when he was ordered to leave. He arrived at the king's headquarters in Tripoli (in modern Lebanon) on August 15, 1255.

Solving the Riddle

William's trip was only a modest political success, but it was an important early exploration of Asia. He described the Volga River and traced its course. His description went on to note that the Caspian Sea was not a part of an ocean as western Europeans had believed. According to William, the sea "is never in contact with the ocean, and is surrounded everywhere by the mainland."

William also solved the mystery of Prester John, the legendary king of a group of Christians in Asia. He found that Prester John was probably the leader of a Turkish people, who called him King John. King John's brother ruled a group of Mongol Christians, giving rise to the European rumors about a kingdom of Asian Christians. William also learned that King John had played a significant role in the rise of the great Mongol ruler, Genghis Khan. Despite William's report, European explorers continued to search for Prester John in Africa, central Asia, and India for more than 200 years.

The friar used his keen eye to describe many sights that were new to Europeans, such as the Mongols' large portable tents. He was the first European to mention the traveling Buddhist priests known as **lamas** and the unique writing system used in China. His account of his travels has been published in English as *The Journey of William of Rubruck to the Eastern Parts of the World, 1253–55.*

SUGGESTED READING Christopher Dawson, *The Mongol Mission: Narratives and Letters of the Franciscan Missionaries in Mongolia and China in the Thirteenth and Fourteenth Centuries* (AMS Press, 1980); Willem van Ruysbroeck, *The Journey of William of Rubruck to the Eastern Parts of the World, 1253-55,* edited by William W. Rockhill (reprint, Kraus Reprint, 1967).

lama Buddhist priest or monk of high rank in Tibet and Mongolia

Wills, William John

Australian
b 1834; Ballarat, Australia
d June 30, 1861; Cooper's Creek, Australia
Crossed Australia from south to north

surveyor one who makes precise measurements of a location's geography

dysentery disease that causes severe diarrhea

William John Wills accompanied Robert O'Hara BURKE on the Great Northern Exploration Expedition of 1860 to 1861. Though successful, it turned out to be one of the most tragic journeys in Australian history. Wills's field notes from the expedition tell a story of bravery under desperate conditions.

Struggles in the Outback

Wills was the son of a surgeon in a town northwest of Melbourne. He was recruited for the expedition as a trained **surveyor** and astronomical observer. Burke also valued Wills's experience in Australia's rural interior, known as the outback. With the goal of crossing Australia from Melbourne in the south to the Gulf of Carpentaria in the north, Burke had assembled a costly and well-equipped expedition.

The party left Melbourne on August 21, 1861. When Burke's second-in-command resigned early in the journey, Wills replaced him. As the explorers headed north, more men turned back or stayed behind to keep watch over supplies. Only four made the entire trip to the gulf: Burke, Wills, Charles Gray, and John King.

A Slow Journey to the End

The return trip south was a nightmare. The four men had few supplies and were drenched by several weeks of rain. Gray fell ill with **dysentery,** but the others believed that he was faking his illness, and Burke beat him severely. When Gray finally died, Wills wrote in his journal: "Poor Gray must have suffered very much when we thought him shamming."

Starving, the three remaining men were forced to kill and eat their horse and camels. When this food ran out, they survived only with the help of local Australian Aborigines, the people native to the outback. Burke's poor judgment then kept the party in the wilderness longer than necessary. Wills was helpless to disagree—at 26, he was much younger than the 40-year-old Burke, and he lacked the assertiveness to challenge his commander. On June 28, 1861, Burke died. Wills wrote: "I may live four or five days if the weather continues to warm . . . my legs and arms are nearly skin and bones." His pen then trailed off, leaving an unreadable scrawl on the page. He died two days after Burke.

Unable to challenge his commander's poor decisions, William John Wills died in the Australian wilderness.

King was found by a group of Aborigines, who cared for him until he was found by a search party. The Australian public, greatly moved by the tragic end of the quest, considered Wills and Burke to be heroes. Their crossing of the continent remains a milestone in the history of Australia.

SUGGESTED READING M. Colwell, *The Journey of Burke and Wills* (P. Hamlyn, 1971).

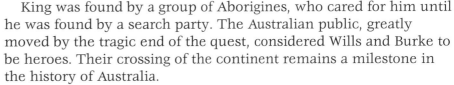

> For a map of Wills's route, see the profile of Robert BURKE in Volume 1.

Wyeth, Nathaniel Jarvis

American
b January 29, 1802; Cambridge, Massachusetts
d August 31, 1856; Cambridge, Massachusetts
Led first American settlers to Oregon

Nathaniel Jarvis Wyeth was a successful Boston businessman who went to the Oregon Territory in hopes of starting a new trading venture. However, bad luck repeatedly frustrated his efforts in the West. Despite those failures, he helped to establish the first permanent American settlement in what is now the state of Oregon.

Answering the Call

Wyeth's interest in the Oregon Territory (now the states of Washington, Oregon, and Idaho) was stirred by Hall J. Kelley of Boston, a vocal supporter of U.S. settlement in the Pacific Northwest. When Kelley failed to follow through on a plan to take settlers to the Oregon Territory, Wyeth organized his own expedition. To avoid the expense of carrying the new community's supplies across the continent, he loaded the goods onto a ship. He intended that the ship would sail around South America's Cape Horn and transport the supplies north to the coast of Oregon. His plan was to gather furs and dried salmon in the West and send them on the same ship back to Boston, where he hoped to sell them at a profit.

Wyeth's party left Boston in March 1832 and met some experienced Mountain Men in Independence, Missouri. The guides led the party to the Green River rendezvous, where fur trappers met to trade their furs for supplies they needed. At that gathering, Wyeth arranged to have the Rocky Mountain Fur Company sell him supplies at the next year's rendezvous. Wyeth then proceeded with a small group to Fort Vancouver, near the mouth of the Columbia River. There he learned that his ship had been wrecked at sea, and he had no choice but to return to Boston and try again the following year.

Perseverance Rewarded

In 1834 Wyeth set out for the Oregon Territory as before, sending a supply ship around Cape Horn. He brought along goods to trade at the rendezvous, but the Rocky Mountain Fur Company refused to take them in exchange for the supplies he needed. Hoping to make up for his losses, Wyeth built Fort Hall, a fur trading post located where the Snake and Portneuf Rivers meet. The fort later became a well-known stop on the route of settlers heading west.

At Fort Vancouver, Wyeth learned that his ship had been delayed for repairs after being hit by lightning. It arrived too late for the salmon season, so Wyeth sought to establish himself in the fur trade. Unable to compete with the Hudson's Bay Company outpost in the area, he returned east in 1836. However, he left behind several settlers and a Methodist minister named Jason Lee. That group formed the first permanent American settlement in what is now the state of Oregon.

Xavier, Francis

Spanish
b April 7, 1506; Navarre (now in Spain)
d December 3, 1552; Shangchuan, China
Traveled to India, Malay Archipelago, and Japan

Francis Xavier worked as a missionary in India, Japan, and other Asian countries, providing detailed observations to European mapmakers and historians.

Jesuit member of the Society of Jesus, a Roman Catholic order founded by Ignatius of Loyola in 1534

cartographer mapmaker

SUGGESTED READING Nathaniel J. Wyeth, *The Journals of Captain Nathaniel J. Wyeth's Expeditions to the Oregon Country, 1831–1836* (reprint, Ye Galleon Press, 1984).

Francis Xavier, sometimes called the "Apostle of the Indies," is considered the greatest Roman Catholic missionary in the modern history of Christianity. One of the founders of the religious order known as the Society of Jesus, he spent 10 years traveling throughout Asia, preaching Christianity to the local people and converting many. His journeys provided Europeans with their first eyewitness account of the island of Japan.

Founding Father

Xavier was one of the younger sons of a Basque nobleman from Navarre (which became a part of Spain in 1515). At the age of 19, he entered the University of Paris, the center of religious teaching in Europe at that time. In Paris he met a fellow student, Ignatius of Loyola. Ignatius wanted Xavier to help him establish a religious order whose members would vow to live according to the example of Jesus Christ. The group's members would also be devoted to missionary work. Xavier was reluctant at first, but he eventually joined Ignatius and five other students in forming the Society of Jesus in 1534.

After they had finished their studies, the seven men went to Venice, where Xavier became a priest in 1537. They then traveled to Rome, hoping that the pope would send them on a mission to a distant land. At the time, Portugal's King John III was looking for priests to minister in the lands under his rule in Asia. Xavier was chosen for that mission, and after stopping in Lisbon, he set sail for India.

A New Strategy

On May 6, 1542, Xavier arrived in Goa, on India's east coast. Goa, the main Portuguese outpost in Asia, was the center of Catholic activity in the region. The church leaders in Goa were responsible for ministering to an area that stretched from China to the Cape of Good Hope at the southern tip of Africa. Xavier spent several years among the Parava, a group of pearl fishers who worked on the southeastern coast of India. There he developed an approach to dealing with the Asians he would meet on his travels. He adapted to the customs and cultures of the people he met, a policy that became standard for later **Jesuit** missionaries such as Matteo RICCI. Xavier traveled from village to village, preaching Christianity. He also wrote detailed descriptions of the people and places he visited. His notes were collected by the Jesuits and were used to teach new missionaries about the geography and customs of those regions. **Cartographers** and historians later made use of the information gathered by Xavier and other Jesuits.

While in India, Xavier also spent a few months with the Macuan, who lived on the southwestern coast of the country. In 1545, reports of opportunities to attract converts to Christianity in the Malay Archipelago prompted Xavier to head east. For two years, he traveled through the islands in the Banda Sea, living among the Malay and other peoples in the region. During that time, Xavier met a Japanese named Anjiro whose intelligence and sophistication impressed him. After that encounter, the priest became convinced that the future of Christianity in Asia depended upon a successful mission to Japan.

The Culture of Japan

After leaving the Malay Archipelago, Xavier returned to Goa for a short time and then departed for Japan. On August 15, 1549, Xavier and several companions arrived at the Japanese port of Kagoshima. Xavier's first letter from Japan demonstrates his limitless enthusiasm for the Japanese, whom he described as "the best people yet discovered." During the two years he spent there, his correspondence gave Europeans their first look at the sophisticated culture of Japan. Xavier returned to India in late 1551.

Xavier came to believe that the Japanese admired the wisdom of the Chinese. He therefore thought that the Japanese would accept Christianity more easily if some of the Chinese were converted first. After attending to his duties at Goa, he set out for China. He traveled to Shangchuan, an island off China's south coast, where he died of a fever on December 3, 1552.

Xavier was one of the most remarkable figures in the early history of Europeans in Asia. His work established the approach and range of Jesuit activity in the area. In recognition of his contributions as an early missionary to Asia, he was made a saint by the Roman Catholic Church in 1622.

SUGGESTED READING Henry James Coleridge, *The Life and Letters of St. Francis Xavier*, second edition (reprint, Asian Educational Services, 1997); Archbishop Alban Goodier, *Saints for Sinners* (Sheed and Ward, 1948); Theodore Maynard, *The Odyssey of Francis Xavier* (Longmans, Green and Company, 1936).

Xenophon

Greek
b 428 B.C.?; Athens, Greece
d 355 B.C.?; Corinth?, Greece
Led Greek army through western Asia

mercenary soldier who is hired to fight, often for a foreign country

About 2,400 years ago, a military disaster marooned thousands of Greek soldiers in the Middle East. A man named Xenophon took command, and over the next year, he led the dispirited troops toward Greece through unfamiliar and hazardous terrain. Twenty years later, Xenophon described their ordeal—and the lands through which they traveled—in a book called the *Anabasis,* which means "The March into the Interior." He went on to a successful but controversial career as a historian of Greece.

The Noble Adventurer

Xenophon belonged to a wealthy family in ancient Athens, a Greek city-state. Like other highborn Athenians of his day, Xenophon probably acquired military experience at an early age, during fighting between Athens and another city-state, Sparta. Tested in battle, he received an invitation from a friend named Proxenus to seek adventure in Persia (present-day Iran).

King Darius II of Persia had recently died, and his sons Artaxerxes and Cyrus were fighting for control of the Persian Empire. Artaxerxes was king, but Cyrus hoped to overthrow him and had decided to hire an army of Greek **mercenaries.** Proxenus had enlisted with Cyrus and suggested that Xenophon join as well. At the time, Xenophon was unpopular with the leaders of Athens, who doubted his commitment to the city's domocratic government.

The ancient Greek soldier and historian Xenophon described how he led thousands of soldiers through the freezing, uncharted mountains of western Asia.

Eager to leave his political troubles behind and to win fame and fortune, Xenophon accepted Proxenus's invitation.

The Death of Cyrus

In Asia Minor, the large Asian peninsula now occupied by Turkey, Cyrus gathered his army and marched south. Covering about 1,700 miles in five months, the force crossed Asia Minor and then headed southeast toward the heart of the Persian Empire. At a place called Cunaxa, not far from the ancient city of Babylon (in present-day Iraq), Cyrus's troops were met by an army loyal to Artaxerxes. Caught by surprise, Cyrus was killed and his army defeated. The victors executed the Greek generals, including Proxenus.

The surviving Greek mercenaries, now known as the Ten Thousand, found themselves in a perilous position. They were far from home, in hostile territory, and without leaders. However, they were permitted to return to Greece, so the soldiers elected new commanders to guide them home. Xenophon was one of those chosen, and he eventually became the leader of the entire force.

The Greeks did not want to return by the route they had followed into Iraq. That journey had taken them across a desert as well as over flat, open plains, where Persian horsemen could easily attack them. Instead they decided to head north toward the Black Sea, where Greek colonies had been established. But between the stranded soldiers and the Black Sea lay 1,500 miles of unknown territory.

The Long Walk Home

The Greeks marched northwest along the Tigris River, which flows from Turkey through Iraq. Persian forces threatened the Greek army as it followed the Tigris past Nineveh (near the site of the present-day Iraqi city of Mosul).

The Greeks then reached the Taurus Mountains, a region inhabited by the ancestors of the Kurds who live in those mountains today. The Greeks fought their way past these fierce warriors and entered the kingdom of Armenia, which included much of what is now eastern Turkey. Facing an Armenian army, the Greeks asked the king of Armenia for permission to continue northward. They had to promise that they would do no damage to the fertile areas of the country. To avoid possible conflict with the Armenian soldiers, the Greeks were forced to cross the region's Pontic Mountains in the middle of winter.

In the *Anabasis,* Xenophon gave a graphic account of this terrible journey. The Greeks waded through the frigid currents of mountain streams and struggled up and down steep, icy slopes. Battered by snowstorms and weakened by hunger, many died from exhaustion and cold. Toes and fingers were lost to frostbite, and snow blindness deprived men of their sight.

According to Xenophon, it was his own outstanding leadership that brought the surviving men through the mountains. He appears to have been well liked by the common soldiers and to have been a sensible, energetic general. On one occasion, he caught a mule driver preparing to bury a soldier who, though very ill, was not yet dead. Xenophon struck the treacherous driver, winning the approval of the other men.

In a well-known passage, Xenophon recalled the end of the grim march through the mountains:

When the men in front reached the summit and caught sight of the sea there was great shouting. . . . Xenophon galloped forward to the front with his cavalry. When he got near he heard what the cry was—The Sea! The Sea! Then they all began to run, the rearguard and all, and drove on the pack animals and horses at full speed; and when they had all got to the top, the soldiers, with tears in their eyes, embraced each other and their generals and captains.

The surviving Greeks—about 6,000—made their way along the coast of the Black Sea to the Greek colony of Trapezus (present-day Trabzon, Turkey) and then on to another colony, Chalcedon (near Byzantium, present-day Istanbul, Turkey). Xenophon, by then the mercenaries' leader, found paid work for them with an army from Sparta, fighting Persians in Asia Minor. Then, knowing that the men could now find their way home, Xenophon left the army and returned to Greece.

Exile and Retirement

Xenophon found that in his absence, Athens had banished him for opposing democracy. Moving to Sparta, he lived with his family for many years on a country estate. There he wrote several books, including a history of Greece, biographies of Cyrus and the philosopher Socrates, and the famous *Anabasis.*

Modern scholars do not consider Xenophon a completely reliable author. He tended to overstate his own importance and downplay the contributions of others. Some of his historical writings are not strictly factual. However, the *Anabasis* has retained its popularity and value over the centuries. Besides being a vivid account of a dramatic adventure, it describes the geography of an isolated region that was seldom visited by outsiders. His descriptions allowed Greek geographers to make new and more complete maps, and later travelers in that region benefited from his notes on its terrain, weather, food, and customs. Like HERODOTUS, PYTHEAS, and ALEXANDER, Xenophon extended the borders of the world known to ancient Greeks.

SUGGESTED READING Ced Adams, *A View of Xenophon's Anabasis* (Vantage Press, 1980); Ann Gaines, *Herodotus and the Explorers of the Classical Age* (Chelsea House, 1993); Geoffrey Household, *The Exploits of Xenophon* (reprint, Linnet Books, 1989).

Xu Hongzu

Chinese
b 1586; Jiangyin, China
d 1641; Jiangyin, China
Explored China

The Chinese travelers FAXIAN, ZHANG Qian, XUAN Zang, and YI JING won fame for their travels in the world outside China. Xu Hongzu, however, explored his own country, and some scholars believe that he may have covered more miles over land than any other Chinese traveler of his time. Inspired by his lifelong passions for geography and mountain scenery, he made a series of journeys to many parts of China. He recorded his travels and observations in a set of detailed journals. On his last and greatest expedition, he visited remote southwestern China and charted the courses of several major rivers.

The Training of an Explorer

Xu Hongzu was born into a prosperous and well-known family living in the province of Jiangsu, near the mouth of the Chang Jiang (also known as the Yangtze River). His parents could afford to provide him with many books, and he devoted himself to the study of history and geography. Normally a young man of Xu's upbringing would have been expected to study for the examinations that, if he passed them, would lead to a post in China's civil service. But Xu ignored the examinations. He studied literature and won a modest reputation as a poet. His greatest desire, however, was to travel.

Chinese literature and art traditionally placed high value on beautiful landscapes. Throughout China were found places, mostly lakes and mountains, that were famous for their beauty. Educated, well-read men would often travel out of their way to view a celebrated landscape. Xu wanted to see them all.

He made his first trip in 1607, visiting a scenic lake and climbing several hills nearby. Over the next 10 years, Xu made seven more journeys, returning home briefly between trips to visit his mother and his wife. He saw waterfalls, caves, and the tomb of an emperor, and he climbed several high, snowy mountain ranges. These adventures toughened Xu and increased his endurance.

After his wife died, Xu remarried and resumed his travels in 1618. He visited friends, climbed mountains, and admired the geographic marvels that he saw. One man who met him during this period wrote that although Xu appeared to be a ragged mountain hermit, "there resides in him a rich spirit and the essence of courage."

Travel Writing

By 1633 Xu Hongzu had made 16 journeys and was a seasoned traveler. He did not go alone—one or two friends, relatives, and servants always accompanied him—nor did he wander aimlessly. He planned his journeys carefully, reading everything he could about the region he planned to visit. He set specific goals, knowing what he meant to see or do when he arrived.

Following a common custom in China, a friend gave him a new personal name that reflected Xu's traveling nature. This name, Xiake, means "one who lives apart and stays only temporarily." Xu's travel diaries were published under the name Xu Xiake (also spelled Hsü Hsia-K'o), and he is often known by that name today.

Writing these diaries was part of Xu's daily routine. Aware that his writings might bring him fame, he never let fatigue prevent him from recording the day's events each night. In his diaries, he described the routes he had followed, the distances he had covered, encounters with local residents or fellow travelers, and any noteworthy sights he had seen along the way. Xu's diaries are carefully crafted works that combine skillful literary language with precise geographical details. By the time he had completed his first 16 journeys, he had written a great deal. Yet most of his writing, like his most ambitious journey, was still to come.

Western Dangers

In 1636 Xu's mother died, so he had more freedom to travel. He started on a journey that he had been planning for a long time—a lengthy expedition to southwestern China. This region is far to the west of the ancient centers of Chinese civilization, which are mostly near the Pacific Ocean. The southwestern lands were known for their harsh terrain and independent, non-Chinese tribes.

During four years of almost constant travel, Xu endured severe hardships and walked thousands of miles. Bad luck plagued him from the beginning of the trip. One servant soon abandoned him. Xu and his companion, a monk, were nearly drowned in a river during an attack by robbers. The monk soon died of the injuries he had suffered in this assault. When Xu and one remaining servant entered the province of Yunnan, they were almost penniless. But various scholars, writers, and government officials provided them with money and hospitality. Through it all, Xu kept his diaries, writing extensive entries as often as possible.

Xu had hoped to enter Tibet, but he had to turn back because the region was controlled by bandits. Heading south, he was also unable to cross the border into Burma. But he did succeed in exploring the upper reaches of two of Southeast Asia's mightiest rivers, the Salween and the Mekong. He proved that the two rivers are not connected.

More troubles followed. Xu found himself with no money at all and had to sell some of the clothes he was wearing in order to buy food. Then his servant fled, stealing most of Xu's few remaining possessions. After that there are no diary entries. Historians do not know whether Xu stopped writing or whether some of his manuscript has been lost. By the time Xu returned home in 1640, he was suffering from skin and foot diseases. The long journey had exhausted his remaining strength, and he died the following year.

Chinese readers of Xu's time treasured his diaries for their fine literary style. Geographers prized them for their wealth of precise details about the lands Xu had visited. The spirit of curiosity in which he traveled, as well as the care with which he recorded his observations, made Xu a model for modern geographers of China.

SUGGESTED READING Li Chi, *The Travel Diaries of Hsü Hsia-K'o* (Chinese University of Hong Kong, 1974).

Xuan Zang

Chinese
b 602; Ch'en-lu (now Kaifeng), China
d 664; China
*Traveled from China to India
to find Buddhist texts*

Xuan Zang (also known as Hsüan-Tsang) was a Chinese Buddhist monk who traveled for 16 years through much of central Asia and India. He did not intend to become an explorer—he wanted to reach India only to find the holy writings of his religion. But Xuan Zang was a brave traveler and a sharp-eyed observer. His journey took place in the 600s, when there was little contact among the widespread peoples of Asia. In his book *Records of the Western Regions of the Great T'ang Dynasty,* he gathered a great deal of information about the geography, cultures, and peoples of the places he visited. Xuan Zang's contribution to China's knowledge of other lands was matched only by the great success of his religious mission. His journey was not, however, free of danger.

Xuan Zang's courageous journey to India won him great reverence and fame for centuries to come.

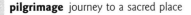

plateau high, flat area of land

pilgrimage journey to a sacred place

khan title of an Asian ruler

A Religious Puzzle

An older brother first introduced Xuan Zang to the teachings of the Buddha—Siddhartha Guatama, the man whose philosophies had founded Buddhism about 1000 years before Xuan Zang's lifetime. Xuan Zang began to study this religion, and his teachers soon realized that the young scholar had great potential. Shortly after becoming a monk himself, Xuan Zang was chosen as one of 14 monks who received financial support from the Chinese emperor while they pursued their studies. Xuan Zang traveled throughout China to study with some of the country's most respected Buddhist scholars.

The young monk quickly mastered even the most difficult philosophical texts, but he soon became troubled. He found contradictions among different writings, and he saw that every scholar interpreted the holy writings in a different way. Xuan Zang decided that the only way to gain a correct and complete understanding of Buddhism would be to travel to India, the homeland of the Buddha. He hoped that by studying the original texts of Buddhism and by visiting holy shrines in India, he would find the answers he needed.

A Dangerous Trip to India

Unfortunately, a trip to India was not easily accomplished in the 600s. Xuan Zang decided to avoid the central **plateau** of Tibet by heading west through central Asia and then southwest into India. At the age of 28, he left the Chinese city of Liang-zhou, a flourishing center of trade. At first he had two companions, but one soon deserted him, and the other was too weak to make the difficult journey.

Traveling alone, Xuan Zang overcame many challenges on the way to India. At one point, he was captured by river pirates, who intended to sacrifice him to the goddess they worshiped. Xuan Zang protested that he was on a holy **pilgrimage,** but the pirates ignored his pleas. As the monk prepared to die, a fierce storm blew up. His captors saw this as a bad omen. Terrified, they released him and begged him for forgiveness.

Xuan Zang proceeded to Turpan (now in the Chinese province of Xinjiang). There a local **khan** was so deeply impressed by him that he invited him to stay and take charge of the city's Buddhist temple. When Xuan Zang declined, the khan insisted. The young monk then went on a hunger strike, refusing food for days to show his determination to continue his mission. The khan not only gave in but also became Xuan Zang's greatest supporter and presented him with enough gold and silver to meet his needs for 20 years. He also provided Xuan Zang with letters and gifts to help ensure his safe passage to India.

The Birthplace of Buddhism

The obstacles that other people put before Xuan Zang were hardly so great as those presented by the deserts of central Asia and the mountains of northern India. But he overcame such difficult terrain and reached India in 633, four years after he had left China. He traveled on both the east and west coasts of the Indian subcontinent, visiting all of the sites in India that were considered holy in

For a map of Xuan Zang's route, see the profile of ZHANG Qian in this volume.

Buddhism. During his travels, he collected many Buddhist images and holy books. He also complied descriptions of the people he met and the places he saw. However, he spent most of his time at Nalanda, where he studied Buddhist philosophy and learned the Sanskrit language, in which the original Buddhist works had been written.

Xuan Zang's fame spread throughout India, and the Buddhist monks there tried to persuade him to stay. They said that China was a land of barbarians. However, Xuan Zang disagreed with the monks, pointing to China's effective and stable system of government as well as to its many advances in astronomy, engineering, and music.

Honor and Influence

Xuan Zang's return journey took him through central Asia once again, and he returned to China in 645, after more than 40,000 miles of travel. The emperor called him to the capital city of Xian to give a detailed report on the climate, resources, and cultures of the lands he had visited. Having previously told the Indians about the wonders of China, Xuan Zang now described India to the Chinese. Some historians believe that his efforts led to the beginning of political relations between China and India.

Xuan Zang set to work translating the hundreds of Sanskrit texts he had brought from India. He was unable to complete this enormous task before his death, but his writings—like his fame—have survived to this day. In 1913 some of his translations were found by Mark Aurel STEIN in a hidden chamber, kept safe by monks in the deserts of western China.

SUGGESTED READING Arthur Waley, *The Real Tripitaka* (Macmillan, 1952).

Yermak, Timofeyevich

Russian
b 1500s; ?
d August 6, 1584; Irtysh River, Siberia (now in Russia)
Led early Russian attempt to conquer Siberia

cossack horseman from southern Russia who served as a mounted soldier in the armies of Russian monarchs

Timofeyevich Yermak was an outlaw who became a hero by extending Russian rule into the heart of northern Asia. He was the first in a series of adventurers who would eventually help Russia to conquer and control over one-fourth of the Asian continent. When the last of these explorers reached the Pacific Ocean, the Russian Empire claimed 10 percent of the world's land.

A Deceptive Request

Little is known of Yermak's early history. He probably grew up among the **cossack** outlaws who lived in the Crimea (now part of Ukraine) and along the banks of the Don and Volga Rivers. Yermak's adventures began when the Stroganov family, rulers of Russia's easternmost province, asked him to lead a force to subdue the Siberians, who were raiding Stroganov lands. To carry out his mission, Yermak would have to cross the Ural Mountains. Known as the Iron Wall, these mountains had long been considered the eastern frontier of Europe. The handful of fur traders who had crossed them had returned with frightening tales about cannibals—or had not returned at all. The Stroganovs hoped that they could not only defeat the Siberians but also get rid of the troublesome Yermak.

The Fight for Power

Yermak was not fearful of the dangerous assignment. It appealed to his recklessness, and it offered him the chance to capture a fortune in Siberian furs. In July 1579, he set out for Siberia with 540 mounted cossacks and 300 of the Stroganovs' soldiers. It took them 10 long months to cross the rugged Urals. Upon reaching the Tobol River, they built rafts to travel farther east. The men spent another year on this difficult, slow journey before they finally reached the central area of Siberia.

The region was ruled by Kuchum, a Tartar warlord whose people had terrorized eastern Russia for 200 years. As Yermak's troops advanced on their enemies, the Tartars resisted. In the crucial final battle, 10,000 cavalry led by Kuchum's nephew fought Yermak's small force for five days. Much of the fighting was hand-to-hand combat, but the superior weapons possessed by the cossacks gave Yermak the victory in the end.

Yermak had captured the Siberian capital, Siber, and wanted to keep its vast supply of furs for himself. However, he realized that his small force alone could never retain control of Siberia. He called upon Ivan IV (also known as Ivan the Terrible), the **czar** of Russia, to send soldiers, telling him that Siberia was his to rule. Even though Ivan considered Yermak a criminal, he sent 500 troops to establish Russian control over Siberia. However, they arrived just as winter came, and they suffered greatly from disease and hunger.

Meanwhile, the Siberians mounted a seemingly endless series of revolts against Yermak's rule. The summer after Ivan's troops arrived, Yermak led a party south in boats along the Irtysh River to fight a band of rebels. But in August 1584, Kuchum's troops made a surprise attack. Yermak tried to fight his way back to the boats. At the time, however, he was wearing a coat of armor that the czar had given to him. He fell into the river and drowned, dragged under by the weight of his armor.

SUGGESTED READING Terence E. Armstrong, compiler, *Yermak's Campaign in Siberia: A Selection of Documents* (Hakluyt Society, 1975).

Yi Jing was a Chinese follower of Buddhism, a religion that originated in northern India. In the A.D. 600s, Yi Jing joined a growing number of Chinese Buddhists who made dangerous and difficult **pilgrimages** to India in search of information about Buddhism. After 24 years in India and Southeast Asia, Yi Jing returned home with a wealth of Buddhist writings. He wrote a detailed description of the little-known lands and peoples south of China.

Religious Inspiration

In 645 the Chinese Buddhist monk XUAN Zang returned from a long pilgrimage to India. His journey inspired many other Chinese Buddhists to attempt pilgrimages of their own. They had two goals: to see the sacred sites of their faith and to ensure that the sacred writings of Chinese Buddhism were correct and complete. In India they could study ancient Buddhist documents and obtain copies to take home to China to be translated into Chinese.

czar title of Russian monarchs from the 1200s to 1917

Yi Jing

Chinese
b 634?; Fanyang, China
d 713; Xi'an, China
Traveled in India and Southeast Asia

pilgrimage journey to a sacred place

Yi Jing was only a boy when Xuan Zang returned from China. Few details exist about Yi Jing's early life, but he apparently came from a wealthy family that lived in a city near Beijing in northern China. When he was 7 years old, his family sent him to live in a Buddhist monastery, where he learned about Buddhism and Chinese literature. Yi Jing continued his studies in Xi'an, which at that time was China's capital, and he may have studied with Xuan Zang. Yi Jing also admired FAXIAN, a Buddhist pilgrim who had traveled to India in the early 400s. At the age of 37, Yi Jing was ready to make his own journey.

Danger by Land and Sea

Unlike pilgrims before him, Yi Jing did not travel the overland route to India through central Asia and across the Himalaya mountain ranges. Warfare had seized central Asia, where Tibetan people were rebelling against Chinese rule and where Islamic armies from the west were conquering Afghanistan. With the overland route so dangerous, travelers looked to the sea. Yi Jing went to the city of Guangzhou (also known as Canton) in southern China, where in 671 he took passage on a Persian trading vessel headed south.

"Huge waves as high as mountains barred the surface of the ocean, sweeping right across the vast abyss; the spray, like clouds, rose full up into the sky," Yi Jing later wrote of this sea voyage. He left the ship at the port of Palembang on Sumatra, an island that is now part of Indonesia.

After six months on the island, Yi Jing traveled on a Sumatran ship to Tamralipti, a port on the eastern coast of India. There he remained for a year while he improved his knowledge of Sanskrit, the ancient language in which Buddhist documents were originally written. He then decided that he was ready to visit the Magadha region of India, on the Ganges River. In Magadha there were several holy sites, including Nalanda, a Buddhist religious center where Xuan Zang had studied.

Risk and Reward

With more than 20 other monks, Yi Jing set out for Nalanda. The monks had to pass through a region of lakes and mountains that was plagued by bandits. "The perils of the road are not easily overcome," Yi Jing wrote later. "Only a party of several persons traveling together can get through because the various members can all help each other; no one should proceed alone." Unfortunately, Yi Jing became ill and fell behind his companions. A party of about 20 bandits waylaid him, stole his clothes, and threatened to kill him. In the end, however, the thieves spared Yi Jing's life. He covered his naked body with mud and leaves and then struggled on to rejoin his fellow travelers.

Yi Jing spent 10 years at Nalanda, studying and collecting copies of Buddhist writings. He also made pilgrimages to many of the holy places of Buddhism. But as the years passed, his homesickness grew. In a poem, he wrote: "I am sad; China is far from here. . . . day followed upon day until, without my realizing it, I have reached the years of my decline, autumn ever having followed upon autumn. . . . Oh, that I might take with me the holy books and set out on my way back to China!"

The Quiet Hero

In 682, having visited more than 30 Indian states, Yi Jing was ready to depart. With more than 10,000 rolls of Sanskrit writings, Yi Jing returned to Palembang in Sumatra and began the work of translation. He made a brief trip to China to enlist the help of other Buddhist scholars. He also arranged the notes that he had kept, describing his travels.

In 695 Yi Jing returned to China to stay. Like Xuan Zang before him, he was treated as a hero. He was even called to relate his experiences at the court of the Chinese empress. Yi Jing spent most of his time working peacefully in a monastery near Xi'an. With the help of several learned monks, he completed the translation of 56 Buddhist texts in 230 volumes. The next emperor became a friend of Yi Jing, visiting the monk often and taking part in the work of translation.

Yi Jing also found time to write a book about the lives of about 60 Chinese and Korean Buddhist pilgrims in India, many of whom he had met. His account of their lives reflects their deep religious devotion and their homesickness for China. He also wrote about India and Southeast Asia. His description of India did not focus on geography, which other Chinese writers had covered. Instead he discussed many aspects of India's social life, especially customs involving food and drink, clothing, bathing, and manners.

His account of his time in Southeast Asia was more geographical, containing valuable information about place names, distances, and governments. He also described the region's weather, customs, and religions. The products he described—such as pineapples, sugarcane, nutmeg, and cloves—came from the tropical islands that European explorers and merchants would compete to reach 700 years later.

SUGGESTED READING Rene Grousset, *In the Footsteps of the Buddha*, translated by J. A. Underwood (Orion Press, 1971); I-Ching, *Chinese Monks in India*, translated by Latika Lahiri (Motilal Banarsidass, 1986).

Younghusband, Francis Edward

English
b May 31, 1863; Murree, India
d July 31, 1942; Lytchett, England
Explored Asia; led British army into Lhasa

Francis Edward Younghusband was a soldier, explorer, and diplomat. He made several dangerous journeys throughout central Asia in the service of the British army. In 1904 Younghusband led a controversial military expedition sent to force Tibet to open relations with Britain. Afterward, he experienced a spiritual awakening and devoted his life to advancing fellowship among the world's peoples.

Mountain Heights

Younghusband was born at a British military station on India's northern frontier. His family had a tradition of military service that dated back hundreds of years. His father was a major general of the British army in India, and his uncle was a respected explorer of Asia.

Educated in England, Younghusband graduated from the British military academy at Sandhurst in 1882 and was sent to serve in

India. Several years later, he took leave of his unit to attempt an extensive exploration of Manchuria in northeastern China. In 1887 he journeyed 1,200 miles west across the Gobi Desert and over the mountains of the Tian Shan in Chinese Turkistan (now part of China). Turning south, he crossed the Karakoram Range of the Himalaya. He proved that the range is the **watershed** between the Indian subcontinent and western China. On two later expeditions to the region, he trekked through the Pamirs, the mountain range known as the "roof of the world," to explore passes and note any Russian activity in the area.

The Use of Force

In the late 1800s, Russia and Britain were active rivals in central Asia. Both nations wanted control over Tibet, which was strategically located between their two empires. However, the **lamas** who ruled Tibet refused to establish diplomatic relations with any foreign countries. Since its capital city, Lhasa, was located deep in the rocky Himalaya, Tibet had been successful in isolating itself from the outside world. The British, however, refused to accept this state of affairs. In 1903 the British governor of India, Lord Curzon, decided to send a military force to Lhasa to negotiate trade and frontier issues. He hoped that by taking such an action, he would be able to limit Russia's own influence in Tibet.

In May 1903, Younghusband was chosen to lead a force of 1,200 British, Indian, and Nepalese soldiers. The troops crossed the border between India and Tibet in December and marched slowly through the mountains. On March 31, 1904, they reached the plains of Guru, where they met a Tibetan army of 1,500 men armed with swords and muskets. The Tibetans carried pictures of their high priest and ruler, the Dalai Lama, believing that his image would make them invincible in battle. However, they were no match for the British, who were armed with machine guns. The slaughter was so awful that the horrified British troops could not continue to fire. About 700 Tibetans were killed. To the Tibetans' amazement, the British then tried to save the wounded.

The Tibetan leaders eventually realized that they could not hope to resist foreign invasion. On August 4, Younghusband's force became the first European army to enter Lhasa. Although the Tibetans did not want to accept British demands, they were eager for the invaders to leave. Therefore, the Dalai Lama signed a treaty under which Tibet was not allowed to enter into foreign **alliances** without British permission. The Tibetans also agreed to pay for the cost of the war and to establish trade relations with Britain. The British government faced intense international protest as a result of its military actions. It eventually compromised some of the requirements that had been written into the treaty. Nevertheless, Younghusband was knighted for his role in the campaign.

Spiritual Awakening

Younghusband later became president of the Royal Geographical Society and sponsored early efforts to climb Mount Everest. But

watershed ridge of high ground forming the boundary between regions where the water of each region flows into a different river system

lama Buddhist priest or monk of high rank in Tibet and Mongolia

alliance formal agreement of friendship or common defense

Francis Younghusband's bloody military campaign in Tibet led him to a spiritual awakening that changed his life.

perhaps the most significant result of his journey to Tibet was his spiritual awakening, which he experienced as he looked at the Dalai Lama's palace, the Potala. Younghusband decided that he would never again be in conflict with others. He came to believe that all the world's major religions are related to Christianity, and he founded the World Congress of Faiths to advance his ideals.

SUGGESTED READING Jan Morris, *Farewell the Trumpets: An Imperial Retreat* (Penguin, 1979); George Seaver, *Francis Younghusband: Explorer and Mystic* (John Murray, 1952); Sir Francis Younghusband, *The Epic of Mount Everest* (Longmans, Green, 1927).

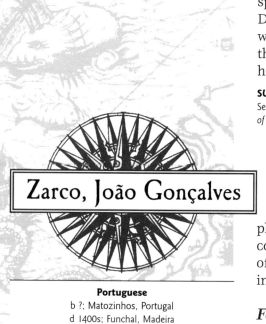

Zarco, João Gonçalves

Portuguese
b ?; Matozinhos, Portugal
d 1400s; Funchal, Madeira
Discovered and settled island of Madeira

João Gonçalves Zarco was one of the first explorers in the service of Prince Henry the Navigator. Zarco's efforts laid the groundwork for Portugal's large-scale voyages of discovery, which took place in the 1400s and 1500s. He explored stretches of Africa's coastline and rediscovered two nearly forgotten islands off the coast of North Africa. Zarco transformed one of these islands, Madeira, into a thriving Portuguese colony.

Food for Explorers and Rabbits

Zarco distinguished himself in the Battle of Ceuta before offering his services to the prince's court in 1418. Eager to explore the west coast of Africa, Prince Henry ordered Zarco to try to reach what is now known as Guinea. Zarco and a soldier named Tristão Vaz Teixeira sailed southwest into the Atlantic Ocean. While seeking refuge from a storm, they landed on a small island that they named Porto Santo, which means Holy Haven in Portuguese. After a three-day visit, the sailors returned to Portugal, reporting the discovery of an island with fresh water and fertile soil.

Prince Henry then instructed the men to return to Porto Santo to start a colony. He hoped that the island would become a supply base for later Portuguese explorers. Zarco and Teixeira were joined by the island's appointed governor, Bartolomeu Perestrello, the future father-in-law of Christopher COLUMBUS. Perestrello brought along a pregnant rabbit, making a mistake that would eventually ruin the colony. The rabbits multiplied rapidly over the next two years, eating every crop that the settlers had planted. When the food supply ran dangerously low, the island had to be abandoned temporarily.

Second Chances

In 1424 Zarco received permission to set sail for an island he had sighted near Porto Santo. He named it Madeira, the Portuguese word for wood, because of its forests. Located less than 400 miles northwest of the coast of Africa, Madeira held great potential as a colony. Zarco decided to make a home there with his wife and children. He also brought convicted criminals whom he had recruited as settlers. In spite of early problems, including a devastating fire, the colony grew rapidly under Zarco's leadership. He founded the capital city of Funchal, and within 20 years, Madeira became a prosperous settlement with several towns and villages. Zarco later took part in another voyage of exploration,

caravel small ship with three masts and both square and triangular sails

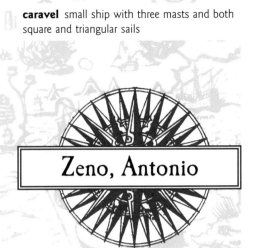

Zeno, Antonio

Italian
b ?; Venice (now in Italy)
d 1406?; Venice? (now in Italy)
May have explored Faeroe Islands, Orkney Islands, and North America

commanding one of 14 **caravels** that sailed down the African coast to Cape Verde.

SUGGESTED READING Charles Raymond Beazley, *Prince Henry the Navigator, The Hero of Portugal and Modern Discovery 1394-1460 A.D.: With An Account of Geographical Progress Throughout the Middle Ages as the Preparation of His Work* (reprint, Cass, 1968); Leonard Everett Fisher, *Prince Henry the Navigator* (Macmillan, 1990).

In 1558 a Venetian named Nicolo Zeno published a manuscript, which he claimed was more than 150 years old, describing the explorations of his ancestor, also named Nicolo Zeno. According to the story, the elder Nicolo traveled to an island called Frisland in the northeastern Atlantic Ocean, where he served under a chief named Zichmni. From there he went to a place called Engroneland. His brother—or son—Antonio, later visited Frisland and journeyed with Zichmni to lands where two fishermen had found the remains of Norse colonies called Estotiland and Drogeo.

Fact or Fiction?

Historians have attempted to identify the people and places presented in this account. Frisland may be in the Faeroe Islands. Engroneland may be Greenland. The name of Zichmni may refer to Scotland's Prince Henry Sinclair, the Earl of Orkney. The Norse colonies may have been parts of North America. However, the original manuscript, reportedly written by Antonio Zeno upon his return to Venice, had never been circulated. The version published in 1558 by the younger Nicolo was a replacement—Nicolo said that as a boy, he had found the original in a trunk and had torn it up just for fun. He claimed that he had reconstructed the account from letters written by his exploring ancestors. He also included a map of the northern Atlantic Ocean that he said he had found with the manuscript. If the story is true, it means that Antonio Zeno visited North America 100 years before Christopher COLUMBUS.

Surrounded by Doubters

The text was widely accepted at the time of its publication, and the map was even incorporated into famous world maps produced by Gerardus Mercator in 1569 and Abraham Ortelius in 1570. Martin FROBISHER, John DAVIS, and William BAFFIN all used Antonio Zeno's map in their travels to what is now Baffin Bay, and all were confused by it. Even so, the map was generally thought to be genuine until the late 1800s. At that time, scholars began to note that much of it had been copied from maps that had been printed before the manuscript was published. Many historians began to think that the story was a fraud, created to bring credit for these discoveries to Venice and the Zenos.

There is no firm proof that the map and manuscript were or were not genuine. In any case, the story serves as a reminder that travelers, merchants, fishermen, and others journeyed to many places that were only later officially discovered and charted by professional explorers.

Zhang Qian

Chinese
b ?; China
d 107 B.C.?; China
Explored lands west of China

---

dynasty succession of rulers from the same family or tribe

alliance formal agreement of friendship or common defense

Seven hundred years apart, Zhang Qian and Xuan Zang made remarkable journeys to lands far from the centers of Chinese civilization.

SUGGESTED READING Niccolò Zeno, *Nicolò and Antonio Zeno, to the Northern Seas in the XIVth Century, Comprising the Latest Known Accounts of the Lost Colony of Greenland and of the Northmen in America Before Columbus*, edited by Richard Henry Major (B. Franklin, 1963).

Zhang Qian was an ancient Chinese diplomat who became an explorer and helped to open trade relations between China and central Asia. In 138 B.C. he was sent by the Chinese emperor Wu-di to what is now Iran, where he hoped to find allies to assist the Chinese in their war with the Huns. Instead he spent years as a prisoner of the Huns. When he finally escaped, he explored lands previously unknown to the Chinese. His explorations eventually led to the establishment of the famous trade route known as the Silk Road.

First Contact with Western Lands

Before 140 B.C., the Chinese knew almost nothing about what lay to the west of their empire. The emperor Wu-di, of the Han **dynasty,** sent out several groups with the mission of extending China's influence to western states. At that time, the Chinese were at war with the Huns, a central Asian people. Zhang Qian was chosen to lead an attempt to find the Yue-chi, a tribe that had been driven out of its homeland by the Huns. The emperor hoped that the Yue-chi would form an **alliance** with China against their common enemy.

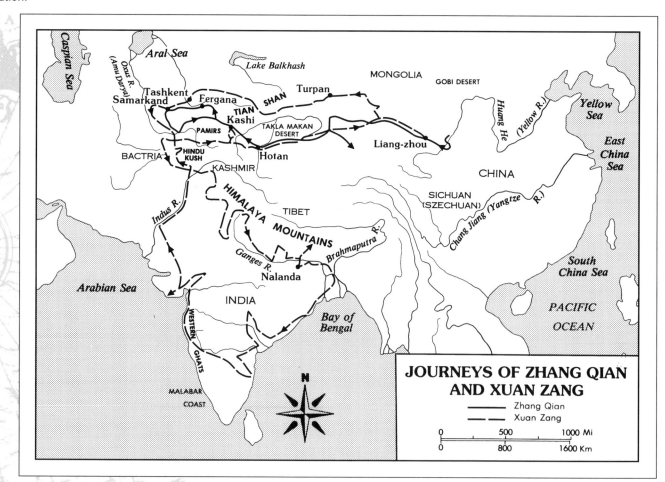

JOURNEYS OF ZHANG QIAN AND XUAN ZANG

——— Zhang Qian
– – – Xuan Zang

0   500   1000 Mi
0   800   1600 Km

Zhang Qian set out with over 100 men, but he and his men were quickly captured by the Huns. He spent the next 10 years in prison but then escaped and made his way to Fergana (in what is now Uzbekistan). There the friendly Ta-yuan people helped him locate the Yue-chi. However, he found that the Yue-chi had recently conquered a new land for themselves, and they had no desire to go back to war with the Huns.

The disappointed Zhang Qian headed back to China by way of Tibet, but the Huns captured him a second time. A few months later, the Huns' ruler died, and his successors began to fight over his throne. Zhang Qian took advantage of this confusion and escaped again, arriving in China in 126 B.C. with only two members of his original party. He could offer the emperor no new allies, but he did bring much information about western lands, such as Fergana, Syria, Babylonia (now Iraq), and Bactria (now Afghanistan).

Opening the Silk Road

Zhang Qian proposed a new approach to making contact with western peoples. He suggested that the Chinese could bypass the lands of the Huns and Tibetans and travel directly to places such as Bactria and Fergana. About 10 years later, the emperor sent Zhang Qian west again to explore this possibility. The expedition proved much more productive than the first. Zhang Qian and his assistants investigated numerous existing trade routes across Asia. He issued a report to the emperor that resulted in the opening of the Silk Road in 105 B.C. The Silk Road became the main overland route between China and Europe, a link that lasted for hundreds of years.

SUGGESTED READING Herbert D. Pierson, *Travelers from Ancient Cathay: An Account of China's Great Explorers* (Joint Publishing Company, 1992).

Zheng He

Chinese
b 1371; Yunnan (now Kunming), China
d 1433?; China?
Commanded sea voyages to southern Asia, Middle East, and East Africa

dynasty succession of rulers from the same family or tribe

courtier attendant at a royal court

Between 1405 and 1433, Zheng He led seven sea expeditions on behalf of the emperors of China's Ming **dynasty.** He sailed with enormous fleets to ports throughout Southeast Asia, India, Arabia, and East Africa. Zheng's mission was to display the power and wealth of the Chinese emperor to neighboring peoples.

A Servant Rises to Power

Zheng He was born to Muslim parents in Yunnan, a Chinese territory that was held by Mongols until the Chinese reconquered it in 1381. The 10-year-old boy, like many others, was captured and made a servant to the Chinese army. Gradually, he impressed his masters, became an officer, and made a name for himself at the court of his commander, a prince named Chu Ti.

In 1400 the prince led a revolt against the emperor, his nephew, and in 1402 Chu Ti took the throne and became known as the Yonglo emperor. Zheng's fortunes rose with those of his commander. He continued to advance his career as a well-known **courtier** and trusted adviser.

The Yonglo emperor began to reassert the greatness of the Ming dynasty. At home he turned Beijing into an impressive new capital.

This Chinese character represents the Ming dynasty, which Zheng He served on seven sea expeditions intended to display China's glory and power.

sultan ruler of a Muslim nation

But he also wanted to demonstrate his glory to foreign countries. He decided to send out fleets that would dazzle and intimidate his neighbors, who would then recognize China as the one and only center of power and culture. The emperor further intended those peoples to offer money and goods as a tribute to China's superiority.

Diplomacy by Ship and Sea

Zheng He was named commander of the largest naval expedition in China's history, with nearly 28,000 people on 62 large ships and 255 smaller boats. The largest vessel had nine masts and was 450 feet long. Many of the ships were several stories high, well built, and beautifully designed and decorated. From 1405 to 1407, the fleet visited the lands that are now Vietnam, Thailand, Indonesia, India, and Sri Lanka.

Zheng's many voyages were often peaceful, but the first came into conflict with a pirate who ruled the city of Palembang on the island of Sumatra. The second fleet faced resistance from the king of Ceylon (present-day Sri Lanka). Zheng defeated both opponents and sent them to the emperor as captives.

Zheng undertook a total of seven expeditions. He and his assistants visited dozens of states. They called on familiar peoples in the islands and coastal rain forests of Southeast Asia, and they anchored in the bustling ports of the Indian subcontinent. Braving the far western waters of the Indian Ocean, the Chinese established relations with Arab states of the Persian Gulf, Arabian Peninsula, and Red Sea, as far west as Egypt. The fleets also sailed down the east coast of Africa, visiting kings, princes, and **sultans** in lands now known as Somalia, Kenya, Tanzania, and Mozambique. Zheng is believed to have died between 1433 and 1435 in either India or China, and he was later buried near Nanjing, China.

Zheng He's expeditions achieved their goals. Many of the states that he visited acknowledged China's power by sending diplomats and gifts to the emperor's court. The contacts he made led to increases in Chinese settlement and trade throughout the Indian Ocean. China's political influence lasted for several more decades, and the trade benefits of Zheng He's efforts lasted until the 1800s.

SUGGESTED READING J. J. L. Duyvendak, *China's Discovery of Africa* (A. Probsthain, 1949).

Glossary

*Words in **boldface** are defined under their own entries in this Glossary.*

adelantado During the 1500s, Spain placed an official called an adelantado in charge of each of its colonies in the Americas. The adelantado controlled all military, civil, and legal affairs of a colony. Spain later replaced the adelantados with alcaldes, who served as mayors or judges.

Admiralty The Board of Admiralty, often known simply as the Admiralty, was the government body in charge of Britain's Royal Navy for over 200 years. Before the 1700s, a high-ranking state official called the Lord High Admiral oversaw the navy. In the early 1700s, that task fell to a committee called the Board of Admiralty, which became a major sponsor of many voyages of exploration, such as those of James Cook. In the early 1800s, the Admiralty also led the charting of coasts and harbors in the British Isles and in other parts of the world. The Admiralty ceased to be an independent body in 1964, when it became part of the British Ministry of Defense.

astrolabe First used by Greek astronomers as early as the 200s B.C., an astrolabe is an instrument designed to measure the height of the sun and stars above the horizon. The first astrolabes consisted of a wooden disk that hung straight down from a ring-shaped handle. The edge of the disk had marks for the 360 degrees of a circle. In the center of the disk was a pointer that spun around a pin. The user of the astrolabe lined up the pointer with the sun or star and saw where the pointer met the degree scale; this reading indicated the sun's or the star's height above the horizon. By applying this information to complex tables and charts, the user could determine the **latitude** of his or her location.

In the Middle Ages, Arab craftsmen designed astrolabes that employed several interchangeable disks for use in sighting various stars. Improved charts allowed the user to determine the time of day as well. The astrolabe was eventually replaced by the **quadrant** and the **sextant.**

astronaut   A member of the U.S. or European space programs who has been selected to travel in space is called an astronaut. The term comes from the Greek words that mean "traveler to the stars." In 1959 **NASA** chose the United States's first seven astronauts, all of whom were military test pilots and most of whom had had valuable experience in flying experimental aircraft. As scientific research came to play a larger role in space exploration, NASA began to recruit scientists to join the pilots on missions. **Space shuttle** crews in the 1980s and 1990s included civilian men and women with backgrounds in science, medicine, journalism, and education.

The European Space Agency was organized in the 1970s. It does not operate crewed spacecraft, but it sometimes sends astronauts to fly on U.S. shuttle missions. People from other countries, such as Canada and Ukraine, have also joined shuttle crews. The space program in Russia (formerly the **Soviet Union**) calls its space travelers **cosmonauts.** All astronauts and cosmonauts must pass demanding tests in order to be selected, trained, and approved for missions.

bandeira/bandeirante   The term *bandeira* is Portuguese for flag, banner, or group. In the 1600s, it referred to a Portuguese raiding expedition into the interior of Brazil. These raids were intended mainly to capture Indians as slaves, although another goal was to locate gold and silver. A bandeira might consist of a few dozen to several thousand men, called bandeirantes, and it could last as long as several years. The bandeirantes moved from place to place in search of villages to raid. Along the way, they sometimes established their own settlements, built roads, farmed, and traded.

Among the bandeirantes' prime targets were Indian villages that had been set up by **Jesuits.** These missionaries became the Indians' greatest allies, petitioning Portuguese officials to outlaw the bandeiras. After the mid-1600s, the aims of the bandeiras shifted away from slavery and more toward the search for precious metals and gemstones.

boat-sledge   Used in the Arctic Ocean, a boat-sledge is a boat that is mounted on runners like a **sledge.** This vessel can therefore travel over either open water or solid ice. It was most often used during the spring, when explorers frequently encountered gaps in the melting Arctic ice.

brig   A brig was a small, fast sailing ship that was popular from about 1700 until 1860. Brigs were used by merchants to carry light goods and by the military to conduct scouting missions. They had two masts and were **square-rigged,** requiring large crews to handle the sails. The brig was gradually replaced by the **brigantine** and the **schooner,** which used triangular sails and thus required fewer crewmen.

brigantine   A brigantine was a two-masted sailing ship. Its front mast was **square-rigged** and the rear mast was **lateen-rigged.**

The brigantine's design served as a transition between the **brig** and the **schooner.**

buccaneer Pirates and **privateers** who were active during the 1500s, 1600s, and 1700s were sometimes called buccaneers. These raiders were especially infamous in the 1600s, when they often attacked Spanish colonies and treasure ships in the Americas.

bush This term applies to undeveloped, sparsely inhabited regions in many parts of the world. Most commonly, it refers to Australia's vast interior, far inland from the settled coasts. Vegetation in the Australian bush is usually limited to dry shrubs or a few small trees.

Canadians refer to their northern backcountry as the bush, although the land has little in common with the Australian bush. In Alaska, the term describes parts of the state that have no roads. A bush pilot is someone who flies an airplane or helicopter into these areas.

cacique A cacique (pronounced "kah-SEEK") is a local Indian chief in Central or South America. When the Spanish arrived in the Caribbean region in the late 1400s, they found island communities governed by rulers whose title the Spanish wrote as *cacique*. The Spanish then carried the term to the mainland. Once the **conquistadors** and colonists had taken control, they established the hereditary office of cacique among the Indians in order to ensure stability and order. As middlemen between the Spanish rulers and the Indian population, caciques collected taxes and organized labor to meet Spanish needs.

capsule The spacecraft that carried the first **astronauts** and **cosmonauts** into space in the 1960s were called capsules. Typically cone-shaped, capsules were not much larger than the one or more people they carried into **orbit** around the earth. When launched, they were mounted atop **rockets,** which detached in space and fell to earth, leaving the capsules in orbit. Capsules could be operated remotely by ground controllers or manually by a pilot. The flat part of the cone was covered with a heat shield to withstand the intense heat of the friction created upon reentering the earth's atmosphere. Capsules deployed parachutes to slow their descent. Those launched by the **Soviet Union** usually landed on the plains of Kazakhstan. Capsules launched by the United States splashed down in ocean waters, where they drifted on inflatable rafts until they could be picked up by a navy vessel.

caravan A caravan is a group of merchants, pilgrims, or other travelers journeying together by land, usually with pack animals and guards. This form of travel helps people to overcome difficult terrain and to protect themselves against bandits or other dangers. Traders can increase their profits by joining with other merchants in organizing such journeys.

Caravans have crossed Asia, North Africa, and the Middle East since ancient times. Today transport of goods by sea, road, and rail has ended most caravan trade, but a few pilgrim caravans still travel the ancient routes. Caravans usually average two to three miles an hour for 8 to 14 hours each day. In hot climates, they travel by night and rest by day. The largest caravans were those organized for special purposes, such as pilgrimages to Mecca or trade across the Sahara, and could include as many as 20,000 camels.

caravel   Early versions of the caravel were built in the 1300s as small merchant ships with two **lateen-rigged** masts. The Portuguese later enlarged the vessel and added a third mast, which carried square sails. These changes made the caravel ideal for ocean exploration. The lateen sails were useful for tricky coastal navigation, whereas the square sails were best for catching the wind on long ocean crossings. The caravel was favored by the Portuguese explorers of the 1400s, such as Bartolomeu DIAS, as well as by Christopher COLUMBUS, whose *Niña* and *Pinta* were both caravels.

chronometer   A chronometer is a clock designed to keep exceptionally precise time—even in the rough weather, changing temperatures, and rolling motion endured on a ship at sea. Precise measurement of time is needed for an accurate calculation of **longitude.** Such a clock was first devised in 1659, but it became truly useful only when perfected by John HARRISON in 1762. Together with a **quadrant** or **sextant**—used to find **latitude**—Harrison's invention allowed navigators to determine their exact position on the earth.

conquistador   This term, which means conqueror in Spanish, refers to the military leaders who explored and claimed much of the Americas for Spain and Portugal during the 1500s. Most conquistadors were men who had not prospered in Europe and had gone overseas to seek fame and fortune. Some became governors and landowners in the colonies they helped to establish. They won praise for their endurance, courage, and skill, but they also were criticized for their often brutal treatment of American Indians.

corsair   A corsair was a fast ship used for piracy, especially along the Mediterranean coast of North Africa, known as the Barbary Coast. The term also referred to a pirate on such a ship. Corsairs sometimes operated with the support of local governments.

cosmonaut   A cosmonaut is someone who has been chosen for space flight as part of the space program founded by the **Soviet Union** in the 1950s and continued in the 1990s by Russia. The term comes from the Greek words meaning "traveler to the universe." The first cosmonauts were male pilots, but in 1963, Valentina TERESHKOVA became the first woman in space. In 1965 the Soviets sent two nonpilots—an engineer and a physician—

into space, and the Soviet cosmonaut program grew to include many more scientists. All cosmonauts receive extensive training before a spaceflight. The U.S. space program calls its own space travelers **astronauts.**

cossack This term comes from the Turkic word *kazak,* which means an adventurer or free man. The word originally referred to the independent peoples who lived in southern Russia, north of the Black and Caspian Seas. By the late 1400s, it also included peasants who had fled the service of their landlords to establish self-governing communities around the Don, Dniepr, and Ural Rivers.

The cossacks became known and feared for their skill as warriors and horsemen. In 1654 the cossacks agreed to serve in the Russian military in exchange for political independence. They guarded Russia's frontiers and pioneered its expansion eastward into Siberia. During the 1800s and early 1900s, Russian rulers deployed the cossacks against revolutionary forces. When the monarchy fell in 1922, the cossacks lost their independence to the new **Soviet Union.**

Council of the Indies The Council of the Indies was the supreme ruling body of Spain's colonial empire. Founded in 1524 by King Charles I of Spain, the council included a president and 4 to 10 other members. It made laws, nominated high colonial officials, collected taxes, and judged legal cases. The council censored all literature read throughout the empire and even controlled the activities of the Roman Catholic Church in the colonies. After 1790 the council merely advised the Spanish monarch, and in 1834 it was dissolved entirely.

Creole Depending on where it is used, the term *Creole* can refer to any of the following: a person of Spanish ancestry, born in Spain's American colonies; a person descended from the French settlers of the southern United States, especially Louisiana; a person descended from the Spanish or Portuguese settlers of land around the Gulf of Mexico; a person of mixed European and African ancestry, born in the Caribbean islands, especially Haiti; or a dialect of French or Spanish spoken in the Caribbean islands.

Crusades The Crusades were a series of wars launched in the Middle Ages by Christians against Muslims in the Middle East. The name comes from the Spanish word *cruzada,* which means "marked with the cross." The Crusades were intended to conquer biblical lands—known as the Holy Land to European Christians—that had come under Islamic rule. Other goals were to unify quarreling European nations under a common cause, to establish the prestige of Christianity and the pope, and to limit the growing power of the Muslims.

The first Crusade was organized in 1095. European forces captured Jerusalem and founded Christian kingdoms in the Holy Land. One by one, however, these kingdoms fell into Islamic hands. The Muslim leader Saladin recaptured Jerusalem in 1187. Several more Crusades failed to regain Christian territory. The last major Crusade took place in 1270, and the last Christian strongholds fell in the early 1300s.

The Crusades brought Europeans into closer contact with the culture and trade of the Islamic world. This exposure led to greater interest in non-European lands and contributed to the burst of European exploration that began in the 1400s.

dhow The dhow is a type of sailing vessel used by Arab traders and fishers since ancient times. Dhows range in size from small coastal boats to large seagoing vessels. They have one or two masts, and their hulls are designed for speed. The ships' most distinctive feature is their triangular, **lateen-rigged** sails. This design was adopted by shipbuilders around the Mediterranean Sea and the Indian Ocean and also influenced the development of European vessels such as the **caravel.**

dirigible A dirigible, also called an airship, is a long, narrow, lighter-than-air craft. Like a hot-air balloon, it is filled with a lighter-than-air gas (usually hydrogen or helium) that causes it to rise from the ground. Unlike a balloon, it has an engine, a steering mechanism, and a rigid frame. When dirigibles were introduced in the mid-1800s, they were the first steerable aircraft that could carry people and make long flights. They were used through the 1930s as military and passenger vehicles. However, they were not reliable in stormy weather, and a series of disasters weakened their reputation. As airplanes became safer and faster, they replaced dirigibles for most purposes, including polar exploration. One type of non-rigid airship, the blimp, is used today to carry cargo, advertise products, and conduct research.

doldrums The doldrums is a belt of calm or light winds around the equator, mainly over the oceans. The lack of wind often stranded sailing ships there for weeks at a time. Occasionally, **trade winds** from the northeast and southeast collide in the doldrums and produce sudden storms.

El Dorado The Spanish **conquistadors** first used this name, meaning "the golden one," to refer to an Indian king who was rumored to have great wealth. Later the name was extended to the king's city or realm. The legend of El Dorado probably came from a ceremony actually performed by an Indian tribe in what is now Colombia. This tribe covered the bodies of its new chiefs with gold dust. The chief then plunged into or floated on a lake, while his people honored him by throwing gold or emeralds into the water. Early European explorers heard of this ceremony and added to the story, creating the legend of a city of gold. The hope of conquering this wealthy kingdom inspired many explorers, including Sebastián de BENALCÁZAR, Francisco PIZARRO, and Walter RALEIGH.

encomendero In Spain's American colonies during the early 1500s, an encomendero was a Spanish soldier or colonist to whom the authorities granted land or a village. The encomendero was expected to protect the Indians on his land and teach them about Christianity. The Indians were expected to provide goods and labor to the encomendero. In many cases, however, encomenderos abused and enslaved the Indians. The efforts of the missionary Bartolomé de LAS CASAS to reform this system led to laws that abolished it in 1542. However, the laws were not enforced for years afterward.

frigate The first frigates were small, oar-driven **galleys** of the 1300s. These often carried messages or scouted waters ahead of a fleet. In the 1600s, a frigate was a small, sail-powered warship. Shipbuilders introduced a new kind of frigate, also a sailing warship, around 1750. These vessels had three masts, square sails, and two decks. They had cannons mounted on just one deck, so that they were smaller and faster than ships with guns on two or three decks. Frigates were ideal for carrying out raids and escorting merchant ships. Steam frigates came into use in the 1800s. Today the term applies to a type of naval vessel that escorts another ship to protect against attacks by submarines.

galleon This term generally refers to a large sailing ship of the 1400s, 1500s, and 1600s, used primarily by England and Spain for both war and trade. Since they were the first ships to carry heavy cannons, galleons revolutionized naval warfare. Before that time, sailors had boarded enemy vessels and fought hand to hand.

A typical galleon had three or four masts and featured both square and triangular sails. The earliest versions had sterncastles, structures at the rear of the ship that could provide as many as four decks of living quarters. Smaller forecastles were built at the front of the ship. Around 1550, shipbuilders reduced the sterncastle to two or three decks and moved the forecastle closer to the middle. This form of galleon became the standard European naval vessel in the late 1500s. It also became famous as the cargo ship used to carry treasure between Spanish colonies in the Americas and the Philippine Islands.

galley The galley, a vessel used for both war and trade, first appeared on the Nile River as early as 3000 B.C., and it remained popular for more than 4,000 years, especially in the Mediterranean Sea. A galley was light, slender, and shallow. Though some galleys had sails, most were propelled by oars. The earliest galleys had only one row of oars on each side, but around 700 B.C., the ancient Phoenicians added a second row. About 200 years later, the Greeks added a third row, and this type of galley eventually became the most important warship in the navy of the Roman Empire. During the Middle Ages, the galley remained the standard battle vessel of Europe, but the **galleon** took its place in the 1500s.

Jesuit Jesuits are members of a Roman Catholic religious order called the Society of Jesus. The society was founded in 1534 by a Spanish priest named Ignatius of Loyola. The order was approved by the pope in 1540, and it soon became noted for its members' roles as teachers, scholars, missionaries, and political advisers. The Jesuits also acquired a reputation for the zeal that they brought to their work, which sometimes brought them into conflict with government officials.

Often among the first Europeans to visit foreign lands, some Jesuits became explorers. Unlike most older religious orders, the Society of Jesus encouraged its missionaries to adapt their methods and customs to suit the countries where they worked. Their various activities were especially influential in the Americas, where they vocally defended the rights of Indians. The yearly records of the order's activities, titled *Jesuit Relations,* remain valuable sources of information about the cultures and history of many parts of the world.

junk The junk is a Chinese sailing vessel used mainly to carry cargo in the waters around China, Southeast Asia, and India. It has a flat or slightly rounded bottom and a high stern. A large rudder not only directs the vessel but also extends deep down into the water to provide stability. A junk can have several masts, each of which carries a single large, rectangular sail, usually a mat made of grass or other fibers. Among the largest junks ever built were those sailed by ZHENG He in the early 1400s—one vessel was 450 feet long and had nine masts.

lateen-rigged A lateen-rigged sailing vessel is one with triangular sails that run along the length of the ship. Such a ship requires relatively few crewmen, because the sails can be adjusted by pulling on ropes that hang down to the deck. The sails can be turned to catch wind on either side of a mast, so that these ships are easier to maneuver than **square-rigged** vessels. Lateen-rigged ships were therefore preferred for sailing along coasts. However, a lateen-rigged sail cannot catch as much wind as a square-rigged sail, so it is less efficient on the open seas.

The first lateen-rigged vessels were sailed as early as the A.D. 100s in the Mediterranean Sea. As a distinctive feature of the **dhow,** the triangular sail was used for many centuries throughout the Mediterranean, the Arabian Sea, the Persian Gulf, and the Indian Ocean. European shipbuilders adopted lateen rigging in vessels such as the **caravel, brigantine,** and **schooner.**

latitude Latitude is a figure that describes how far north or south of the equator a place is located. Latitude is measured in degrees, with the equator at 0°, the North Pole at 90° north, and the South Pole at 90° south. One degree of latitude equals about 69 miles. Each degree is subdivided into 60 smaller units of distance called minutes, and each minute is subdivided into 60 seconds. On maps, latitude is shown by east-west lines called parallels.

Latitude is one of the two measurements that are needed to pinpoint a location on the earth's surface—the other is **longitude.** Together, latitude and longitude give a place's coordinates on the grid of imaginary lines drawn on maps. Mapmakers and explorers once used the **astrolabe** or the **quadrant** to measure latitude. Today computerized instruments use signals from **satellites** in space to give quick, extremely precise readings.

league This unit of distance has varied in length at different times and in different countries. In modern English-speaking countries, a statute (land) league is usually estimated at 3 statute miles. However, the league is most commonly used at sea, where it is formally called a nautical league. A nautical league equals 3 nautical miles, or approximately 3.45 statute miles.

longitude On maps, longitude is shown by north-south lines called meridians. A place's longitude is its distance east or west of one of these lines, called the prime meridian. For centuries mapmakers disagreed about the position of this line. Spanish mapmakers, for example, used a prime meridian that ran through Madrid, while French mapmakers used one through Paris. In 1884, however, recognizing the need for a common mapmaking system, the International Geographical Congress agreed on a prime meridian that runs through Greenwich, England.

Longitude is measured in degrees, with the prime meridian marking 0°. There are 180 degrees west of the prime meridian and 180 east of it. Each degree is subdivided into 60 smaller units of distance called minutes, and each minute is subdivided into 60 seconds. The length of a degree of longitude is greatest at the equator, where the earth's circumference is greatest. Farther north or south, the length becomes smaller, reaching zero at the poles.

Longitude is one of the two measurements needed to pinpoint any location on the earth's surface; the other is **latitude.** The latitude and longitude of a place are its coordinates on the grid of imaginary lines drawn on maps. The difficulty of determining longitude while at sea was a problem for explorers and navigators until 1762, when John HARRISON perfected a **chronometer** that allowed them to make accurate measurements.

mission A mission is an outpost or settlement that a church or religious order creates to spread Christianity among the people of another culture. The establishment of missions was closely tied to exploration. Missions were often established by priests who explored an uncharted territory, and these outposts in turn served as bases for other exploring expeditions.

As early as the 1300s, the Roman Catholic Church founded missions in Asia, but their most active role in exploration was in the Spanish colonial empire in the Americas. The Spanish made religious conversion of Indians an official objective. Along with military forts and civilian estates, missions played a key role in the colonization of the Americas. Some missionaries tried to protect the Indians from abuse by Spanish authorities. However, the goal was not to preserve the Indians' way of life but to convert them to a Christian one.

NASA The National Aeronautics and Space Administration (NASA) is the government agency that manages the U.S. space program. In July 1958, the U.S. Congress created NASA, which absorbed an earlier agency called the National Advisory Committee for Aeronautics (NACA). NASA took over the supervision of various programs created by the American armed forces to develop **rockets** and spacecraft. Since that time, NASA has directed the U.S. space program from its early launches of **satellites** and **capsules** to its lunar landings, **space stations,** and **space shuttles.**

New France New France was originally the name given to all lands claimed and explored by France in North America. Gradually, it came to refer more specifically to the area of French settlement in the St. Lawrence River valley. The other main French territories in North America were Acadia, on the Atlantic coast of Canada, and Louisiana, in the Mississippi River basin.

In 1524 Giovanni da Verrazano explored the coast of North America for France, and five years later, his brother drew a map that was the first to name New France. In 1608 Samuel de Champlain founded Québec, the first permanent French settlement in the territory. Québec fell to the English in 1629, but a treaty restored it to France three years later. The French colony grew slowly under the ineffective leadership of the Company of New France, but in 1663 the French king Louis XIV brought the region under his direct control. Three years later, French troops defeated the Iroquois Indians, making the lands around New France easier to settle and develop. In the 30 years that followed, thousands of new settlers arrived. Explorers such as René Robert Cavelier de La Salle and Daniel Greysolon Dulhut expanded French influence over the Great Lakes and the Mississippi River basin.

In 1689 France and England began a long period of rivalry that led to four wars. England won control of Acadia in 1713 and of New France in 1763. The French sold Louisiana to the United States in 1803, bringing an end to the French empire on the North American continent.

New Spain Established in 1530, New Spain was the first of Spain's four viceroyalties, which were territories governed by **viceroys.** As Spain extended its rule, New Spain came to include Central America, Mexico, and the northern borderlands of California, Arizona, New Mexico, and Texas. In theory the viceroy of New Spain also held authority over Spain's colonies in the Caribbean Sea, Florida, and the Philippine Islands. However, the governors of these regions had a great deal of independence, and for all practical purposes, New Spain consisted of Mexico and its northern frontier. Most of New Spain became part of the independent nation of Mexico in 1821, but neither the Spanish nor the Mexicans succeeded in establishing a large colonial population in the borderlands. Settlers and traders from the United States began moving in during the early 1800s, and after the Mexican-American War, the region became U.S. territory in 1848.

orbit A spacecraft that travels in a circular path around a planet or moon is said to orbit, or to be in orbit around, that body. Each trip around is referred to as one orbit. A spacecraft achieves a stable orbit when its speed and distance from the earth are balanced against the earth's gravity. In such a balance, the spacecraft is pulled in a circular orbit instead of flying out into space or spiraling down toward the earth. Except for missions to the moon, orbit of the earth has been the goal of nearly all spaceflights with crews aboard. Once in orbit, a craft can remain in space for a long time. Many **satellites** also have been launched into permanent orbit.

packet Packets were small, speedy vessels used during the 1800s. They carried mail, freight, and passengers on regular schedules along fixed routes—a new practice in shipping at the time. The first packets were sailing ships, but these were later replaced by steam-powered vessels.

pinnace This term refers to a light sailing ship that accompanied a larger merchant vessel or warship. It can also mean any of several kinds of small boats that larger ships often carried on board. The boats were used to perform various tasks such as taking landing parties to shore and sailing in waters that were too shallow or dangerous for the larger vessel.

portage The verb *to portage* means to carry boats and supplies over land between two waterways. When used as a noun, the term refers to the land route taken. Explorers of continental river systems often had to portage when they reached a stretch of river that was too dangerous for travel in canoes or other boats. Waterfalls and rapids were common obstacles. The travelers usually returned to the river farther upstream or downstream. In some cases, they would portage from one river to another.

privateer During times of war, governments sometimes hired privately owned ships to attack enemy vessels. These ships—and their crew members—were called privateers. The term can also be used as a verb, and the activity is referred to as privateering. In some ways, privateering was a legal form of piracy.

pueblo This word is Spanish for people or nation. It usually refers to a large, shared dwelling built by certain Indian tribes in what is now the southwestern United States. Made of brick or adobe (a mixture of mud and straw), pueblos may stand up to five stories high. They were sometimes built into the sides of cliffs. The term can also refer to the Pueblo Indian tribes who built such communities or to any other Indian or Spanish village in the Southwest.

quadrant A quadrant is a device used since about 1600 to measure the altitudes of the sun and stars. Several kinds of quadrants existed, but most included a quarter-circle arc marked with 90 degrees. The user lined up sights, holes, or mirrors with the horizon and the sun or star. A pointer, weighted string, or the sun's shadow would then intersect with the arc. After reading the degree figure from the arc, the user could consult a chart to determine **latitude.**

Quadrants were developed in the 1500s and 1600s from earlier, similar instruments called the cross-staff and the backstaff. In 1730 John HADLEY invented an improved quadrant that led to the modern **sextant.**

rocket A rocket is a type of jet engine propelled by the force of exploding fuel. Some rockets, called launch vehicles, carry spacecraft into space. Launch vehicles are often well over 200 feet tall and sometimes have several stages that fire in sequence. Rockets can function in space because they carry with them the oxygen needed for combustion. Smaller rockets built into spacecraft allow pilots to steer the craft in space and return to earth.

The science of rocketry originated in China, where military uses for rockets propelled by gunpowder were developed in the 1200s. Rocketry spread to Europe, where it became a military science by the mid-1800s. In the early 1900s, a Russian schoolteacher named Konstantin Tsiolkovsky developed the idea of using rockets as space vehicles. He also proposed the use of liquid instead of solid fuel. The American physicist Robert Goddard launched the first liquid-fuel rocket in 1926. During World War II, German scientists developed a powerful military rocket called the A-4, which led directly to the first rockets used in the space programs of the United States and the **Soviet Union.**

satellite A satellite is any body that **orbits** a larger body, as the moon circles the earth. Modern space exploration began with the launching of artificial satellites. In 1957 the **Soviet Union** succeeded in launching a 184-pound radio transmitter named *Sputnik 1*, the first artificial earth satellite. Since that time, satellites have grown in size and complexity, and today hundreds orbit the earth for military, scientific, and other purposes. Satellites called probes have orbited or flown past other planets and moons in the solar system.

schooner A schooner is a sailing vessel with two or more masts, featuring triangular sails that ran along the length of the ship. These **lateen-rigged** ships were commonly used in the 1700s and 1800s. They were faster, easier to maneuver, and needed fewer crewmen than similar **square-rigged** ships of the day, such as the **brig.**

scurvy A disease once common at sea, scurvy is caused by a lack of vitamin C in a person's diet. Its symptoms include bleeding under the skin, around the bones, in the joints, and from the gums. Scurvy leaves its victims extremely weak. Tissue swells, wounds do not heal, teeth loosen, and bones become brittle. The condition can be fatal. Since sailors at sea might go without fresh food for weeks, scurvy could wipe out an entire crew. Sea voyages had to include frequent stops on land or be kept as short as possible.

In the late 1700s, Captain James COOK of the British navy began experimenting with and enforcing diets at sea that included sauerkraut and citrus fruits. As a result of his efforts, all British naval vessels started carrying supplies of lime juice in 1795, leading to the nickname *limey* for a British sailor. Scurvy can also be prevented with supplies of fresh meat, as explorers of the Arctic Ocean learned.

sextant A sextant is an instrument used by navigators to measure the altitude of the sun or stars. With that information, the user can consult a chart to determine **latitude.** The sextant's name comes from its main feature, a metal arc in the shape of one-sixth of a circle, marked with 60 degrees. This device is an improvement on the quadrant and began to replace it in the mid-1700s. Small telescopes and mirrors on the sextant help the user to measure the height of stars above the horizon more easily and precisely. In more modern forms, sextants are still in use today. Similar instruments called octants have arcs of 45 degrees, one-eighth of a circle.

shallop A shallop was a small open boat equipped with oars, sails, or both, intended for use in shallow water. The term was most commonly used in the 1600s and 1700s.

sledge A sledge is a vehicle mounted on parallel runners instead of wheels. Used mainly to transport supplies over snow or ice, a sledge can be pulled by teams of people, animals such as dogs or reindeer, or motorized vehicles such as snow tractors. The earliest sledges were made from logs that were tied together and dragged along the ground. Runners were added later to allow the sledge to slide more easily. Sledges have been a major means of transportation in the exploration of the polar regions.

sloop A sloop is a small, **lateen-rigged** vessel with one mast. Valued for their speed, agility, and light weight, sloops were employed for many purposes, and some were fitted with about 20 cannons for battle. Today sloops are mainly used for recreational sailing.

Soviet Union The Union of Soviet Socialist Republics (USSR), also called the Soviet Union, existed as a nation from 1922 until 1991. By 1940 it consisted of Russia and 14 neighboring republics: Armenia, Azerbaijan, Byelorussia, Estonia, Georgia, Kazakhstan, Kyrgyzstan, Latvia, Lithuania, Moldova, Tajikistan, Turkmenistan,

Ukraine, and Uzbekistan. Of these Russia was by far the largest and most populous. The USSR's capital was Moscow, in Russia.

The Soviet Union's origin lay in the Russian Revolution of 1917, in which the monarchy was overthrown by followers of a political and economic philosophy known as communism. In the new system of government, the state—rather than private citizens—owned or controlled all land, factories, and other industries.

In the years that followed the end of World War II in 1945, the Soviet Union was locked in a hostile relationship—called the Cold War—with the United States, which perceived communism as a threat. Although the two powers never actually went to war, they competed in other ways, including the "space race," a rivalry in space exploration lasting from the 1950s through the 1970s.

In 1991 the ruling Communist Party allowed open elections that resulted in the breakup of the Soviet Union. The republics became independent nations, although most retained close ties.

space shuttle   In the 1970s, the U.S. space agency, **NASA,** began to develop a reusable spacecraft called the Space Transportation System (STS), or space shuttle. NASA launched the first shuttle, *Columbia,* in 1981. Space shuttles quickly became the standard U.S. vehicle for taking **astronauts** into earth **orbit.** Their crews can conduct scientific research and launch **satellites** during missions that can last as long as two weeks. The shuttles are expected to play a major role in the construction of an international **space station.**

The STS consists of three parts: an external tank that contains fuel for the main engines and is used only once, during launch; two **rocket** boosters that assist the main rockets during liftoff and then drop to earth for recovery and reuse; and the orbiter, a winged, rocket-propelled craft that flies in space and then returns to earth by landing on a runway like a glider.

space station   A spacecraft intended to carry a human crew in **orbit** around the earth for an extended period is called a space station. Such craft have living quarters for the crew, as well as laboratory space for scientific experiments. They are typically occupied by a series of crews over time.

Between 1971 and 1982, the **Soviet Union** launched seven Salyut stations, and the United States carried out three missions to its *Skylab* station. The final Salyut station was last inhabited in 1986, although it remained aloft until 1991, when—like all stations before it—it fell back into the earth's atmosphere and burned up. In 1986 the Soviets launched the main parts of the *Mir* station and then added new sections until it grew to five times its original size. Crew members of *Mir* have included several American **astronauts.**

In the 1990s, the United States, Russia, and other nations agreed to build an international space station to serve as a base for research and as a platform for further exploration of the solar system.

space suit Because people cannot survive in the airless vacuum of space, **astronauts** and **cosmonauts** must wear protective gear called a space suit. Early space explorers wore space suits throughout their missions in case of a leak in their spacecraft. The suits were equipped with devices to regulate temperature and airflow and to allow the wearers to eat, drink, and eliminate body wastes.

More recently, crews aboard **space shuttles** or **space stations** have worn lightweight clothing most of the time. They put on space suits only during launches, dangerous maneuvers, or extravehicular activities (EVAs, also known as space walks).

Modern space suits are lighter and less awkward than the first models. A life-support system mounted on the back of the suit can keep a person alive for eight hours. It contains oxygen, rechargeable batteries, an air treatment system, and water for a cooling system. In the mid-1980s, **NASA** experimented with the manned maneuvering unit (MMU), a large device attached to the back of a space suit. The MMU contains small gas thrusters that allow the wearer to move independently through space. However, it has rarely been used.

Spanish Main This name was given to parts of the Spanish colonial empire in the Americas from the 1500s to the 1700s. The term first referred to the north coast of South America, from the mouth of the Orinoco River to what is now Panama. It later included the Caribbean coast of Central America and the Caribbean Sea itself. These waters were often sailed by Spanish treasure **galleons** and by the English, Dutch, and French **buccaneers** who preyed on them, so the Spanish Main had a reputation for piracy.

square-rigged Square-rigged ships have rectangular sails that hang from yards, which are long pieces of wood attached to a mast and running across the width of a ship. These kinds of sails are intended for sailing with the wind directly behind a ship. On the open sea, strong, constant winds propel square-rigged ships more quickly than **lateen-rigged** ships. In waters that are more difficult to navigate, however, square-rigged vessels are not as easy to maneuver. They require many crewmen to climb up the masts and out on the yards in order to adjust the sails. One type of square-rigged ship was the **brig;** the **brigantine** and the **galleon** used both square and lateen rigging.

trade winds The trade winds (also called trades) are winds that are nearly constant and blow in an easterly direction at **latitudes** between 30° North and 30° South. They blow toward the equator from the northeast in the Northern Hemisphere and from the southeast in the Southern Hemisphere. Eventually, they die out around the equator, in a region called the **doldrums.** Because these winds have fairly consistent direction and speed, sailors referred to them using the word *trade,* which meant a path or course. Trade winds carried Christopher COLUMBUS from Europe to the Caribbean Sea, and sailors of his time and after greatly depended on them for ocean crossings.

Treaty of Tordesillas This historic agreement, signed in 1494 by Spain and Portugal, was intended to settle disputes over the right to claim newly discovered lands. Sailing in the service of Spain, Christopher COLUMBUS had reached islands in the Caribbean Sea in 1492. Spain then asked Pope Alexander VI, who was Spanish, to grant Spain the right to all trade in the western Atlantic Ocean. In response, the pope created an imaginary north-south line 100 **leagues** to the west of the Azores, a group of islands about halfway between Europe and North America. Spain was given the right to control non-Christian lands to the west of the line. Portugal received the right to lands to the east of the line, including Africa, where Portuguese explorers had recently made significant progress.

However, Portugal's king, John II, demanded to deal directly with Spain. In 1494, ambassadors from each country met in the town of Tordesillas, in northwestern Spain. They agreed to move the north-south line to 370 leagues west of the Azores. The new line gave Portuguese navigators more room to sail around the bulge of West Africa on their way toward the southern tip of the continent. It also gave Portugal a chance to explore the Americas. In 1500 Pedro Álvares CABRAL landed in what is now eastern Brazil and established a legal Portuguese claim in the Americas.

viceroy A viceroy governs a country, province, or colony as the representative of a monarch. The title has been used in many parts of the world, but its most famous holders were the governors of the four viceroyalties of Spanish America—New Spain, Peru, New Granada, and Río de la Plata. Their responsibilities included collecting taxes, enforcing laws, and converting Indians to Christianity. The viceroys often came into conflict with Spanish monarchs, other colonial officials, and the colonial courts known as *audiencias*.

voyageur This term, the French word for traveler, was often used to refer to the expert woodsmen, boatmen, and guides who ranged across the North American wilderness in the 1700s and 1800s. Many voyageurs were employed by fur companies to transport beaver furs and supplies between remote stations in the United States and Canada.

westerlies Sometimes called the prevailing westerlies, these two belts of winds are located between the **latitudes** of 30° and 60° in both hemispheres. Between them lie the **trade winds.** The westerlies blow from west to east. More storms occur in the westerlies than in any of the other wind belts.

List of Explorers by Nationality

American

Akeley, Delia Denning

Akeley, Mary Lee Jobe

Armstrong, Neil Alden

Ashley, William Henry

Bartram, John

Bennett, Floyd

Bingham, Hiram

Bonneville, Benjamin Louis Eulalie de

Boone, Daniel

Boyd, Louise Arner

Bridger, James

Byrd, Richard Evelyn

Carson, Christopher

Chaillé-Long, Charles

Clark, William

Colter, John

Cook, Frederick Albert

De Long, George Washington

Ellsworth, Lincoln

Frémont, John Charles

Glenn, John Herschel, Jr.

Gray, Robert

Hall, Charles Francis

Henson, Matthew Alexander

Hunt, Wilson Price

Kane, Elisha Kent

King, Clarence

Lewis, Meriwether

Long, Stephen Harriman

Lucid, Shannon Wells

MacMillan, Donald Baxter

Maury, Matthew Fontaine

Peary, Robert Edwin

Pike, Zebulon Montgomery

Pond, Peter

Powell, John Wesley

Ride, Sally Kristen

Roosevelt, Theodore

Sheldon, May French

Shepard, Alan Bartlett, Jr.

Smith, Jedediah Strong

Walker, Joseph Reddeford

Wheeler, George Montague

Wilkes, Charles

Wyeth, Nathaniel Jarvis

Anglo-Irish

McClintock, Francis Leopold

McClure, Robert John Le Mesurier

Shackleton, Ernest Henry

Arab

Ibn Battuta

Ibn Hawqal

Idrisi, al-

Leo Africanus

Mas'udi, al-

Australian

Giles, Ernest

Hume, Hamilton

Mawson, Douglas

Wentworth, William Charles

Wilkins, George Hubert

Wills, William John

Austrian

Payer, Julius von

Belgian

Hennepin, Louis

Brazilian

Rondón, Cândido Mariano da Silva

Canadian

Fraser, Simon

Hind, Henry Youle

Ogden, Peter Skene

Canadian-American

Stefansson, Vilhjalmur

Carthaginian

Hanno

Chinese

Faxian

Xu Hongzu

Xuan Zang

Yi Jing

Zhang Qian

Zheng He

Danish

Bering, Vitus Jonassen

Rasmussen, Knud Johan Victor

Dutch

Barents, Willem

Hartog, Dirck

Jansz, Willem

Linschoten, Jan Huyghen van

Roggeveen, Jacob

Schouten, Willem Corneliszoon

Tasman, Abel Janszoon

Tinné, Alexine

English

Anson, George

Back, George

Baffin, William

Baker, Samuel White

Banks, Joseph

Barrow, John

Bates, Henry Walter

Bell, Gertrude Margaret Lowthian

Bishop, Isabella Bird

Blaxland, Gregory

Bligh, William

Burton, Richard Francis

Bylot, Robert

Byron, John

Cameron, Verney Lovett

Carteret, Philip

Cavendish, Thomas

Chancellor, Richard

Cook, James

Dampier, William Cecil

Darwin, Charles Robert

Davis, John

Doughty, Charles Montagu

Drake, Francis

Everest, George

Eyre, Edward John

Fitzroy, Robert

Flinders, Matthew

Foxe, Luke

Franklin, John

Frobisher, Martin

Fuchs, Vivian Ernest

Gilbert, Humphrey

Hadley, John

Hakluyt, Richard

Hargraves, Edward Hammond

Harrison, John

Hearne, Samuel

Herbert, Walter William

Hudson, Henry

Kelsey, Henry

Kingsley, Mary Henrietta

Lander, Richard Lemon

Parry, William Edward

Purchas, Samuel

Raleigh, Walter

Ross, James Clark

Schomburgk, Robert Hermann

Scoresby, William

Scott, Robert Falcon

Smith, John

Smith, William

Speke, John Hanning

Stark, Freya

Sturt, Charles

Thesiger, Wilfred Patrick

Thompson, David

Vancouver, George

Wallace, Alfred Russel

Wallis, Samuel

Whymper, Edward

Younghusband, Francis Edward

French

Audubon, John James

Baudin, Nicolas

Bethencourt, Jean de

Bougainville, Louis-Antoine de

Brulé, Etienne

Caillié, René-Auguste

Cartier, Jacques

Champlain, Samuel de

Charlevoix, Pierre François Xavier de

Cousteau, Jacques-Yves

David-Neel, Alexandra

Dulhut, Daniel Greysolon

Dumont d'Urville, Jules-Sébastien-César

Duveyrier, Henri

Entrecasteaux, Antoine Raymond Joseph de Bruni d'

Foucauld, Charles-Eugène de

Garnier, Francis

Groseilliers, Médard Chouart des

La Condamine, Charles-Marie de

La Pérouse, Jean François de Galaup de

La Salle, René Robert Cavelier de

Marchand, Jean-Baptiste

Marcos de Niza

Marquette, Jacques

Nicollet de Belleborne, Jean

Pavie, Auguste-Jean-Marie

Radisson, Pierre Esprit

William of Rubruck

French-American

Du Chaillu, Paul Belloni

French-Canadian

Drouillard, George

Iberville, Pierre Le Moyne d'

Jolliet, Louis

La Vérendrye, Pierre Gaultier de Varennes de

German

Barth, Heinrich

Drygalski, Erich Dagobert von

Federmann, Nikolaus

Forster, Johann Georg Adam

Forster, Johann Reinhold

Hornemann, Friedrich Konrad

Humboldt, Alexander von

Leichhardt, Friedrich Wilhelm Ludwig

Messerschmidt, Daniel Gottlieb

Nachtigal, Gustav

Richthofen, Ferdinand Paul Wilhelm von

Rohlfs, Friedrich Gerhard

Schiltberger, Johann

Schnitzer, Eduard

Schweinfurth, Georg August

Wegener, Alfred Lothar

Greek

Alexander the Great (Macedonian)

Eratosthenes

Herodotus of Halicarnassus

Hipparchus

Nearchus

Ptolemy

Pytheas

Xenophon

Hungarian

Stein, Mark Aurel

Indian

Kintup

Singh, Kishen

Singh, Nain

Irish

Brendan

Burke, Robert O'Hara

Houghton, Daniel

Palliser, John

Italian

Cabot, John

Cabot, Sebastian

Cadamosto, Alvise da

Carpini, Giovanni de Plano

Columbus, Christopher

Conti, Nicolò de

Kino, Eusebio Francisco

Malaspina, Alejandro

Nobile, Umberto

Odoric of Pordenone

Pigafetta, Antonio Francesco

Polo, Marco

Ricci, Matteo

Varthema, Ludovico di

Verrazano, Giovanni da

Vespucci, Amerigo

Zeno, Antonio

Italian-French

Brazza, Pierre-Paul-François-Camille Savorgnan de

Mesopotamian

Ibn Fadlan, Ahmad

New Zealander

Hillary, Edmund Percival

Norse

Erikson, Leif

Erik the Red

Herjolfsson, Bjarni

Karlsefni, Thorfinn

Norwegian

Amundsen, Roald Engelbregt Gravning

Borchgrevink, Carstens Egeberg

Heyerdahl, Thor

Nansen, Fridtjof

Sverdrup, Otto Neumann

Norwegian-Canadian

Larsen, Henry Asbjorn

Portuguese

Albuquerque, Afonso de

Alvares, Francisco

Barbosa, Duarte

Cabral, Pedro Álvares

Cabrillo, Juan Rodriguez

Cão, Diogo

Covilhã, Pêro da

Dias, Bartolomeu

Eannes, Gil

Gama, Vasco da

Goes, Bento de

Lobo, Jerome

Lopes de Sequeira, Diogo

Magellan, Ferdinand

Quirós, Pedro Fernandez de

Rapôso de Tavares, Antonio

Sintra, Pedro de

Teixeira, Pedro de

Torres, Luis Vaez de

Tristão, Nuño

Zarco, João Gonçalves

Russian

Bellingshausen, Fabian Gottlieb von

Chirikov, Aleksei

Dezhnev, Semyon Ivanov

Gagarin, Yuri Alekseyevich

Khabarov, Yerofei Pavlovich

Kotzebue, Otto von

Krusenstern, Adam Ivan von

Leonov, Aleksei Arkhipovich

Lütke, Fyodor Petrovich

Przhevalski, Nikolai Mikhaylovich

Tereshkova, Valentina Vladimirovna

Yermak, Timofeyevich

Scottish

Bruce, James

Campbell, Robert

Clapperton, Hugh

Dalrymple, Alexander

Laing, Alexander Gordon

Livingstone, David

Mackenzie, Alexander

McKenzie, Donald

Park, Mungo

Rae, John

Simpson, Thomas
Stuart, John McDouall
Thomson, Joseph

Scottish-American

Stuart, Robert

Spanish

Acuña, Cristóbal de
Almagro, Diego de
Alvarado, Pedro de
Alvarez de Pineda, Alonso
Anza, Juan Bautista de
Balboa, Vasco Nuñez de
Bastidas, Rodrigo de
Benalcázar, Sebastián de
Benjamin of Tudela
Bodega y Quadra, Juan Francisco de la
Cabeza de Vaca, Álvar Núñez
Coronado, Francisco Vásquez de
Cortés, Hernán
Elcano, Juan Sebastián de
Escalante, Silvestre Vélez de
Garcés, Francisco Tomas Hermenegildo
Hezeta, Bruno de
Irala, Domingo Martínez de
Jiménez de Quesada, Gonzalo
La Cosa, Juan de
Las Casas, Bartolomé de
Legazpi, Miguel López de
Martínez, Estéban José
Mendaña de Nehra, Alvaro de

Narváez, Pánfilo de
Ojeda, Alonso de
Oñate, Juan de
Orellana, Francisco de
Pérez Hernández, Juan Josef
Pinzón, Martín Alonso
Pinzón, Vicente Yáñez
Pizarro, Francisco
Ponce de León, Juan
Rivera, Juan Maria de
Serra, Junípero
Soto, Hernando de
Urdaneta, Andrés de
Vial, Pedro
Viscaíno, Sebastián
Xavier, Francis

Swedish

Andrée, Salomon August
Hedin, Sven Anders

Swedish-Finnish

Nordenskiöld, Nils Adolf Erik

Swiss

Burckhardt, Johann Ludwig

Welsh

Button, Thomas

Welsh-American

Stanley, Henry Morton

List of Explorers by Area of Exploration

Under the broad geographic headings below, explorers are listed alphabetically. The specific areas visited by an explorer are listed after his or her name. This list uses present-day place names. Question marks indicate cases where doubt exists as to the area explored.

Africa South of the Sahara

Akeley, Delia Denning: *Kenya; Zaire*

Akeley, Mary Lee Jobe: *central Africa*

Alvares, Francisco: *Ethiopia*

Baker, Samuel White: *White Nile River; Sudan*

Barth, Heinrich: *central Africa; West Africa*

Brazza, Pierre-Paul-François-Camille Savorgnan de: *central Africa*

Bruce, James: *Blue Nile River*

Burckhardt, Johann Ludwig: *East Africa*

Burton, Richard Francis: *central Africa; West Africa*

Cadamosto, Alvise da: *west coast*

Caillié, René-Auguste: *central Africa; Timbuktu*

Cameron, Verney Lovett: *central Africa*

Cão, Diogo: *west coast*

Chaillé-Long, Charles: *central Africa; East Africa*

Clapperton, Hugh: *Lake Chad; Niger River; West Africa*

Covilhã, Pêro da: *Ethiopia*

Dias, Bartolomeu: *Cape of Good Hope; west coast*

Du Chaillu, Paul Belloni: *central Africa*

Hanno: *West Africa*

Herodotus of Halicarnassus: *Nile River*

Houghton, Daniel: *Niger River*

Ibn Battuta: *East Africa; Timbuktu*

Ibn Hawqal: *Sudan*

Kingsley, Mary Henrietta: *central Africa; West Africa*

Laing, Alexander Gordon: *Timbuktu*

Lander, Richard Lemon: *Niger River; West Africa*

Leo Africanus: *West Africa*

Livingstone, David: *central Africa; southern Africa*

Lobo, Jerome: *East Africa*

Marchand, Jean-Baptiste: *Ivory Coast; Niger River; Sudan*

Mas'udi, al-: *East Africa*

Nachtigal, Gustav: *North Africa*

Park, Mungo: *Niger River*

Schnitzer, Eduard: *East Africa*

Schweinfurth, Georg August: *central Africa; East Africa*

Sheldon, May French: *East Africa*

Sintra, Pedro de: *coast of West Africa*

Speke, John Hanning: *central Africa; Lake Victoria*

Stanley, Henry Morton: *central Africa*

Thomson, Joseph: *central Africa*

Tinné, Alexine: *central Africa; Nile River*

Zheng He: *East Africa*

Antarctica

Amundsen, Roald Engelbregt Gravning: *South Pole*

Bellingshausen, Fabian Gottlieb von: *Queen Maud Land*

Borchgrevink, Carstens Egeberg: *Cape Adare; Ross Ice Shelf*

Byrd, Richard Evelyn: *South Pole*

Drygalski, Erich Dagobert von: *Gaussberg Range*

Dumont d'Urville, Jules-Sébastien-César: *Adélie Coast*

Ellsworth, Lincoln: *Ellsworth Land, Marie Byrd Land*

Fuchs, Vivian Ernest: *South Pole*

Hillary, Edmund Percival: *South Pole*

Mawson, Douglas: *Wilkes Land; Mac Robertson Land*

Ross, James Clark: *Ross Sea; Victoria Land*

Scott, Robert Falcon: *South Pole*

Shackleton, Ernest Henry: *Queen Maud Mountains; Ross Sea*

Smith, William: *Graham Land; South Shetland Islands*

Wilkes, Charles: *Graham Land; Wilkes Land*

Wilkins, George Hubert: *Graham Land*

Arctic Ocean

Amundsen, Roald Engelbregt Gravning: *Northwest Passage*

Andrée, Salomon August: *Svalbard*

Back, George: *Canadian Arctic*

Baffin, William: *Greenland; Baffin Bay; Northwest Passage*

Barents, Willem: *Northeast Passage; Norwegian Arctic*

Bennett, Floyd: *North Pole*

Bering, Vitus Jonassen: *Bering Strait; Alaska*

Boyd, Louise Arner: *Greenland*

Button, Thomas: *Northwest Passage*

Bylot, Robert: *Baffin Bay; Northwest Passage*

Byrd, Richard Evelyn: *North Pole*

Cabot, Sebastian: *Northwest Passage*

Chancellor, Richard: *Northeast Passage*

Chirikov, Aleksei: *Alaska; Siberia*

Cook, Frederick Albert: *Greenland; North Pole?*

Cook, James: *Bering Strait; Northwest Passage*

Davis, John: *Baffin Island; Greenland; Northwest Passage*

De Long, George Washington: *Alaskan Arctic; Russian Arctic*

Dezhnev, Semyon Ivanov: *Bering Strait; Siberia*

Drygalski, Erich Dagobert von: *Greenland*

Ellsworth, Lincoln: *North Pole*

Erik the Red: *Greenland*

Foxe, Luke: *Northwest Passage*

Franklin, John: *Northwest Passage*

Frobisher, Martin: *Greenland; Northwest Passage*

Hall, Charles Francis: *King William Island; Greenland*

Henson, Matthew Alexander: *Greenland; North Pole*

Herbert, Walter William: *North Pole*

Hudson, Henry: *Northeast Passage; Northwest Passage*

Kane, Elisha Kent: *Canadian Arctic*

Larsen, Henry Asbjorn: *Northwest Passage*

Linschoten, Jan Huyghen van: *Northeast Passage*

Lütke, Fyodor Petrovich: *Bering Sea*

MacMillan, Donald Baxter: *Baffin Island; Ellesmere Island*

McClintock, Francis Leopold: *Canadian Arctic*

McClure, Robert John Le Mesurier: *Northwest Passage*

Nansen, Fridtjof: *Greenland; Russian Arctic*

Nobile, Umberto: *North Pole*

Nordenskiöld, Nils Adolf Erik: *Greenland; Northeast Passage*

Parry, William Edward: *Northwest Passage; Norwegian Arctic*

Payer, Julius von: *Franz Josef Land*

Peary, Robert Edwin: *Greenland; North Pole*

Pytheas: *British Isles?; Scandinavia?*

Rae, John: *Canadian Arctic*

Rasmussen, Knud Johan Victor: *Canadian Arctic; Greenland*

Ross, James Clark: *Canadian Arctic; Northwest Passage*

Scoresby, William: *Greenland; Norwegian Arctic*

Simpson, Thomas: *Canadian Arctic; Northwest Passage*

Stefansson, Vilhjalmur: *Canadian Arctic*

Sverdrup, Otto Neumann: *Canadian Arctic; Greenland*

Wegener, Alfred Lothar: *Greenland*

Wilkins, George Hubert: *Canadian Arctic Ocean*

Asia

Albuquerque, Afonso de: *India; Malay Peninsula*

Alexander the Great: *central Asia; India; Turkey*

Barbosa, Duarte: *India; Philippine Islands; Sumatra*

Bering, Vitus Jonassen: *Siberia; Kamchatka*

Carpini, Giovanni de Plano: *central Asia*

Conti, Nicolò de: *southern Asia*

Covilhã, Pêro da: *India*

David-Neel, Alexandra: *Tibet; western China*

Drake, Francis: *Indonesia*

Elcano, Juan Sebastián de: *Indonesia, Moluccas*

Everest, George: *India*

Faxian: *central Asia; India*

Gama, Vasco da: *India*

Garnier, Francis: *Southeast Asia*

Goes, Bento de: *India; central Asia*

Hedin, Sven Anders: *central Asia*

Ibn Battuta: *China; India; Turkey*

Ibn Fadlan, Ahmad: *southern Russia; central Asia*

Ibn Hawqal: *central Asia*

Khabarov, Yerofei Pavlovich: *Siberia*

Kintup: *Tibet*

Krusenstern, Adam Ivan von: *China; Japan*

La Pérouse, Jean François de Galaup de: *China; Japan*

Linschoten, Jan Huyghen van: *India*

Lopes de Sequeira, Diogo: *Malay Archipelago*

Mas'udi, al-: *central Asia*

Messerschmidt, Daniel Gottlieb: *Siberia*

Nearchus: *India*

Odoric of Pordenone: *central Asia; China; Tibet*

Pavie, Auguste-Jean-Marie: *Laos*

Polo, Marco: *central Asia; China; southern Asia*

Przhevalski, Nikolai Mikhaylovich: *central Asia*

Ricci, Matteo: *China*

Richthofen, Ferdinand Paul Wilhelm von: *China*

Schiltberger, Johann: *Turkey; central Asia; Siberia*

Singh, Kishen: *Tibet*

Singh, Nain: *Tibet*

Stein, Mark Aurel: *central Asia*

Varthema, Ludovico di: *India; Southeast Asia*

Wallace, Alfred Russel: *Malay Archipelago*

William of Rubruck: *Central Asia*

Xavier, Francis: *India; Japan; Malay Archipelago*

Xenophon: *western Asia*

Xu Hongzu: *China*

Xuan Zang: *central Asia; India*

Yermak, Timofeyevich: *Siberia*

Yi Jing: *India; Southeast Asia*

Younghusband, Francis Edward: *India; Tibet*

Zhang Qian: *central Asia*

Zheng He: *southern Asia*

Australia

Banks, Joseph: *Botany Bay; New Guinea; New Zealand*

Baudin, Nicolas: *southern coast*

Blaxland, Gregory: *Blue Mountains*

Bligh, William: *northeast coast*

Burke, Robert O'Hara: *eastern interior*

Cook, James: *Botany Bay; New Guinea; New Zealand*

Dampier, William Cecil: *northwest coast; New Zealand*

Entrecasteaux, Antoine Raymond Joseph de Bruni d': *south coast; Tasmania*

Eyre, Edward John: *South Australia*

Flinders, Matthew: *Gulf of Carpentaria; South Australia; Tasmania*

Giles, Ernest: *interior*

Hargraves, Edward Hammond: *New South Wales*

Hartog, Dirck: *west coast*

Hume, Hamilton: *New South Wales; Victoria*

Jansz, Willem: *north and west coasts*

Leichhardt, Friedrich Wilhelm Ludwig: *Queensland*

Stuart, John McDouall: *South Australia; Northern Territory*

Sturt, Charles: *New South Wales; Simpson Desert*

Tasman, Abel Janszoon: *north coast; Tasmania; New Zealand*

Torres, Luis Vaez de: *Torres Strait*

Wentworth, William Charles: *Blue Mountains*

Wills, William John: *eastern interior*

Central America, Mexico, and the Caribbean

Alvarado, Pedro de: *El Salvador; Guatemala; Mexico*

Alvarez de Pineda, Alonso: *Gulf of Mexico*

Balboa, Vasco Nuñez de: *Panama*

Bastidas, Rodrigo de: *Panama*

Brendan: *Caribbean islands?*

Cabeza de Vaca, Álvar Núñez: *northern Mexico*

Cabrillo, Juan Rodriguez: *Central America; Mexico*

Columbus, Christopher: *Caribbean islands; coast of Central America*

Cortés, Hernán: *Mexico*

Dampier, William Cecil: *Central America*

Humboldt, Alexander von: *Mexico*

La Cosa, Juan de: *Panama*

Las Casas, Bartolomé de: *Mexico*

Narváez, Pánfilo de: *Cuba; Mexico*

Pinzón, Martín Alonzo: *Caribbean islands*

Pinzón, Vicente Yáñez: *Honduras; Yucatán*

Ponce de León, Juan: *Puerto Rico*

Middle East

Albuquerque, Afonso de: *Persian Gulf*

Alexander the Great: *Iran; Iraq; Lebanon; Syria*

Bell, Gertrude Margaret Lowthian: *Saudi Arabia; Iran; Syria*

Benjamin of Tudela: *Iraq; Israel; Syria*

Burckhardt, Johann Ludwig: *Arabian Peninsula*

Burton, Richard Francis: *Arabian Peninsula*

Covilhã, Pêro da: *Arabian Peninsula*

Doughty, Charles Montagu: *Arabian Peninsula*

Herodotus of Halicarnassus: *Iran*

Ibn Battuta: *Arabian Peninsula*

Mas'udi, al-: *Iran; Iraq; Israel; Syria; Yemen*

Nearchus: *Arabian Peninsula*

Schiltberger, Johann: *Saudi Arabia*

Stark, Freya: *Arabia; Iran; Iraq; Syria*

Thesiger, Wilfred Patrick: *Saudi Arabia*

Varthema, Ludovico di: *Saudi Arabia; Syria*

Zheng He: *Arabian Peninsula; Persian Gulf*

North Africa

Alexander the Great: *Egypt*

Barth, Heinrich: *Libya*

Benjamin of Tudela: *Egypt; Sahara*

Bethencourt, Jean de: *Canary Islands*

Caillié, René-Auguste: *Sahara*

Chaillé-Long, Charles: *Egypt*

Duveyrier, Henri: *Sahara*

Eannes, Gil: *west coast*

Foucauld, Charles-Eugène de: *Algeria; Morocco*

Hanno: *Morocco; Western Sahara*

Herodotus of Halicarnassus: *Egypt; Libya*

Hornemann, Friedrich Konrad: *Libya; Sahara*

Ibn Battuta: *Egypt; Sahara*

Ibn Hawqal: *Mediterranean; Morocco; Sahara*

Idrisi, al-: *Algeria; Morocco*

Laing, Alexander Gordon: *Sahara*

Mas'udi, al-: *Egypt*

Nachtigal, Gustav: *Libya*

Rohlfs, Friedrich Gerhard: *Libya; Morocco; Sahara*

Schiltberger, Johann: *Egypt*

Tinné, Alexine: *Sahara*

Tristão, Nuño: *northwest coast*

Zarco, João Gonçalves: *Madeira; northwest coast*

North America

Akeley, Mary Lee Jobe: *northwestern Canada*

Anza, Juan Bautista de: *California; southwestern U.S.*

Ashley, William Henry: *western U.S.*

Audubon, John James: *Florida; Labrador; Texas; Missouri River*

Bartram, John: *eastern U.S.*

Bodega y Quadra, Juan Francisco de la: *northwest coast*

Bonneville, Benjamin Louis Eulalie de: *Rocky Mountains*

Boone, Daniel: *Kentucky*

Bridger, James: *western U.S.*

Brulé, Etienne: *Chesapeake Bay; Great Lakes*

Button, Thomas: *Hudson Bay*

Bylot, Robert: *Hudson Bay*

Cabeza de Vaca, Álvar Núñez: *southeastern U.S.*

Cabot, John: *coast of Newfoundland*

Cabot, Sebastian: *Hudson Bay*

Cabrillo, Juan Rodriguez: *coast of California*

Campbell, Robert: *Yukon*

Carson, Christopher: *western U.S.*

Cartier, Jacques: *Gulf of St. Lawrence; St. Lawrence River*

Champlain, Samuel de: *New England; Great Lakes*

Charlevoix, Pierre François Xavier de: *Great Lakes; Mississippi River*

Clark, William: *Missouri River; northwestern U.S.*

Colter, John: *Idaho; Montana; Wyoming*

Cook, James: *northwest coast*

Coronado, Francisco Vásquez de: *southwestern U.S.*

Drake, Francis: *west coast*

Drouillard, George: *Rocky Mountains*

Dulhut, Daniel Greysolon: *Great Lakes*

Erikson, Leif: *northeast coast*

Escalante, Silvestre Vélez de: *southwestern U.S.*

Foxe, Luke: *Hudson Bay*

Fraser, Simon: *western Canada*

Frémont, John Charles: *western U.S.*

Garcés, Francisco Tomas Hermenegildo: *southwestern U.S.*

Gilbert, Humphrey: *Newfoundland*

Gray, Robert: *Columbia River; northwest coast*

Groseilliers, Médard Chouart des: *Hudson Bay; Great Lakes*

Hearne, Samuel: *northwestern Canada*

Hennepin, Louis: *Niagara Falls; Minnesota*

Herjolfsson, Bjarni: *northeast coast*

Hezeta, Bruno de: *northwest coast*

Hind, Henry Youle: *Labrador; Manitoba; Saskatchewan*

Hudson, Henry: *east coast; Hudson Bay; Hudson River*

Hunt, Wilson Price: *western U.S.*

Iberville, Pierre Le Moyne d': *Hudson Bay; Mississippi River*

Jolliet, Louis: *Mississippi River*

Karlsefni, Thorfinn: *northeast coast*

Kelsey, Henry: *Saskatchewan*

King, Clarence: *western U.S.*

Kino, Eusebio Francisco: *California; southwestern U.S.*

Kotzebue, Otto von: *west coast*

La Salle, René Robert Cavelier de: *Great Lakes; Mississippi River*

La Vérendrye, Pierre Gaultier de Varennes de: *central Canada; north central U.S.*

Lewis, Meriwether: *Missouri River; northwestern U.S.*

Long, Stephen Harriman: *western U.S.*

Mackenzie, Alexander: *western Canada*

Malaspina, Alejandro: *west coast of U.S.*

Marcos de Niza: *Arizona; New Mexico*

Marquette, Jacques: *Mississippi River*

Martínez, Estéban José: *northwest coast*

McKenzie, Donald: *Idaho*

Narváez, Pánfilo de: *Florida*

Nicollet de Belleborne, Jean: *Great Lakes*

Ogden, Peter Skene: *western U.S.*

Oñate, Juan de: *southwestern U.S.*

Palliser, John: *western Canada*

Pérez Hernández, Juan Josef: *northwest coast*

Pike, Zebulon Montgomery: *southwestern U.S.*

Ponce de León, Juan: *Florida*

Pond, Peter: *central Canada*

Powell, John Wesley: *Colorado River; Grand Canyon*

Radisson, Pierre Esprit: *Hudson Bay*

Raleigh, Walter: *North Carolina*

Rivera, Juan Maria de: *southwestern U.S.*

Serra, Junípero: *California*

Smith, Jedediah Strong: *western U.S.*

Smith, John: *New England; Virginia*

Soto, Hernando de: *southeastern U.S.*

Stuart, Robert: *western U.S.*

Thompson, David: *Columbia River; southwestern Canada*

Vancouver, George: *northwest coast*

Verrazano, Giovanni da: *east coast*

Vial, Pedro: *southwestern U.S.*

Vizcaíno, Sebastián: *coast of California*

Walker, Joseph Reddeford: *California; Nevada; Utah*

Wheeler, George Montague: *western U.S.*

Whymper, Edward: *Rocky Mountains*

Wyeth, Nathaniel Jarvis: *northwestern U.S.*

Zeno, Antonio: *northeast coast?*

Pacific Islands

Banks, Joseph: *French Polynesia*

Bligh, William: *Tahiti*

Bougainville, Louis-Antoine de: *French Polynesia; Samoa; Vanuatu*

Byron, John: *French Polynesia; Kiribati*

Carteret, Philip: *Pitcairn; Solomon Islands; Bismarck Archipelago*

Cook, James: *French Polynesia; Tonga; Vanuatu; New Caledonia; Cook Islands; Hawaii*

Dampier, William Cecil: *New Britain Island*

Drake, Francis: *Philippines*

Dumont d'Urville, Jules-Sébastien-César: *Melanesia*

Forster, Johann Georg Adam: *New Caledonia; French Polynesia*

Forster, Johann Reinhold: *New Caledonia; French Polynesia*

Kotzebue, Otto von: *French Polynesia; Kiribati*

Krusenstern, Adam Ivan von: *Marquesas*

La Pérouse, Jean François de Galaup de: *Tonga; New Caledonia; Solomon Islands*

Legazpi, Miguel López de: *Philippines*

Lütke, Fyodor Petrovich: *Caroline Islands*

Magellan, Ferdinand: *Guam; Philippines; Tuamotus?; Marianas?*

Malaspina, Alejandro: *Philippines; Tonga*

Mendaña de Nehra, Alvaro de: *Marquesas; Santa Cruz Islands; Solomon Islands*

Pigafetta, Antonio Francesco: *Guam; Philippines*

Quirós, Pedro Fernandez de: *Vanuatu*

Roggeveen, Jacob: *Easter Island*

Schouten, Willem Corneliszoon: *Tuamotus; Fiji; Samoa; Futuna*

Tasman, Abel Janszoon: *Tonga, Fiji, Melanesia*

Urdaneta, Andrés de: *Philippines*

Wallis, Samuel: *French Polynesia; Tonga; Wallis Islands*

Wilkes, Charles: *Fiji; Hawaii*

South America

Acuña, Cristóbal de: *Amazon River*

Almagro, Diego de: *Chile; Peru*

Alvarado, Pedro de: *Ecuador*

Banks, Joseph: *Tierra del Fuego*

Bastidas, Rodrigo de: *Colombia*

Bates, Henry Walter: *Amazon River basin*

Benalcázar, Sebastián de: *Colombia; Ecuador; Peru*

Bingham, Hiram: *Peru*

Bougainville, Louis-Antoine de: *Falkland Islands*

Byron, John: *Falkland Islands; Patagonia*

Cabeza de Vaca, Álvar Núñez: *Brazil; Paraguay*

Cabot, Sebastian: *Río de la Plata*

Cabral, Pedro Álvares: *Brazil*

Cavendish, Thomas: *Patagonia*

Columbus, Christopher: *coast of Venezuela*

Darwin, Charles Robert: *Argentina; Chile; Galápagos Islands*

Federmann, Nikolaus: *Colombia; Venezuela*

Fitzroy, Robert: *Argentina; Chile; Galápagos Islands*

Humboldt, Alexander von: *Colombia; Ecuador; Peru; Venezuela*

Irala, Domingo Martínez de: *Paraguay; Argentina; Bolivia; Brazil; Chile; Uruguay*

Jiménez de Quesada, Gonzalo: *Colombia*

La Condamine, Charles-Marie de: *Amazon River; Ecuador*

La Cosa, Juan de: *Colombia; Venezuela*

Las Casas, Bartolomé de: *Peru*

Magellan, Ferdinand: *southeast coast; Patagonia*

Malaspina, Alejandro: *east and west coasts*

Ojeda, Alonso de: *Colombia; Venezuela*

Orellana, Francisco de: *Amazon River*

Pinzón, Vicente Yáñez: *Brazil*

Pizarro, Francisco: *Ecuador; Peru*

Raleigh, Walter: *Orinoco River*

Rapôso de Tavares, Antonio: *Argentina; Bolivia; Brazil; Paraguay; Peru; Uruguay*

Rondón, Cândido Mariano da Silva: *Brazil*

Roosevelt, Theodore: *Rio Roosevelt*

Schomburgk, Robert Hermann: *Guyana*

Schouten, Willem Corneliszoon: *Le Maire Strait*

Teixeira, Pedro de: *Amazon River*

Vespucci, Amerigo: *east and north coasts*

Wallace, Alfred Russel: *Amazon River basin*

Whymper, Edward: *Andes*

Space

Armstrong, Neil Alden: *first on moon*

Gagarin, Yuri Alekseyevich: *first in orbit*

Glenn, John Herschel, Jr.: *first American in orbit*

Leonov, Aleksei Arkhipovich: *first space walk*

Lucid, Shannon Wells: *set records for time in space*

Ride, Sally Kristen: *first American woman in space*

Shepard, Alan Bartlett, Jr.: *first American in space*

Tereshkova, Valentina Vladimirovna: *first woman in space*

Bibliography

The Bibliography is divided into two main sections: General Works and Works by Region of Exploration. Entries marked with an asterisk (*) are written especially for a Young Adult audience. However, many of the other sources listed here are also suitable for students.

General Works

Albion, Robert J., editor. *Exploration and Discovery.* New York: Macmillan, 1965.

Armstrong, Richard. *The History of Seafaring.* Volume 2, *The Discoverers.* New York: Frederick A. Praeger, 1969.

Baker, J. N. L. *A History of Geographical Discovery and Exploration.* Revised edition. New York: Cooper Square, 1967.

Bettex, Albert. *The Discovery of the World.* New York: Simon and Schuster, 1960.

Bohlander, Richard E., editor. *World Explorers and Discoverers.* 1992. Reprint, New York: Da Capo Press, 1998.

Boorstin, Daniel J. *The Discoverers.* New York: Random House, 1983.

Boxer, Charles R. *The Dutch Seaborne Empire, 1600–1800.* New York: Alfred A. Knopf, 1965.

——. *The Portuguese Seaborne Empire, 1415–1825.* London: Hutchinson, 1969.

Brendon, John Adams. *Great Navigators and Discoverers.* 1929. Reprint, Salem, N.H.: Ayer, 1977.

Burrage, Henry S., editor. *Early English and French Voyages Chiefly from Hakluyt 1534–1608.* New York: Barnes and Noble, 1959.

Cameron, Ian. *Lodestone and Evening Star: The Epic Voyages of Discovery, 1493 B.C.–1896 A.D.* New York: E. P. Dutton, 1965.

——. *To the Farthest Ends of the Earth: 150 Years of World Exploration by the Royal Geographical Society.* New York: E. P. Dutton, 1980.

Cary, M., and E. H. Warmington. *The Ancient Explorers.* London: Methuen, 1929.

*Cavendish, Richard, et al. *Journeys of the Great Explorers.* New York: Facts on File, 1992.

Clark, William Ronald. *Explorers of the World.* Garden City, N.Y.: Natural History Press, 1964.

Connell, Evan S. *A Long Desire.* New York: Holt, Rinehart and Winston, 1979.

Crone, G. R. *The Explorers: Great Adventurers Tell Their Own Stories of Discovery.* New York: Thomas Y. Crowell, 1962.

David, Richard, compiler. *Hakluyt's Voyages.* London: Chatto and Windus, 1981.

Debenham, Frank. *Discovery and Exploration: An Atlas-History of Man's Journeys into the Unknown.* New York: Crescent Books, 1960.

Delpar, Helen, editor. *The Discoverers: An Encyclopedia of Explorers and Exploration.* New York: McGraw-Hill, 1980.

Divine, David. *The Opening of the World: The Great Age of Maritime Exploration.* New York: G. P. Putnam's Sons, 1973.

Dos Passos, John. *The Portugal Story: Three Centuries of Exploration and Discovery.* Garden City, N.Y.: Doubleday, 1969.

Downs, Robert B. *In Search of New Horizons: Epic Tales of Travel and Exploration.* Chicago: American Library Association, 1978.

Editors of Time-Life Books. *Voyages of Discovery: Time Frame A.D. 1400–1500.* Alexandria, Va.: Time-Life Books, 1989.

Finger, Charles. *Valiant Vagabonds.* 1936. Reprint, Salem, N.H.: Ayer, 1977.

Fleischer, Suri, and Arleen Keylin. *Exploration and Discovery: As Reported by the New York Times.* Salem, N.H.: Ayer, 1976.

Gaines, Ann. *Herodotus and the Explorers of the Classical Age.* New York: Chelsea House, 1994.

Gersi, Douchan. *Explorer.* Los Angeles: Jeremy P. Tarcher, 1987.

The Glorious Age of Exploration. Garden City, N.Y.: Doubleday, 1973.

Grolier Student Library of Explorers and Exploration. Danbury, Conn.: Grolier Educational, 1998.

*Grosseck, Joyce C. *Great Explorers.* Grand Rapids, Mich.: Gateway Press, 1988.

Grosvenor, Melville Bell, editor. *Great Adventures with National Geographic: Exploring Land, Sea, and Sky.* Washington, D.C.: National Geographic Society, 1963.

Gvodzdetsky, N. A. *Soviet Geographical Explorations and Discoveries: In the U.S.S.R., Antarctica, and World Oceans.* Woodstock, N.Y.: Beekman, 1975.

*Hacker, Carlotta. *Explorers.* New York: Crabtree Publishing, 1998.

Hakluyt, Richard. *The Principal Navigations, Voyages, Traffiques, and Discoveries of the English Nation,* 10 volumes. Edited by John Masefield. New York: E. P. Dutton, 1927.

Hale, J. R. *Age of Exploration.* New York: Time-Life Books, 1966.

Hamalian, Leo, editor. *Ladies on the Loose: Women Travellers of the Eighteenth and Nineteenth Centuries.* New York: Dodd, Mead, 1981.

Hampden, John, editor. *New Worlds Ahead: First-hand Accounts of English Voyages.* New York: Farrar, Straus, and Giroux, 1968.

Hanbury-Tenison, Robin, compiler. *The Oxford Book of Exploration.* New York: Oxford University Press, 1993.

Hart, Henry H. *Sea Road to the Indies.* 1950. Reprint, Westport, Conn.: Greenwood, 1971.

Heawood, Edward. *A History of Geographical Discovery in the Seventeenth and Eighteenth Centuries.* 1912. Reprint, New York: Octagon Books, 1965.

Herrmann, Paul. *Conquest by Man.* Translated by Michael Bullock. New York: Harper and Brothers, 1954.

——. *The Great Age of Discovery.* Translated by Arnold J. Pomerans. 1958. Reprint, Westport, Conn.: Greenwood, 1974.

Humble, Richard. *The Explorers.* The Seafarers. Alexandria, Va.: Time-Life Books, 1978.

Jackson, Donald Dale. *The Explorers.* The Epic of Flight. Alexandria, Va.: Time-Life Books, 1983.

Keay, John. *Explorers Extraordinary.* Los Angeles, Calif.: Jeremy P. Tarcher, 1986.

Knight, Frank. *Stories of Famous Explorers by Land.* Philadelphia: Westminster Press, 1965.

Lacey, Peter, editor. *Great Adventures That Changed Our World: The World's Great Explorers, Their Triumphs and Tragedies.* Pleasantville, N.Y.: Reader's Digest Association, 1978.

Lamb, Ursula, editor. *The Globe Encircled and the World Revealed.* Brookfield, Vt.: Variorum, 1995.

Langnas, I. A. *Dictionary of Discoveries.* New York: Philosophical Library, 1959.

Leed, Eric J. *Shores of Discovery: How Expeditionaries Have Constructed the World.* New York: Basic Books, 1995.

Leithäuser, Joachim G. *Worlds Beyond the Horizon.* Translated by Hugh Merrick. New York: Alfred A. Knopf, 1955.

*Leon, George de Lucenay. *Explorers of the Americas Before Columbus.* New York: Franklin Watts, 1990.

Ley, Charles David, editor. *Portuguese Voyages, 1498–1663.* London: E. P. Dutton, 1947.

Lucas, Mary Seymour. *Vast Horizons.* Toronto: Macmillan of Canada, 1943.

Mackay, David. *In the Wake of Cook: Exploration, Science, and Empire 1780–1801.* New York: St. Martin's, 1985.

*Maestro, Betsy. *The Discovery of the Americas.* New York: Lothrop, Lee and Shepard Books, 1990.

Mallery, Richard D., editor. *Masterworks of Travel and Exploration: Digests of Thirteen Great Classics.* 1948. Reprint, Freeport, N.Y.: Books for Libraries, 1970.

The Marshall Cavendish Illustrated Encyclopedia of Discovery and Exploration. New York: Marshall Cavendish, 1990.

Neider, Charles. *Man Against Nature: Tales of Adventure and Exploration.* New York: Harper and Brothers, 1954.

Newby, Eric. *The World Atlas of Exploration.* New York: Crescent Books, 1985.

Newton, Arthur Percival, editor. *The Great Age of Discovery.* 1932. Reprint, New York: B. Franklin, 1970.

——. *Travel and Travellers of the Middle Ages.* New York: Alfred A. Knopf, 1950.

Novaresio, Paolo. *The Explorers: From the Ancient World to the Present.* New York: Stewart, Tabori and Chang, 1996.

Olds, Elizabeth Flagg. *Women of the Four Winds.* Boston: Houghton Mifflin, 1985.

Outhwaite, Leonard. *Unrolling the Map: The Story of Exploration.* Revised edition. New York: John Day, 1972.

Parry, John Horace. *The Age of Reconnaissance: Discovery, Exploration and Settlement, 1450–1650.* Revised edition. Berkeley and Los Angeles, Calif.: University of California Press, 1982.

———. *The Discovery of the Sea.* 1974. Reprint, Berkeley and Los Angeles, Calif.: University of California Press, 1981.

———. *The European Reconnaissance: Selected Documents.* New York: Harper Torchbooks, 1968.

———. *The Spanish Seaborne Empire.* London: Hutchinson, 1966.

———. *Trade and Dominion.* London: Weidenfeld and Nicolson, 1971.

Penrose, Boies. *Travel and Discovery in the Renaissance, 1420–1620.* 1952. Reprint, New York: Atheneum, 1962.

*Podell, Janet, and Steven Anzovin. *Old Worlds to New: The Age of Exploration and Discovery.* Bronx, N.Y.: H. W. Wilson, 1993.

Pohl, Frederick J. *Atlantic Crossings Before Columbus.* New York: W. W. Norton, 1961.

Pond, Seymour G. *The History and Romance of Exploration, Told with Pictures.* New York: Cooper Square, 1966.

Prestage, Edgar. *The Portuguese Pioneers.* 1933. Reprint, New York: Barnes and Noble, 1967.

Reid, Alan. *Discovery and Exploration: A Concise History.* London: Gentry Books, 1980.

Rittenhouse, Mignon. *Seven Women Explorers.* Philadelphia: J. B. Lippincott, 1964.

Riverain, Jean. *Concise Encyclopedia of Explorations.* Chicago: Follett, 1969.

Roberts, David. *Great Exploration Hoaxes.* San Francisco: Sierra Club Books, 1982.

Roberts, Gail. *Atlas of Discovery.* New York: Crown, 1973.

Ronan, Colin A. *The Astronomers.* New York: Hill and Wang, 1964.

———. *Discovering the Universe.* New York: Basic Books, 1971.

Rowse, Alfred Leslie. *The Expansion of Elizabethan England.* New York: Macmillan, 1955.

Royal Geographical Society. *The Oxford Atlas of Exploration.* New York: Oxford University Press, 1997.

*Saari, Peggy. *Explorers and Discoverers: From Alexander the Great to Sally Ride.* New York: UXL, 1995.

*Schraff, Anne E. *American Heroes of Exploration and Flight.* Springfield, N.J.: Enslow Publishers, 1996.

Schurz, William L. *The Manila Galleon.* 1939. Reprint, New York: E. P. Dutton, 1959.

Silverberg, Robert. *The Longest Voyage: Circumnavigators in the Age of Discovery.* Athens, Ohio: Ohio University Press, 1997.

Skelton, R. A. *Explorers' Maps: Chapters in the Cartographic Record of Geographical Discovery.* New York: Spring Books, 1958.

Stefansson, Vilhjalmur, editor. *Great Adventures and Explorations: From the Earliest Times to the Present, as Told by the Explorers Themselves.* Revised edition. 1949. Reprint, New York: Telegraph Books, 1985.

*Stefoff, Rebecca. *Women of the World: Women Travelers and Explorers.* New York: Oxford University Press, 1993.

*———. *The Young Oxford Companion to Maps and Mapmaking.* New York: Oxford University Press, 1995.

Sykes, Sir Percy. *A History of Exploration from the Earliest Times to the Present Day.* 3rd edition. 1949. Reprint, Westport, Conn.: Greenwood, 1976.

Thomson, J. Oliver. *History of Ancient Geography.* 1948. Reprint, New York: Biblo and Tannen, 1965.

Tinling, Marion. *Women into the Unknown: A Sourcebook on Women Explorers and Travelers.* New York: Greenwood, 1989.

*Waldman, Carl, and Alan Wexler. *Who Was Who in World Exploration.* New York: Facts on File, 1992.

Whitfield, Peter. *New Found Lands.* New York: Routledge, 1998.

Wilford, John Noble. *The Mapmakers.* New York: Vintage Books, 1982.

*Williams, Brian. *Voyages of Discovery.* Austin, Tex.: Steck-Vaughn Library, 1990.

Williams, Neville. *The Sea Dogs: Privateers, Plunder, and Piracy in the Elizabethan Age.* New York: Macmillan, 1975.

Williamson, James A. *The Age of Drake.* 5th edition. New York: Meridian Books, 1965.

Wood, H. J. *Exploration and Discovery.* London: Hutchinson, 1951.

Woodbridge, David. *The History of Cartography.* Chicago: University of Chicago Press, 1987.

Wright, Helen, and Samuel Rapport. *The Great Explorers.* New York: Harper and Brothers, 1957.

Wright, Louis B. *Gold, Glory, and the Gospel: The Adventurous Lives and Times of the Renaissance Explorers.* New York: Atheneum, 1970.

Works by Region

Africa

Axelson, Eric Victor. *Congo to Cape.* New York: Harper and Row, 1973.

——. *Portugal and the Scramble for Africa, 1875–1891.* Johannesburg, South Africa: Witwatersrand University Press, 1967.

——, editor. *South African Explorers.* New York: Oxford University Press, 1954.

Birmingham, David. *The Portuguese Conquest of Angola.* London: Oxford University Press, 1965.

Bovill, Edward William. *The Golden Trade of the Moors.* New York: Oxford University Press, 1958.

——. *The Niger Explored.* London: Oxford University Press, 1968.

Duffy, James. *Portuguese Africa.* Cambridge, Mass.: Harvard University Press, 1968.

Exploring Africa and Asia. Garden City, N.Y.: Doubleday, 1973.

Forbath, Peter. *The River Congo.* New York: Harper and Row, 1977.

Gardner, Brian. *The Quest for Timbuctoo.* New York: Harcourt, Brace, and World, 1969.

Guadalupi, Gianni. *The Discovery of the Nile.* New York: Stewart, Tabori and Chang, 1997.

Hallett, Robin. *The Penetration of Africa to 1815.* New York: Frederick A. Praeger, 1965.

——, editor. *Records of the African Association, 1788–1821.* London: Thomas Nelson and Sons, 1964.

Hammond, Richard James. *Portugal and Africa, 1815–1910: A Study in Uneconomic Imperialism.* Stanford, Calif.: Stanford University Press, 1966.

Hibbert, Christopher. *Africa Explored.* New York: W. W. Norton, 1983.

Howard, C., and J. H. Plumb, editors. *West African Explorers.* New York: Oxford University Press, 1952.

Hugon, Anne. *The Exploration of Africa: From Cairo to the Cape.* New York: Abrams, 1993.

Livingstone and the Victorian Encounter with Africa. London: National Portrait Gallery, 1996.

Lloyd, Christopher. *The Search for the Niger.* London: Collins, 1973.

*Martell, Hazel. *Exploring Africa.* New York: Peter Bedrick Books, 1997.

McLynn, F. J. *Hearts of Darkness: The European Exploration of Africa.* New York: Carroll and Graf Publishers, 1993.

Miller, C. *The Lunatic Express.* New York: Macmillan, 1971.

Moorehead, Alan. *The Blue Nile.* Revised edition. New York: Vintage Books, 1983.

——. *The White Nile.* Revised edition. New York: Harper and Row, 1971.

Moorhouse, Geoffrey. *The Fearful Void.* Philadelphia: J. B. Lippincott, 1974.

Mountfield, David. *A History of African Exploration.* Northbrook, Ill.: Domus Books, 1976.

Oliver, Caroline. *Western Women in Colonial Africa.* Westport, Conn.: Greenwood, 1982.

Oliver, Roland Anthony, and Caroline Oliver. *Africa in the Days of Exploration.* Englewood Cliffs, N.J.: Prentice-Hall, 1965.

Perham, Margery, and Jack Simmons, compilers. *African Discovery: An Anthology of Exploration.* 2nd edition. London: Faber and Faber, 1957.

Porch, Douglas. *The Conquest of the Sahara.* New York: Alfred A. Knopf, 1984.

Richards, Charles Anthony Langdon, and James Place, editors. *East African Explorers.* New York: Oxford University Press, 1959.

Robinson, Ronald, John Gallacher, and Alice Denny. *Africa and the Victorians: The Climax of Imperialism in the Dark Continent.* 1961. Reprint, Garden City, N.Y.: Doubleday, 1968.

Rotberg, Robert I., editor. *Africa and Its Explorers: Motives, Methods, and Impact.* Cambridge, Mass.: Harvard University Press, 1970.

Severin, Timothy. *The African Adventure.* New York: E. P. Dutton, 1973.

*Sherman, Steven. *Henry Stanley and the European Explorers of Africa.* New York: Chelsea House, 1993.

Silverberg, Robert. *The Realm of Prester John.* Garden City, N.Y.: Doubleday, 1972.

*Stefoff, Rebecca. *Vasco da Gama and the Portuguese Explorers.* New York: Chelsea House, 1993.

Welland, James. *The Great Sahara.* New York: E. P. Dutton, 1965.

West, Richard. *Congo.* New York: Holt, Rinehart and Winston, 1972.

Antarctica

Andrist, Ralph K. *Heroes of Polar Exploration.* New York: American Heritage, 1962.

Bertrand, Kenneth J. *Americans in Antarctica, 1775–1948.* New York: American Geographical Society, 1971.

Bowman, Gerald. *Men of Antarctica.* New York: Fleet, 1958.

Chapman, Walker. *The Loneliest Continent.* Boston: New York Graphic Society, 1964.

Cooper, Paul Fenimore. *Island of the Lost.* New York: Putnam, 1961.

Debenham, Frank. *Antarctica: The Story of a Continent.* New York: Macmillan, 1961.

Fedorov, Y. *Polar Diaries.* Chicago: Imported Publications, 1983.

Friis, Herman R., and Shelby G. Bale, editors. *United States Polar Exploration.* Athens, Ohio: Ohio University Press, 1970.

Giaver, John. *The White Desert: The Official Account of the Norwegian-British-Swedish Antarctic Expedition.* New York: E. P. Dutton, 1954.

Gurney, Alan. *Below the Convergence: Voyages Toward Antarctica, 1699–1839.* New York: Norton, 1997.

Hobbs, William Herbert. *Explorers of the Antarctic.* New York: House of Field, 1941.

Hunt, William R. *To Stand at the Pole.* New York: Stein and Day, 1981.

Kirwan, Lawrence Park. *A History of Polar Exploration.* New York: W. W. Norton, 1959.

Lamb, Harold. *New Found World.* New York: Doubleday, 1955.

Land, Barbara. *The New Explorers: Women in Antarctica.* New York: Dodd, Mead, 1981.

The Last Frontiers. Garden City, N.Y.: Doubleday, 1973.

Ley, Willy. *The Poles.* New York: Time, 1962.

*McLoone, Margo. *Women Explorers in Polar Regions.* Mankato, Minn.: Capstone Press, 1997.

Mickleburgh, Edwin. *Beyond the Frozen Sea: Visions of Antarctica.* New York: St. Martin's, 1987.

Mountfield, David. *A History of Polar Exploration.* New York: Dial, 1974.

Mowat, Farley, editor. *Ordeal By Ice.* Boston: Little, Brown, 1961.

Neatby, Leslie Hilda. *Conquest of the Last Frontier.* Athens, Ohio: Ohio University Press, 1966.

Neider, Charles, editor. *Antarctica: Authentic Accounts of Life and Exploration in the World's Highest, Driest, Windiest, Coldest, and Most Remote Continent.* New York: Random House, 1972.

Pyne, Stephen J. *The Ice: A Journey to Antarctica.* Seattle, Wash.: University of Washington Press, 1998.

Sullivan, Walter. *Quest for a Continent.* New York: McGraw-Hill, 1957.

Victor, Paul-Emile. *Man and the Conquest of the Poles.* New York: Simon and Schuster, 1964.

Weems, John Edward. *Race for the Pole.* New York: Henry Holt, 1960.

The Arctic

Barrow, John. *A Chronological History of Voyages into the Arctic Regions.* 1818. Reprint, Newton Abbot, U.K.: David and Charles Reprints, 1971.

Berton, Pierre. *The Arctic Grail: The Quest for the North West Passage and the North Pole, 1818–1909.* New York: Viking, 1988.

Burpee, Lawrence J. *The Search for the Western Sea: The Story of the Exploration of Northwestern America.* Revised edition. Toronto: Macmillan of Canada, 1935.

Cantwell, Robert. *The Hidden Northwest.* Philadelphia: J. B. Lippincott, 1972.

Caswell, John E. *Arctic Frontiers.* Norman, Okla.: University of Oklahoma Press, 1956.

Cooke, Alan, and Clive Holland. *The Exploration of Northern Canada, 500–1920.* Toronto: Arctic History Press, 1978.

Cooper, Paul Fenimore. *Island of the Lost.* New York: Putnam, 1961.

Crouse, Nellis M. *The Search for the North Pole.* New York: Richard R. Smith, 1947.

——. *The Search for the North-West Passage.* New York: Columbia University Press, 1934.

*Curlee, Lynn. *Into the Ice: The Story of Arctic Exploration.* Boston: Houghton Mifflin, 1997.

Davies, K. G. *The North Atlantic World in the Seventeenth Century.* Minneapolis, Minn.: University of Minnesota Press, 1974.

Day, Alan Edwin. *Search for the Northwest Passage: An Annotated Bibliography.* New York: Garland, 1986.

Dodge, E. S. *Northwest by Sea.* New York: Oxford University Press, 1961.

*Dwyer, Christopher. *Robert Peary and the Quest for the North Pole.* New York: Chelsea House, 1992.

Euller, John. *Arctic World.* New York: Abelard-Schuman, 1958.

Fedorov, Y. *Polar Diaries.* Chicago: Imported Publications, 1983.

Freuchen, Peter. *Book of Arctic Exploration.* New York: Coward-McCann, 1962.

Friis, Herman R., and Shelby G. Bale, editors. *United States Polar Exploration.* Athens, Ohio: Ohio University Press, 1970.

Golder, Frank Alfred. *Russian Expansion on the Pacific, 1641–1850.* 1914. Reprint, Gloucester, Mass.: Peter Smith, 1960.

Herbert, Wally. *Across the Top of the World: The Last Great Journey on Earth.* New York: Putnam, 1971.

Hunt, William R. *To Stand at the Pole.* New York: Stein and Day, 1981.

Jones, Gwyn. *A History of the Vikings.* New York: Oxford University Press, 1968.

———. *The Norse Atlantic Saga: Being the Norse Voyages of Discovery and Settlement to Iceland, Greenland, America.* London: Oxford University Press, 1964.

Jones, Lawrence F., and George Lonn. *Pathfinders of the North.* Toronto: Pitt, 1969.

Keating, Bern. *The Northwest Passage: From the Mathew to the Manhattan: 1497 to 1969.* Chicago: Rand McNally, 1970.

Kirwan, Lawrence Park. *A History of Polar Exploration.* New York: W. W. Norton, 1959.

Lamb, Harold. *New Found World.* New York: Doubleday, 1955.

The Last Frontiers. Garden City, N.Y.: Doubleday, 1973.

Leacock, Stephen. *Adventurers of the Far North.* Toronto: University of Toronto Press, 1964.

Lehane, Brendan. *The Northwest Passage.* Alexandria, Va.: Time-Life Books, 1981.

Ley, Willy. *The Poles.* 2nd edition. Alexandria, V.A.: Time-Life Books, 1977.

*McLoone, Margo. *Women Explorers in Polar Regions.* Mankato, Minn.: Capstone Press, 1997.

Mirsky, Jeannette. *To the Arctic! The Story of Northern Exploration from Earliest Times to the Present.* Chicago: University of Chicago Press, 1970.

Mountfield, David. *A History of Polar Exploration.* New York: Dial, 1974.

Mowat, Farley. *Canada North.* Boston: Little, Brown, 1968.

———, editor. *Ordeal By Ice.* Boston: Little, Brown, 1961.

———, editor. *The Polar Passion: The Quest for the North Pole, with Selections from Arctic Journals.* Boston: Little, Brown, 1968.

Neatby, Leslie Hilda. *Conquest of the Last Frontier.* Athens, Ohio: Ohio University Press, 1966.

———. *Discovery in Russian and Siberian Waters.* Athens, Ohio: Ohio University Press, 1973.

———. *In Quest of the North-West Passage.* New York: Thomas Y. Crowell, 1958.

———. *Search for Franklin.* New York: Walker, 1970.

Oleson, Tryggvi J. *Early Voyages and Northern Approaches, 1000–1632.* New York: Oxford University Press, 1964.

Orlob, Helen. *The Northeast Passage: Black Water, White Ice.* New York: Thomas Nelson, 1977.

Ortzen, Len. *Famous Arctic Adventures.* London: Barker, 1972.

Rasky, Frank. *The North Pole or Bust: Explorers of the North.* Toronto: McGraw-Hill Ryerson, 1977.

Ross, Frank Xavier. *Frozen Frontier: The Story of the Arctic.* New York: Thomas Y. Crowell, 1961.

Sauer, Carl O. *Northern Mists.* Berkeley and Los Angeles, Calif.: University of California Press, 1968.

Smith, William D. *Northwest Passage.* New York: American Heritage, 1970.

Speck, Gordon. *Northwest Explorations.* 2nd edition. Portland, Ore.: Binford-Metropolitan, 1970.

Stefansson, Vilhjalmur. *Greenland.* New York: Doubleday, Doran, 1942.

———. *Northwest to Fortune.* New York: Duell, Sloan and Pearce, 1958.

———. *Unsolved Mysteries of the Arctic.* New York: Macmillan, 1939.

Thomson, George Malcolm. *The Search for the North-West Passage.* New York: Macmillan, 1975.

Victor, Paul-Emile. *Man and the Conquest of the Poles.* New York: Simon and Schuster, 1964.

Weems, John Edward. *Race for the Pole.* New York: Henry Holt, 1960.

Wilkinson, Doug. *Arctic Fever.* Toronto: Clarke, Irwin, 1971.

Williams, Glyndwr. *The British Search for the Northwest Passage in the Eighteenth Century.* London: Longmans, Green, 1962.

Zaslow, Morris. *A Century of Canada's Arctic Islands, 1800–1980.* Ottawa: Royal Society of Canada, 1981.
——. *The Opening of the Canadian North.* Toronto: McClelland and Stewart, 1971.

Asia

Bishop, Peter. *The Myth of Shangri-la: Tibet, Travel Writing and the Western Creation of Sacred Landscape.* Berkeley and Los Angeles, Calif.: University of California Press, 1989.

Dmytryshyn, Basil, et al., editors and translators. *Russia's Conquest of Siberia, 1558–1700: A Documentary Record.* Portland, Ore.: Western Imprints, The Press of the Oregon Historical Society, 1985.

Dunne, George H. *Generation of Giants: The Story of the Jesuits in China in the Last Decades of the Ming Dynasty.* Notre Dame, Ind.: University of Notre Dame Press, 1962.

Exploring Africa and Asia. Garden City, N.Y.: Doubleday, 1973.

Gullick, J. M. *Adventures and Encounters: Europeans in South-East Asia.* New York: Oxford University Press, 1995.

Hopkirk, Peter. *Trespassers on the Roof of the World: The Secret Exploration of Tibet.* Los Angeles, Calif.: Jeremy P. Tarcher, 1982.

Keay, John. *When Men and Mountains Meet: The Explorers of the Western Himalayas, 1820–75.* Hamden, Conn.: Shoe String, 1981.

King, Victor T., editor. *Explorers of South-East Asia: Six Lives.* New York: Oxford University Press, 1995.

Lach, Donald. *Asia in the Making of Europe.* Chicago: University of Chicago Press, 1965.

Landström, Björn. *The Quest for India.* Garden City, N.Y.: Doubleday, 1964.

Lattimore, Owen, and Eleanor Lattimore. *Silks, Spices, and Empire: Asia Seen Through the Eyes of Its Discoverers.* New York: Delacorte, 1968.

Macgregor, John. *Tibet: A Chronicle of Exploration.* New York: Frederick A. Praeger, 1970.

March, G. Patrick. *Eastern Destiny: Russia in Asia and the North Pacific.* Westport, Conn.: Praeger Publishers, 1996.

Mason, Kenneth. *Abode of Snow: A History of Himalayan Exploration and Mountaineering.* New York: E. P. Dutton, 1955.

*McLoone, Margo. *Women Explorers in Asia.* Mankato, Minn.: Capstone Press, 1997.

Miller, Luree. *On Top of the World: Five Women Explorers in Tibet.* Seattle, Wash.: Mountaineers, 1984.

Mirsky, Jeannette, editor. *The Great Chinese Travelers: An Anthology.* New York: Pantheon Books, 1964.

Semyonov, Yuri. *Siberia: Its Conquest and Development.* Translated by J. R. Foster. Montreal: International Publishers Representatives, 1963.

Severin, Timothy. *The Oriental Adventure: Explorers of the East.* Boston: Little, Brown, 1976.

*Stefoff, Rebecca. *Marco Polo and the Medieval Explorers.* New York: Chelsea House, 1992.

*——. *Vasco da Gama and the Portuguese Explorers.* New York: Chelsea House, 1993.

Waller, Derek. *The Pundits: British Exploration of Tibet and Central Asia.* Lexington, Ky.: University Press of Kentucky, 1990.

Wood, Frances. *Did Marco Polo Go to China?* London: Secker and Warburg, 1995.

Australia

Cameron, Roderick. *Australia: History and Horizons.* New York: Columbia University Press, 1971.

Carter, Jeff. *In the Steps of the Explorers.* Sydney, Australia: Angus and Robertson, 1970.

Carter, Paul. *The Road to Botany Bay: An Exploration of Landscape and History.* New York: Alfred A. Knopf, 1987.

Feeken, Erwin H. J., G. E. E. Feeken, and O. H. K. Spate. *The Discovery and Exploration of Australia.* London: Thomas Nelson and Sons, 1971.

McLaren, Glen. *Beyond Leichhardt: Bushcraft and the Exploration of Australia.* South Fremantle, Wash.: Fremantle Arts Centre Press, 1996.

Moorehead, Alan. *Cooper's Creek.* 1963. Reprint, New York: Atlantic Monthly, 1987.

Scott, Ernest, editor. *Australian Discovery,* 2 volumes. 1929. Reprint, New York: Johnson Reprint, 1966.

Sharp, Andrew. *The Discovery of Australia.* New York: Oxford University Press, 1963.

Shaw, Alan George Lewers. *The Story of Australia.* 2nd edition. Mystic, Conn.: Lawrence Verry, 1966.

Sigmond, J. P. *Dutch Discoveries of Australia: Shipwrecks, Treasures, and Early Voyages Off the West Coast.* Amsterdam, Netherlands: Batavian Lion, 1995.

Central America, Mexico, and the Caribbean

Andrews, Kenneth R. *The Spanish Caribbean: Trade and Plunder, 1530–1630*. New Haven, Conn.: Yale University Press, 1978.

Carter, Hodding W. *Doomed Road to Empire: The Spanish Trail of Conquest*. New York: McGraw-Hill, 1963.

Descola, Jean. *The Conquistadors*. Translated by Malcolm Barnes. 1954. Reprint, Fairfield, N.J.: Augustus M. Kelley, 1970.

Hamskere, Cyril. *The British in the Caribbean*. Cambridge, Mass.: Harvard University Press, 1972.

Kirkpatrick, Frederick A. *The Spanish Conquistadors*. 3rd edition. Gloucester, Mass.: Peter Smith, 1963.

Lang, James. *Conquest and Commerce: Spain and England in the Americas*. New York: Academic Press, 1975.

*Machado, Ana Maria. *Exploration into Latin America*. Parsippany, N.J.: New Discovery Books, 1995.

Maslow, Jonathan Evan. *Footsteps in the Jungle: Adventures in the Scientific Exploration of the American Tropics*. Chicago: Ivan R. Dee, 1996.

Milanih, Jerald T., and Susan Milbrath, editors. *First Encounters: Spanish Explorations in the Caribbean and the United States, 1492–1570*. Gainesville, Fla.: University of Florida Press, 1989.

Prescott, William H. *The Complete and Unexpurgated History of the Conquest of Mexico and History of the Conquest of Peru*. New York: Random House, 1936.

Tanaka, Shelley. *The Lost Temple of the Aztecs: What it Was When the Spaniards Invaded Mexico*. New York: Hyperion/Madison Press Books, 1998.

Weddle, Robert S. *Spanish Sea: The Gulf of Mexico in North American Discovery, 1500–1685*. College Station, Tex.: Texas A&M University Press, 1985.

Middle East

Beckingham, C. F. *Between Islam and Christendom: Travellers, Facts, and Legends in the Middle Ages and the Renaissance*. London: Variorum Reprints, 1983.

Bidwell, Robin. *Travellers in Arabia*. London: Hamlyn, 1976.

Donini, Pier Giovanni. *Arab Travelers and Geographers*. London: Immel Publishing, 1991.

Freeth, Zahra, and Victor Winstone. *Explorers of Arabia*. New York: Holmes and Meier, 1978.

Hogarth, D. G. *The Penetration of Arabia*. Westport, Conn.: Hyperion Press, 1981.

Kiernan, R. H. *The Unveiling of Arabia*. New York: AMS Press, 1975.

Simmons, James C. *Passionate Pilgrims: English Travelers to the World of the Desert Arabs*. New York: William Morrow, 1987.

North America

Adamson, Hans Christian. *Lands of New World Neighbors*. New York: Whittlesey House, 1941.

Allen, John Logan. *North American Exploration*, 3 volumes. Lincoln, Nebr.: University of Nebraska Press, 1997.

*Asikinack, Bill. *Exploration into North America*. Parsippany, N.J.: New Discovery Books, 1996.

Bakeless, John Edwin. *The Eyes of Discovery: The Pageant of North America as Seen by the First Explorers*. 1950. Reprint, New York: Dover, 1961.

Bartlett, Richard A. *Great Surveys of the American West*. Norman, Okla.: University of Oklahoma Press, 1962.

Batman, Richard. *The Outer Coast*. San Diego, Calif.: Harcourt Brace Jovanovich, 1985.

Becker, Robert E., Henry R. Wagner, and Charles L. Camp, editors. *The Plains and Rockies: A Critical Bibliography of Exploration, Adventure, and Travel in the American West, 1800–1865*. 4th edition. San Francisco: John Howell Books, 1982.

Berry, Don. *A Majority of Scoundrels: An Informal History of the Rocky Mountain Fur Company*. New York: Harper, 1961.

Beston, Henry. *The St. Lawrence*. New York: Farrar and Rinehart, 1942.

Billington, Ray Allen. *The Far Western Frontier 1830–1860*. New York: Harper and Row, 1956.

———. *Westward Expansion: A History of the American Frontier*. 2nd edition. New York: Macmillan, 1960.

Blegen, Theodore C., editor. *Five Fur Traders of the Northwest*. St. Paul, Minn.: Minnesota Historical Society, 1965.

Bourne, Edward Gaylord. *Spain in America, 1450–1580*. New York: Barnes and Noble, 1962.

Brebner, John Bartlet. *The Explorers of North America, 1492–1806*. 2nd edition. Magnolia, Mass.: Peter Smith, 1965.

Bry, Theodore de. *Discovering the New World.* Edited by Michael Alexander. New York: Harper and Row, 1976.

Burpee, Lawrence J. *The Discovery of Canada.* 1929. Reprint, Salem, N.H.: Books for Libraries, 1976.

——. *The Search for the Western Sea: The Story of the Exploration of Northwestern America.* Revised edition. Toronto: Macmillan of Canada, 1935.

Campbell, Marjorie Wilkins. *The North West Company.* Toronto: Macmillan of Canada, 1957.

Carse, Robert. *The River Men.* New York: Charles Scribner's Sons, 1969.

Carson, Phil. *Across the Northern Frontier: Spanish Explorations in Colorado.* Boulder, Colo.: Johnson Books, 1998.

Carter, Hodding W. *Doomed Road to Empire: The Spanish Trail of Conquest.* New York: McGraw-Hill, 1963.

The Conquest of North America. Garden City, N.Y.: Doubleday, 1973.

Cook, Warren L. *Flood Tide of Empire.* New Haven, Conn.: Yale University Press, 1973.

Cooke, Alan, and Clive Holland. *The Exploration of Northern Canada, 500–1920.* Toronto: Arctic History Press, 1978.

Corney, Peter. *Early Voyages in the North Pacific, 1815–1818.* Fairfield, Wash.: Ye Galleon Press, 1965.

*Coulter, Tony. *Jacques Cartier, Samuel de Champlain, and the Explorers of Canada.* New York: Chelsea House, 1993.

*Coulter, Tony, et al. *LaSalle and the Explorers of the Mississippi.* New York: Chelsea House, 1993.

Craner, Verner W. *The Southern Frontier, 1760–1782.* Ann Arbor, Mich.: University of Michigan Press, 1956.

Crone, G. R. *The Discovery of America.* New York: Weybright and Talley, 1969.

Cumming, William P., S. E. Hillier, David Beers Quinn, and G. Williams. *The Exploration of North America, 1630–1776.* New York: G. P. Putnam's Sons, 1974.

Cumming, William P., R. A. Skelton, and David Beers Quinn. *The Discovery of North America.* New York: American Heritage Press, 1972.

Cutter, Donald C. *The California Coast.* Norman, Okla.: University of Oklahoma Press, 1969.

Descola, Jean. *The Conquistadors.* Translated by Malcolm Barnes. 1954. Reprint, Fairfield, N.J.: Augustus M. Kelley, 1970.

DeVoto, Bernard. *The Course of Empire.* Boston: Houghton Mifflin, 1952.

Discoverers of the New World. New York: American Heritage, 1960.

Dreppard, Carl. *Pioneer America: Its First Three Centuries.* Garden City, N.Y.: Doubleday, 1949.

Driver, H. E., editor. *The Americas on the Eve of Discovery.* Englewood Cliffs, N.J.: Prentice-Hall, 1964.

Duffus, R. L. *The Santa Fe Trail.* New York: Longmans, Green, 1930.

Duncan, David Ewing. *Hernando De Soto: A Savage Quest in the Americas.* Norman, Okla.: University of Oklahoma Press, 1997.

Eccles, W. J. *The Canadian Frontier, 1534–1760.* New York: Holt, Rinehart and Winston, 1969.

Elliott, J. H. *The Old World and the New, 1492–1650.* Cambridge, U.K.: Cambridge University Press, 1970.

*Faber, Harold. *The Discoverers of America.* New York: Scribner, 1992.

Faulk, O. B. *Land of Many Frontiers: A History of the American Southwest.* New York: Oxford University Press, 1968.

Gerhard, Peter. *The North Frontier of New Spain.* Princeton, N.J.: Princeton University Press, 1982.

Gibson, Charles. *Spain in America.* New York: Harper and Row, 1966.

Gibson, James R. *Otter Skins, Boston Ships, and China Goods: The Maritime Fur Trade of the Northwest Coast, 1785–1841.* Seattle, Wash.: University of Washington Press, 1992.

Gilbert, Bil. *The Trailblazers.* New York: Time-Life Books, 1973.

Gilbert, E. W. *The Exploration of Western America, 1800–1850.* Cambridge, U.K.: Cambridge University Press, 1933.

Goetzmann, William H. *Army Exploration in the American West, 1803–1863.* Austin, Tex.: Texas State Historical Association, 1991.

——. *Exploration and Empire: The Explorer and the Scientist in the Winning of the American West.* New York: Vintage Books, 1966.

——. *Exploring the American West, 1803–1879.* Washington, D.C.: Division of Publications, National Park Service, U.S. Department of the Interior, 1982.

——. *New Lands, New Men: America and the Second Great Age of Discovery.* New York: Viking, 1986.

Goetzmann, William, and Glyndwr Williams. *The Atlas of North American Exploration: From the Norse Voyages to the Race to the Pole.* New York: Prentice-Hall General Reference, 1992.

Golding, Morton J. *The Mystery of the Vikings in America.* Philadelphia: J. B. Lippincott, 1973.

Gough, Barry M. *Distant Dominion: Britain and the Northwest Coast of North America, 1579–1809.* Vancouver, Canada: University of British Columbia Press, 1980.

Hafen, LeRoy, editor. *Mountain Men and Fur Traders.* Lincoln, Nebr.: University of Nebraska Press, 1982.

Hafen, LeRoy, and Ann W. Hafen. *The Old Spanish Trail.* Glendale, Calif.: Arthur H. Clark Company, 1954.

Hammer, Trudy J. *The St. Lawrence.* New York: Franklin Watts, 1984.

Hannon, Leslie F. *The Discoverers.* Toronto: McClelland and Stewart, 1971.

Haring, C. H. *The Spanish Empire in America.* New York: Harcourt Brace Jovanovich, 1963.

Helps, Sir Arthur. *The Spanish Conquest in America.* Revised edition. New York: AMS Press, 1966.

Hodge, Frederick Webb, and Theodore H. Lewis, editors. *Spanish Explorers in the Southern United States, 1528–1543.* 1965. Reprint, Austin, Tex.: Texas State Historical Association, 1984.

Hoffman, Bernard G. *Cabot to Cartier: Sources for a Historical Ethnography of Northeastern North America, 1497–1550.* Toronto: University of Toronto Press, 1961.

Horgan, Paul. *Conquistadors in North American History.* New York: Farrar, Straus, and Giroux, 1963.

Johnson, Adrian. *America Explored: A Cartographical History of the Exploration of North America.* New York: Viking/Studio Books, 1974.

Johnston, Lissa Jones. *Crossing a Continent: The Incredible Journey of Cabeza de Vaca.* Austin, Tex.: Eakin Press, 1997.

Jones, Gwyn. *A History of the Vikings.* New York: Oxford University Press, 1968.

——. *The Norse Atlantic Saga: Being the Norse Voyages of Discovery and Settlement to Iceland, Greenland, America.* London: Oxford University Press, 1964.

Karamanski, Theodore J. *Fur Trade and Exploration: Opening the Far Northwest, 1821–1852.* Norman, Okla.: University of Oklahoma Press, 1983.

Kendrick, Sir Thomas Downing. *A History of the Vikings.* New York: Barnes and Noble, 1968.

Kirkpatrick, Frederick A. *The Spanish Conquistadors.* 3rd edition. Gloucester, Mass.: Peter Smith, 1963.

LaFeber, Walter. *The New Empire: An Interpretation of American Expansion, 1860–1898.* Ithaca, N.Y.: Cornell University Press, 1963.

Lang, James. *Conquest and Commerce: Spain and England in the Americas.* New York: Academic Press, 1975.

Laut, Agnes. *The Adventurers of England on Hudson Bay.* Toronto: University of Toronto Press, 1964.

Lavender, David. *The Rockies.* New York: Harper and Row, 1968.

——. *The Way to the Western Sea.* New York: Harper and Row, 1988.

——. *Westward Vision: The Oregon Trail.* New York: McGraw-Hill, 1963.

Leach, Douglas E. *The Northern Colonial Frontier, 1607–1763.* New York: Holt, Rinehart and Winston, 1966.

Logan, Donald F. *The Vikings in History.* New York: Barnes and Noble, 1983.

*Marrin, Albert. *Empires Lost and Won: The Spanish Heritage in the Southwest.* New York: Atheneum Books for Young Readers, 1997.

Masselman, George. *The Cradle of Colonialism.* New Haven, Conn.: Yale University Press, 1963.

*Matthews, Leonard. *Pioneers and Trailblazers.* New York: Derrydale Press, 1990.

*McLoone, Margo. *Women Explorers in North America and South America.* Mankato, Minn.: Capstone Press, 1997.

Meredith, Roberts, and E. Brooks Smith, editors. *Exploring the Great River: Early Voyagers on the Mississippi from DeSoto to LaSalle.* Boston: Little, Brown, 1969.

Milanih, Jerald T., and Susan Milbrath, editors. *First Encounters: Spanish Explorations in the Caribbean and the United States, 1492–1570.* Gainesville, Fla.: University of Florida Press, 1989.

Mirsky, Jeannette. *The Westward Crossings: Balboa, Mackenzie, Lewis and Clark.* 1946. Reprint, Philadelphia: Richard West, 1978.

Moring, John. *Men with Sand: Great Explorers of the North American West.* Helena, Mont.: Falcon Publishing, 1998.

Morison, Samuel Eliot. *The European Discovery of America: The Northern Voyages, A.D. 500–1600.* New York: Oxford University Press, 1971.

——. *The Great Explorers: The European Discovery of America.* New York: Oxford University Press, 1978.

——. *Portuguese Voyages to America in the Fifteenth Century.* Cambridge, Mass.: Harvard University Press, 1940.

*Morris, John Miller. *From Coronado to Escalante: The Explorers of the Spanish Southwest.* New York: Chelsea House, 1992.

Muller, Gerhard F. *Voyages from Asia to America.* Amsterdam, Netherlands: N. Israel, 1967.

Newman, Peter C. *Caesars of the Wilderness.* New York: Viking, 1987.

——. *Company of Adventurers.* New York: Viking, 1985.

Norman, Charles. *Discoverers of America.* New York: Thomas Y. Crowell, 1968.

Nuffield, E. W. *The Discovery of Canada.* Vancouver, Canada: Haro, 1996.

Parkman, Francis. *France and England in America.* New York: The Library of America, 1983.

Pelta, Kathy. *The Royal Roads: Spanish Trails in North America.* Austin, Tex.: Raintree Steck-Vaughn, 1997.

Pethick, Derek. *First Approaches to the Northwest Coast.* Vancouver, Canada: J. J. Douglas, 1976.

Phillips, Fred M. *Desert People and Mountain Men: Exploration of the Great Basin, 1824–1865.* Bishop, Calif.: Chalfant Press, 1977.

Quinn, David Beers. *England and the Discovery of America, 1481–1620.* New York: Alfred A. Knopf, 1973.

——. *North America from Earliest Discovery to First Settlements: The Norse Voyages to 1612.* New York: Harper and Row, 1977.

——, editor. *North American Discovery Circa 1000–1612.* Columbia, S.C.: University of South Carolina Press, 1971.

Rasky, Frank. *The Taming of the Canadian West.* Toronto: McClelland and Stewart, 1967.

Rawling, Gerald. *The Pathfinders.* New York: Macmillan, 1964.

Rich, E. E. *The Fur Trade and the Northwest to 1857.* Toronto: McClelland and Stewart, 1967.

Sauer, Carl O. *The Early Spanish Main.* Berkeley and Los Angeles, Calif.: University of California Press, 1966.

——. *Sixteenth-Century North America: The Land and the Peoples as Seen by the Europeans.* Berkeley and Los Angeles, Calif.: University of California Press, 1971.

Savage, Henry, Jr. *Discovering America, Seventeen Hundred to Eighteen Seventy-Five.* New York: Harper and Row, 1979.

Severin, Timothy. *Explorers of the Mississippi.* New York: Alfred A. Knopf, 1967.

Sherwood, Morgan B. *Exploration of Alaska, 1865–1900.* New Haven, Conn.: Yale University Press, 1965.

Smith, Carter, editor. *Exploring the Frontier: A Sourcebook on the American West.* Brookfield, Conn.: Millbrook Press, 1997.

Smith, I. Norman. *The Unbelievable Land.* Ottawa: Queen's Printer, 1965.

Snell, Tee Loftin. *The Wild Shores: America's Beginnings.* Washington, D.C.: National Geographic Society, 1974.

Steensel, Maja Van. *People of Light and Dark.* Ottawa: Queen's Printer, 1966.

*Stefoff, Rebecca. *The Viking Explorers.* New York: Chelsea House, 1993.

Stewart, George. *The California Trail.* New York: McGraw-Hill, 1962.

Terrell, John Upton. *Furs by Astor.* New York: William Morrow, 1963.

Todorov, Tzvetan. *The Conquest of America: The Question of the Other.* Translated by Richard Howard. New York: Harper and Row, 1984.

Townsend, John K. *Across the Rockies to the Columbia.* Lincoln, Nebr.: University of Nebraska Press, 1978.

Toye, William. *The St. Lawrence.* Toronto: Oxford University Press, 1959.

Trappers and Mountain Men. New York: American Heritage, 1961.

Utley, Robert M. *A Life Wild and Perilous: Mountain Men and the Paths to the Pacific.* New York: Henry Holt and Company, 1997.

Viola, Herman J. *Exploring the West.* Washington, D.C.: Smithsonian Books, 1987.

Weddle, Robert S. *Spanish Sea: The Gulf of Mexico in North American Discovery, 1500–1685.* College Station, Tex.: Texas A&M University Press, 1985.

*Wilbur, C. Keith. *Early Explorers of North America.* Philadelphia: Chelsea House, 1996.

Winsor, Justin. *Cartier to Frontenac: Geographical Discovery in the Interior of North America, 1534–1700.* New York: Cooper Square, 1970.

Wood, Peter. *The Spanish Main.* Alexandria, Va.: Time-Life Books, 1979.

Wright, Louis B., and Elaine W. Fowler, editors. *The Moving Frontier: North America Seen Through the Eyes of Its Pioneer Discoverers.* New York: Delacorte, 1972.

——. *West and By North: North America Seen Through the Eyes of Its Seafaring Discoverers.* New York: Delacorte, 1971.

*Xydes, Georgia. *Alexander MacKenzie and the Explorers of Canada.* New York: Chelsea House, 1992.

The Pacific Ocean

Allen, Oliver E. *The Pacific Navigators.* Alexandria, Va.: Time-Life Books, 1980.

Beaglehole, John C. *The Exploration of the Pacific.* 3rd edition. Palo Alto, Calif.: Stanford University Press, 1966.

——. *The Life of Captain James Cook.* Stanford, Calif: Stanford University Press, 1974.

——, editor. *The Journals of Captain James Cook on His Voyages of Discovery,* 3 volumes. Cambridge, U.K.: Hakluyt Society, 1955–1967.

Brosse, Jacques. *Great Voyages of Discovery: Circumnavigators and Scientists, 1764–1843.* Translated by Stanley Hochman. New York: Facts on File, 1983.

Cameron, Ian. *Magellan and the First Circumnavigators of the World.* New York: Saturday Review Press, 1973.

Day, Arthur Grove. *Adventurers of the Pacific.* New York: Meredith Press, 1969.

——. *Explorers of the Pacific.* New York: Duell, Sloan and Pearce, 1966.

Dodge, Ernest S. *Beyond the Capes: Pacific Exploration from Captain Cook to the Challenger, 1776–1877.* Boston: Little, Brown, 1971.

Dos Passos, John. *Easter Island.* Garden City, N.Y.: Doubleday, 1971.

Dousset, Roselene, and Etienne Taillemite. *The Great Book of the Pacific.* Translated by Andrew Mouravieff-Apostal and Edita Lausanne. Secaucus, N.J.: Chartwell Books, 1979.

Dunmore, John. *French Explorers in the Pacific.* Oxford: Oxford University Press, 1965.

Friis, Herman R., editor. *The Pacific Basin: A History of Its Geographical Exploration.* New York: American Geographical Society, 1967.

Gilbert, William Napier John, and Julian Holland. *Pacific Voyages.* Garden City, N.Y.: Doubleday, 1971.

Golder, F. A. *Russian Expansion on the Pacific, 1641–1850.* 1914. Reprint, Gloucester, Mass.: Peter Smith, 1960.

*Haney, David. *Captain James Cook and the Explorers of the Pacific.* New York: Chelsea House, 1992.

Kemp, P. K., and Christopher Lloyd. *The Brethren of the Coast.* London: Heinemann, 1960.

Kirker, James. *Adventures to China: Americans in the Southern Oceans, 1792–1812.* New York: Oxford University Press, 1970.

Moorehead, Alan. *The Fatal Impact: An Account of the Invasion of the South Pacific, 1767–1840.* New York: Penguin Books, 1968.

Oliver, Douglas L. *The Pacific Islands.* Cambridge, Mass.: Harvard University Press, 1962.

Scammell, G. V. *The World Encompassed: The First European Maritime Enterprises c. 800–1650.* Berkeley and Los Angeles, Calif.: University of California Press, 1981.

Schurz, W. L. *The Manila Galleon.* 1939. Reprint, New York: E. P. Dutton, 1959.

Sharp, Andrew. *Ancient Voyages in the Pacific.* London: Polynesian Society, 1957.

——. *The Discovery of the Pacific Islands.* Oxford: Oxford University Press, 1960.

Silverberg, Robert. *The Longest Voyage: Circumnavigators in the Age of Discovery.* New York: Bobbs-Merrill, 1972.

Smith, Bernard. *European Vision and the South Pacific, 1768–1850.* Oxford: Clarendon, 1960.

Van Loon, Hendrik Willem. *The Golden Book of the Dutch Navigators.* 1916. Reprint, Salem, N.H.: Ayer, 1977.

Ward, Ralph T. *Pirates in History.* Baltimore, Md.: York Press, 1974.

Williams, Glyndwr. *The Great South Sea: English Voyages and Encounters, 1570–1750.* New Haven, Conn.: Yale University Press, 1997.

Withey, Lynne. *Voyages of Discovery: Captain Cook and the Exploration of the Pacific.* New York: William Morrow, 1987.

South America

Arciniegas, Germán. *Germans in the Conquest of America: A 16th Century Venture.* Translated by Angel Flores. New York: Macmillan, 1943.

*Bernhard, Brendon. *Pizarro, Orellana, and the Exploration of the Amazon.* New York: Chelsea House, 1991.

Boxer, Charles R. *The Golden Age of Brazil, 1695–1750.* Berkeley and Los Angeles, Calif.: University of California Press, 1962.

Crone, G. R. *The Discovery of America.* New York: Weybright and Talley, 1969.

Cutright, Paul Russell. *The Great Naturalists Explore South America.* New York: Macmillan, 1940.

Descola, Jean. *The Conquistadors.* Translated by Malcolm Barnes. 1954. Reprint, Fairfield, N.J.: Augustus M. Kelley, 1970.

Driver, H. E., editor. *The Americas on the Eve of Discovery.* Englewood Cliffs, N.J.: Prentice-Hall, 1964.

Goodman, Edward J. *The Explorers of South America.* Norman, Okla.: University of Oklahoma Press, 1992.

Hanson, Earl Parker, editor. *South from the Spanish Main: South America Seen Through the Eyes of Its Discoverers.* New York: Delacorte, 1967.

Haskins, Caryl P. *The Amazon.* New York: Doubleday, 1943.

Hemming, John. *The Conquest of the Incas.* London: Macmillan, 1970.

———. *Red Gold: The Conquest of the Brazilian Indians.* Cambridge, Mass.: Harvard University Press, 1978.

Kelly, Brian, and Mark London. *Amazon.* San Diego, Calif.: Harcourt Brace Jovanovich, 1983.

Kirkpatrick, Frederick A. *The Spanish Conquistadors.* 3rd edition. Gloucester, Mass.: Peter Smith, 1962.

Lang, James. *Conquest and Commerce: Spain and England in the Americas.* New York: Academic Press, 1975.

Lockhart, James. *The Men of Cajamarca: A Social and Biographical Study of the First Conquerors of Peru.* Austin, Tex.: University of Texas Press, 1972.

Markham, Sir Clements. *The Conquest of New Granada.* London: Elder, 1912.

———, editor. *Early Spanish Voyages to the Strait of Magellan.* London: Hakluyt Society, 1911.

*McLoone, Margo. *Women Explorers in North America and South America.* Mankato, Minn.: Capstone Press, 1997.

Morison, Samuel Eliot. *The European Discovery of America: The Southern Voyages, 1492–1616.* New York: Oxford University Press, 1974.

———. *Portuguese Voyages to America in the Fifteenth Century.* Cambridge, Mass.: Harvard University Press, 1940.

Morse, Richard M., editor. *The Bandeirantes: The Historical Role of the Brazilian Pathfinders.* New York: Alfred A. Knopf, 1965.

Pocock, H. R. S. *The Conquest of Chile.* New York: Stein and Day, 1967.

Prescott, William H. *The History of the Conquest of Peru.* Abridged edition. New York: New American Library, 1961.

Severin, Timothy. *The Golden Antilles.* New York: Alfred A. Knopf, 1970.

Silverberg, Robert. *The Golden Dream: Seekers of El Dorado.* Athens, Ohio: Ohio University Press, 1996.

Smith, Anthony. *Explorers of the Amazon.* New York: Viking, 1990.

Vigneras, Louis-André. *The Discovery of South America and the Andalusian Voyages.* Chicago: University of Chicago Press, 1976.

Von Hagen, Victor W. *The Golden Man: A Quest for El Dorado.* Lexington, Mass.: D. C. Heath, 1974.

———. *Realm of the Incas.* Revised edition. New York: New American Library, 1961.

———. *South America Called Them.* New York: Alfred A. Knopf, 1945.

Space

Burrows, William E. *Exploring Space: Voyages in the Solar System and Beyond.* New York: Random House, 1990.

———. *This New Ocean: The Story of the Space Age.* New York: Random House, 1998.

Clark, Philip. *The Soviet Manned Space Program.* New York: Orion Books, 1988.

Collins, Michael. *Liftoff: The Story of America's Adventure in Space.* New York: Grove Press, 1988.

Cooper, Gordon L., John H. Glenn, et al. *We Seven: By the Astronauts Themselves.* New York: Simon and Schuster, 1962.

Davies, J. K. *Space Exploration.* New York: Chambers, 1992.

Elias, George Henry. *Breakout into Space: Mission for a Generation.* New York: Morrow, 1990.

Gibson, Roy. *Space.* New York: Oxford University Press, 1992.

*Kennedy, Gregory P. *Apollo to the Moon.* New York: Chelsea House, 1992.

*———. *First Men in Space.* New York: Chelsea House, 1991.

Launius, Roger D. *Frontiers of Space Exploration.* Westport, Conn.: Greenwood Press, 1998.

MacKinnon, Douglas, and Joseph Baldanza. *Footprints.* Washington, D.C.: Acropolis Books, 1989.

Reeves, Robert. *The Superpower Space Race: An Explosive Rivalry Through the Solar System.* New York: Plenum Press, 1994.

Sagan, Carl. *Cosmos.* New York: Random House, 1990.

Walter, William J. *Space Age.* New York: Random House, 1992.

Photo Credits

Volume 1

Color Plates

for *Ancient Times and Middle Ages* between pages 116 and 117:

1: Paul Dupuy Museum, Toulouse, France/Lauros-Giraudon, Paris/SuperStock; **2:** The Granger Collection, New York; **3:** The Granger Collection, New York; **4:** The Granger Collection, New York; **5:** The Granger Collection, New York; **6:** Bibliothèque Nationale, Paris/Bridegman Art Library, London/SuperStock; **7:** Library of Congress; **8:** The Granger Collection, New York; **9:** Library of Congress; **10:** Newberry Library, Chicago/SuperStock; **11:** The Granger Collection, New York; **12:** The Granger Collection, New York; **13:** Corbis; **14:** The Granger Collection, New York

Black-and-White Photographs

1: Corbis; **3:** Corbis; **5:** Corbis; **6:** NASA; **7:** Corbis; **10:** Library of Congress; **12:** Library of Congress; **13:** Corbis; **15:** Corbis; **17:** National Archives of Canada; **18:** Corbis; **19:** National Archives; **21:** Ewing Galloway; **23:** Mansell/Time Inc.; **25:** John Beatty/Tony Stone Images; **27:** Ewing Galloway; **29:** Ward; Baldwin/Corbis; **31:** © Wolfgang Kaehler Provia; **35:** UPI/Corbis; **37:** NASA; **41:** Mansell/Time Inc.; **43:** UPI/Corbis; **44:** UPI/Corbis; **45:** Corbis; **46:** North Wind Picture Archives; **49:** North Wind Picture Archives; **51:** The Granger Collection, New York; **53:** Archivo General de Indias, Seville; **55:** Mansell/Time Inc.; **57:** Library of Congress; **60:** The Flag Research Center, Winchester, Mass.; **62:** Library of Congress; **63:** Corbis; **65:** Corbis; **67:** NASA; **68:** Library of Congress; **71:** Corbis; **72:** By courtesy of the National Portrait Gallery, London; **75:** Corbis; **77:** Library of Congress; **78:** The Flag Research Center, Winchester, Mass.; **79:** Bibliothèque Nationale, Paris; **83:** Corbis; **84:** By courtesy of the National Portrait Gallery, London; **85:** Corbis; **89:** Library of Congress; **92:** Hulton Getty/Tony Stone Images; **93:** National Library of Australia; **96:** Culver Pictures, Inc.; **97:** Library of Congress; **99:** The Granger Collection, New York; **100:** The Flag Research Center, Winchester, Mass.; **101:** Corbis; **102:** Peabody Museum of Natural History, Yale University; **105:** Library of Congress; **107:** Peabody Museum of Salem; **110:** Utah State Historical Society; **112:** North Wind Picture Archives; **115:** Ward; Baldwin/Corbis; **115:** UPI/Corbis; **116:** Corbis; **117:** Library of Congress; **118:** Library of Congress; **120:** Corbis; **121:** The Granger Collection, New York; **123:** Bibliothèque Nationale, Paris; **124:** Australian Foreign Affairs and Trade Department; **126:** Corbis; **131:** National Archives; **133:** Library of Congress; **134:** Corbis; **137:** Corbis; **142:** Corbis; **144:** Library of Congress; **148:** The Granger Collection, New York; **150:** North Wind Picture Archives; **156:** Library of Congress; **158:** Corbis; **160:** North Wind Picture Archives; **166:** Library of Congress; **167:** Library of Congress; **169:** Library of Congress; **171:** The Flag Research Center, Winchester, Mass.; **174:** Library of Congress; **177:** Library of Congress; **178:** Independence National Historical Park Collection; **179:** The Flag Research Center, Winchester, Mass.; **185:** Scala/Art Resource, N.Y.; **188:** Corbis; **189:** The Flag Research Center, Winchester, Mass.; **194:** North Wind Picture Archives; **196:** North Wind Picture Archives; **200:** National Gallery of Victoria;

Volume 2

Color Plates

for *The Renaissance* between pages 124 and 125:

Black-and-White Photographs

Volume 3

Color Plates

for *Modern Times* between pages 124 and 125:

1: The Granger Collection, New York; **2:** Library of Congress; **3:** © Royal Geographical Society; **4:** The Granger Collection, New York; **5:** © Royal Geographical Society; **6:** NASA; **7:** The Granger Collection, New York; **8:** The Newberry Library/Stock Montage, Inc.; **9:** © Royal Geographical Society; **10:** © Royal Geographical Society; **11:** © Royal Geographical Society; **12:** NASA; **13:** NASA; **14:** NASA; **15:** AP/Wide World Photos; **16:** NASA

Black-and-White Photographs

1: Library of Congress; **3:** Hulton Getty/Tony Stone Images; **7:** Library of Congress; **10:** Naval Museum, Madrid; **11:** Naval Museum, Madrid; **13:** Brown Brothers; **16:** Corbis; **20:** Library of Congress; **22:** Corbis; **25:** Library of Congress; **26:** Corbis; **29:** Corbis; **30:** Library of Congress; **31:** Library of Congress; **32:** Culver Pictures, Inc.; **34:** The Granger Collection, New York; **35:** Corbis; **37:** Hulton Getty/Tony Stone Images; **39:** Corbis; **42:** UPI/Corbis; **44:** Bibliothèque Nationale, Paris; **46:** UPI/Corbis; **49:** National Library of Australia; **50:** Corbis; **53:** Library of Congress; **55:** National Maritime Museum; **59:** By courtesy of the National Portrait Gallery, London; **61:** Corbis; **62:** By courtesy of the National Portrait Gallery, London; **63:** Library of Congress; **64:** Archive Photos; **66:** Library of Congress; **68:** Library of Congress; **69:** Library of Congress; **70:** Library of Congress; **71:** NASA; **72:** By courtesy of the National Portrait Gallery, London; **73:** © Royal Geographical Society; **75:** © Royal Geographical Society; **78:** Denver Public Library, Western History Department; **80:** Library of Congress; **82:** Library of Congress; **86:** Corbis; **88:** Corbis; **90:** Culver Pictures, Inc.; **91:** © Royal Geographical Society; **92:** © Royal Geographical Society; **93:** Library of Congress; **95:** Hulton Getty/Tony Stone Images; **97:** The Granger Collection, New York; **100:** The Granger Collection, New York; **104:** National Library of Australia; **109:** Library of Congress; **114:** Brown Brothers; **115:** Library of Congress; **120:** Library of Congress; **124:** Library of Congress; **126:** Architect of the Capitol; **131:** Joslyn Art Museum, Omaha, Nebr.; **133:** Library of Congress; **135:** National Library of Australia; **136:** UPI/Corbis; **137:** Hulton Getty/Tony Stone Images; **138:** Library of Congress; **139:** Corbis; **140:** Corbis; **143:** UPI/Corbis; **144:** Corbis; **145:** The Parker Library, Corpus Christi College, Cambridge University; **146:** National Library of Australia; **148:** Mansell/Time Inc.; **150:** Corbis; **154:** The Granger Collection, New York; **159:** Hulton Getty/Tony Stone Images

Index